DIRECTORS, DILEMMAS AND DEBT

THE GREAT NORTH OF SCOTLAND AND HIGHLAND RAILWAYS IN THE MID-NINETEENTH CENTURY

PETER FLETCHER

Published by the
GREAT NORTH OF SCOTLAND RAILWAY ASSOCIATION
in conjunction with the
HIGHLAND RAILWAY SOCIETY

CONTENTS

Front Cover : The River Spey was about half-way between Aberdeen and Inverness and required a substantial bridge for the line between Keith and Elgin. The Spey crossing was originally proposed as the point at which the two companies building the through route between Aberdeen and Inverness would meet, but the junction was more conveniently made at Keith. The construction of the bridge itself was not without problems; its engineer, William Fairbairn, had great difficulty in persuading the Board of Trade inspector that it was sufficiently sound to carry passenger trains. In this early view, a train from Inverness to Keith is crossing the bridge, with a flagman watching its progress.
                                                                   (Courtesy Anne-Mary Wharton)

ACKNOWLEDGEMENTS

The genesis of this book stretches back many years to the time when, as a teenager, I first encountered the dramatic railways which cross the rugged and stunning landscapes of the west and north highlands of Scotland. I wondered why these remote lines were built, who conceived them and provided their funds, and how the routes had managed to survive in such sparsely populated areas. The opportunity to delve into their economic history occurred much later in life at a point when, coincidentally, the Institute of Railway Studies and Transport History had become well-established through the partnership between the University of York and the National Railway Museum. My research has been assisted not only by the staff of those institutions, but also by the excellent service given by the staff in the West Search Room of the National Archives of Scotland in Edinburgh.

The Great North of Scotland Railway Association and the Highland Railway Society have both earned a reputation for encouraging and disseminating research into the history of these two notable railway companies. The publication of this book, which explores the inter-related development of each company during the three decades following the great railway mania of 1845, would not have been possible without the generous support of these Societies.

I am indebted to the individuals and organisations acknowledged within the following pages for permission to use photographs and drawings from their collections. Keith Fenwick has not only sourced these illustrations, prepared the coloured map and worked assiduously on the layout of the book, but, with John Roake, has offered many helpful comments on the text; I am most grateful to them both.

I hope that this book will extend the knowledge, understanding and appreciation of the development of railways in northern Scotland, and the Great North of Scotland and Highland companies in particular.

Peter Fletcher
York
February 2010.

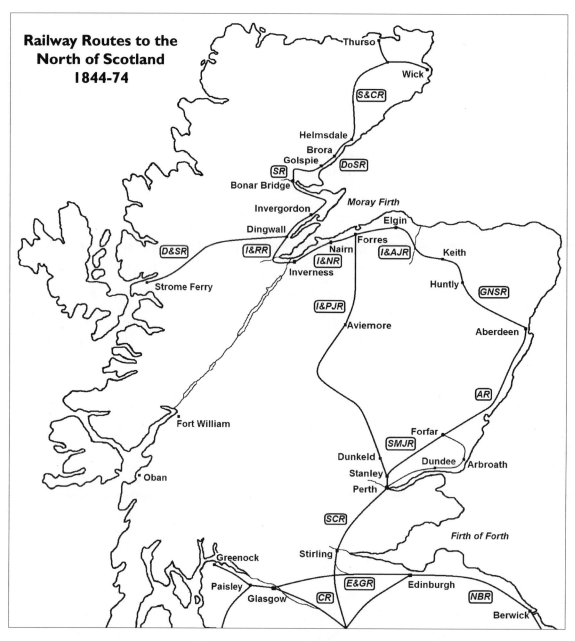

Railway Routes to the North of Scotland 1844-74

Key			
Railways authorised, 1844-46		**Later authorisations**	
AR	Aberdeen Railway	D&SR	Dingwall and Skye Railway
CR	Caledonian Railway	DoSR	Duke of Sutherland's Railway
E&GR	Edinburgh and Glasgow Railway	I&AJR	Inverness and Aberdeen Junction Railway
E&NR	Edinburgh and Northern Railway	I&NR	Inverness and Nairn Railway
GNSR	Great North of Scotland Railway	I&PJR	Inverness and Perth Junction Railway
NBR	North British Railway	I&RR	Inverness and Ross-shire Railway
SCR	Scottish Central Railway	SR	Sutherland Railway
SMJR	Scottish Midland Junction Railway	S&CR	Sutherland and Caithness Railway

CHAPTER 1

INTRODUCTION

Take care of the capital account and the revenue will take care of itself.
Herapath's Railway Journal, 21 April 1855

William Lowndes, secretary to the Treasury in the early years of the eighteenth century, penned the well-known adage which runs 'Take care of the pence, and the pounds will take care of themselves'. The leader writer in *Herapath's Railway Journal* neatly adapted this well-known quotation as the headline to an article which suggested to its readers that attractive dividends were more likely to be obtained from investment in railway companies where capital expenditure was carefully controlled:

> It is a remarkable and most instructive fact that those lines in England which pay remunerative dividends are those whose capital cost is light.

> It is a curious fact, that shareholders generally busy themselves with matters of trifling importance ... and neglect the all-important subject of capital expenditure.[1]

The difficulties of raising capital and managing finance had already severely taxed the minds of many of those on railway boards in Britain even before the collapse in confidence in railway shares following the great railway mania of 1845 which added further to their problems. The need for strict financial control within railway companies was a theme to which the national railway journals regularly returned throughout the century.

Finance is not usually a topic which immediately attracts the interest of railway historians, but the story of its sourcing and management underpins the often hesitant progress of the Great North of Scotland and Highland Railways and their constituent companies throughout the nineteenth century. The intuition, ingenuity and determination shown within these northern boardrooms to tackle and overcome their particular financial hurdles offers a different and intriguing perspective on the history of these two small Scottish railway companies. The severe financial difficulties, which starkly faced the boards of both companies by the mid 1860s and which threatened the very independent existence of each, provide the focus for this book. Using company records and the reports published in the national railway journals of the period, it recounts how these problems arose, describes the relatively bleak prospects faced by the new Highland Railway and the re-constituted Great North of Scotland Railway as the national financial crisis of 1866 erupted, and shows how each company managed successfully to extricate itself from the palpable prospect of financial collapse.

Over the years, the value of money and the structure of the British currency have changed. British currency units in the nineteenth century comprised pounds sterling, shillings (twenty to the pound), pence (twelve to the shilling), half-pence (two to the penny) and farthings (four to the penny). One shilling is now represented by five pence of our present currency. An analysis of historical monetary values suggests that one pound sterling in 1845 would have been equivalent to £55.30 by 1995, and one pound sterling in 1866 would be worth £50.69 by this same date.[2] Although inflation has continued to erode the value of money since 1995, the reader can apply a multiplier of 50 to nineteenth century monetary values given in the text to gain a simple and approximate indication of a current equivalent value.

In the twenty-first century, good financial management of any company usually operates in the background and does not attract much attention from either shareholders or the media until problems emerge which threaten the payment of dividends or even the very future of the business itself. Such was the case for the Great North of Scotland Railway and the constituent companies of the Highland Railway in the early 1860s until their mounting financial difficulties came under closer scrutiny in the middle of the decade. The following chapters lift the lid on this fundamental aspect of the history of these northern railway companies during their critical years of development.

CHAPTER 2

A REGION OF CONTRASTS

In 1835, the *Inverness Courier* published an optimistic view of the highland economy as a result of changes made in the use of land. It reported a recent Edinburgh sale of the Cromartie lands in Ross-shire in which the Fannich lot sold for £6,550 and the Lochbroom lot for £9,200, prices which the editor considered would have been regarded as 'ruinous' only a few years earlier. The *Courier* commented:

> Even unconquerable barrenness is now turned to good account. At the present moment, we believe, many Highland proprietors derive a greater revenue from their moors alone, for grouse shooting, than their whole rental amounted to sixty years since. The passion entertained by English gentlemen for field-sports has been fostered by the increased means of communication northwards, and up and down the country, from the highest hill to the deepest and most distant glen. The sportsman throws himself into a steamer at London, and in forty-eight hours or less he is in Edinburgh or Aberdeen. Another day and he is in the heart of the moor and mountain, where he may shoot, saunter, or angle to his heart's content.
>
> (*Inverness Courier*, 28 October 1835)

Landowners were reaping the rewards of the economic and social revolution that began to sweep through northern Scotland at the end of the eighteenth century, but the severe impact of these changes on the native highlander escaped the attention of the *Courier's* editor on this occasion. Even before the railway arrived in northern Scotland to cast its influence on the pattern and development of trade, there was a marked contrast between the regional economies of east and west.

To the east, Aberdeen was becoming well established as the prosperous mercantile centre of north-east Scotland, surrounded by counties which provided rich and improved agricultural land to meet the increasing demand for its products from the industrialising south. To the west, the highland region was being dragged from a semi-feudal and largely self-sufficient society into a new role as an economic satellite of the markets of the Scottish Lowlands and England.[3] Between 6,000 and 10,000 people were removed from inland parishes in the county of Sutherland in 1807-21 to new coastal settlements in what has been described as 'the most extra-ordinary example of social engineering in early nineteenth century Britain'.[4] James Loch, Commissioner to the Marquis of Stafford, published a pamphlet in 1820 in which he sought to justify the improvements made to his employer's estates in Sutherland and to counter the criticism levelled against the displacement of tenants. In it, he wrote strongly of 'those malicious and false statements and insinuations' about the highland clearances circulated through the public press, and attributed some of this reaction to the 'romantic feeling' evoked by the highlands of Scotland and its connection to the ill-fated cause of Prince Charles Edward Stuart.[5]

Loch and his acolytes had been castigated in the press for numerous incidents in which tenants were forcibly removed from the land in order to create the necessary size of farms required for large flocks of sheep, but the inescapable dilemma facing northern landowners was that the agricultural inefficiency of the feudal clan system conflicted with the increased commercialisation of agriculture. The old agricultural system of 'runrig', the farming of strips between a quarter and half an acre each, continued in parts of the highlands well into the nineteenth century. Highland land was also of variable quality in contrast to the fertile land in the hinterlands of Aberdeen and its neighbouring counties. A description of the interior of Sutherland in 1850 painted a somewhat bleak picture:

> … extensive tracts of great bog, – broken into mountains, and rocks and wild scenery, and interspersed here and there with patches of land, under imperfect tillage, near the riverbanks.[6]

Coastal land in Sutherland and Caithness, to which many displaced tenants were directed, was of poor quality, but the increasing reliance on the potato as the staple diet allowed a large population to be supported by a relatively small area of land of indifferent quality. The arrival of potato blight in 1846, however, devastated the staple diet of the highland population for several years and, by December 1846, almost two-fifths of families living in Inverness-shire were identified as destitute with two thirds of highland districts reporting an entire failure of the potato crop.[7] As a result of these economic and social catastrophes, many highlanders had within half a century lost their land, their homes, their livelihood and their means of sustenance. So, at the very time industrialisation was driving the development of the Scottish economy and new investment was being sought to expand its embryo railway system, large parts of northern Scotland were subject to severe poverty and regular famine.

Public interest in the highlands was revived by news of Queen Victoria's journey through the Crinan Canal in 1847 on board one of David Hutcheson's steamers, which led to Hutcheson's company marketing its network of services between Glasgow and Inverness as the 'Royal Route'.[8] The popularity of the region was further enhanced by Queen Victoria's use of Balmoral as a holiday home from 1848, while Sir Walter Scott's 'Waverley' novels continued to keep the romance of the highlands firmly in the minds of the British public throughout the century.[9] Fifty years after Scott's death in 1832, *Railway News* was still able to comment on the 'many tours opened up in the districts which the genius of Sir Walter Scott has invested with so much value in public estimation'.[10]

The coming of the railway to northern Scotland allowed this inherent romanticism to become more tangible and accessible to the increasing numbers of tourists in mid-nineteenth century Britain. These romantic sentiments have also, perhaps, contributed to the continuing strong interest shown in the history of the two main railway companies that served these northern districts. The Great North of Scotland and Highland Railways represented the rivalry between the two important trading centres of northern Scotland, Aberdeen and Inverness. Throughout much of the nineteenth century, this company rivalry was epitomised by a deep-seated mistrust one between the other, which occasionally manifested itself in openly hostile actions designed to defend and extend their individual spheres of influence and control.

The rival claims of Aberdeen and Inverness for control of the traffic of northern Scotland were apparent in the prospectuses of the Great North of Scotland and Perth and Inverness Railways, published in 1845 as the great railway mania was gathering pace across Britain:

It will be seen that the line passes through the rich and flourishing counties of Aberdeen, Banff, Moray, Nairn and Inverness – most fertile districts and of the highest Agricultural and Manufacturing importance. (*Prospectus of the Great North of Scotland Railway, 1845*)

"As Perth", in the words of the Board of Trade, "is evidently the point of convergence for the traffic of the northern part of the kingdom", so is Inverness, in like manner, the point at which the traffic of the whole counties to the north and west, and for a considerable distance to the east, must necessarily converge. (*Prospectus of the Perth and Inverness Railway, 1845*)

In some respects, research into the history of the Great North of Scotland and Highland railway companies and their constituents has, like these two competitive promotions of their predecessors in 1845, adopted a similar independence and rivalry in that publications have tended to focus on aspects of the development of one company or the other. Yet both companies faced comparable and severe financial predicaments by the third quarter of the nineteenth century, which were caused, not only by the results of the intense enterprise of each during the preceding quarter to develop its network of lines and to secure its territory, but also by the common impact upon them of national economic events. It is this story of the Great North of Scotland and the Highland Railways which is to be explored.

The River Ness drains the Great Glen and runs through Inverness to the Moray Firth. The main part of the town is to the right, with the river at this point running northwards. Bridges across the river connect to the roads southwest to Fort William and north to Dingwall. The railway bridge on the line to Dingwall and the Far North is further down river, just round the bend to the right in the distance. The town grew considerably after the railway came in the middle of the nineteenth century when most of the buildings visible in this photograph, taken in May 1973, were built. It has grown again in the last thirty years to service the north sea oil industry.

(Keith Fenwick)

CHAPTER 3

THE FINANCIAL FRAMEWORK OF RAILWAYS

Governments in nineteenth century Britain were strongly influenced by the principles of *laissez-faire* capitalism and its reliance upon free market forces to control the economic destiny of the nation. The State was therefore reluctant to become involved in any strategic planning or management of railways and so the British railway network evolved from a multitude of uncoordinated plans proposed and financed by private enterprise. By 1845, the size of many railway companies dwarfed those of previous commercial enterprises and it was not long before the inexperience in many railway boardrooms to manage the scale of finance involved became apparent.[11] The Caledonian Railway, approved by Parliament in 1845 to build the trunk route from Carlisle to Glasgow and Edinburgh, was granted powers to raise £2.1 million by the sale of shares to the public and a further £0.7 million from loans. By contrast, just four years earlier in 1841, the paid-up capital of the important and influential Bank of Scotland was £1 million, less than half that of this new railway company.[12]

Early railways in Scotland tended to be relatively short local lines, designed primarily to link coalfields to a water-based system of transport. The money required for their construction was raised principally from industrialists and individuals resident in the districts which were to be served. By the mid 1830s, however, the pace of railway development in England accelerated; seventy-five lines were authorised by Parliament in 1835-37, but just fifteen railway acts were approved for Scottish schemes in the same period.[13] Of these, only the Glasgow, Paisley and Greenock Railway (22 miles) and the Glasgow, Paisley, Kilmarnock and Ayr Railway (50 miles) were of any significant length. By 1838, England had 497 miles of railway; Scotland had just 49, which comprised a series of short lines in the central belt and three short local lines centred on the port of Dundee.[14] Nevertheless, competitive financial returns to private investors in railways were available in Scotland. When the Liverpool and Manchester Railway in England was paying a steady 9% dividend during the 1830s, some of the Scottish mineral lines were paying at least as much. The Ballochney Railway, only five miles long, paid between 14% and 16% in 1838-42, while the Monkland and Kirkintilloch Railway, opened in 1826, paid between 10% and 12% during this same period.[15]

RAILWAY CAPITAL

Railway companies were incorporated by a private act of Parliament, which also granted power to acquire land by compulsory purchase and authority to raise share capital and loans within specified limits. As the scale of new railway promotions increased, larger sums of capital were required to construct the routes and equip the companies with the necessary plant to work the lines. Estimated costs usually determined the level of share capital authorised in the act of incorporation, with additional borrowing powers approved to meet any immediate difficulties in raising share capital or to cover cost increases. From 1836, parliamentary standing orders required that borrowing powers contained in railway legislation were restricted to one-third of the authorised share capital and, furthermore, such powers could not be exercised until half of the share capital had been paid up.[16] Borrowing was intended by Parliament to be a temporary feature of railway finance and not a long term source of funds, but this aspiration of policy was not to be reflected in practice.

Even before the growth of the speculative bubble of 1845, which has become known as the great railway mania, borrowing had became an alternative, rather than the expected complementary, source of finance for many railway companies due to the difficulties experienced in raising sufficient ordinary share capital.[17] As a result, loans often assumed a greater proportion of the total capital raised than Parliament expected, especially in the period before lines opened and generated revenue. This trend was to continue after 1845, when the collapse in confidence in railway shares severely restricted the availability of new capital. The railway companies established in northern Scotland in the two decades following the great railway mania faced additional disadvantage in attempting to raise capital from a national market because of the their small scale and remoteness.[18]

The promotion and construction of many railways in both England and Scotland revealed serious inaccuracies in the estimation of costs, the causes of which included inexperience in planning and managing large scale projects, undue extravagance in the scale of construction, engineering difficulties encountered during construction of the lines, the legal and parliamentary costs of obtaining a parliamentary bill, and the high prices exacted by landowners for the route required. With widespread errors in calculating such costs, many railway companies were forced to seek new capital powers or loans, or both, which in turn tended to depress the returns that could be paid to their shareholders because any profit earned had then to be spread over a larger capital sum.[19]

When a railway company was promoted, it advertised for subscriptions by means of a published prospectus. After shares were allotted and a deposit paid on them, subscribers were issued with a scrip certificate, which was exchanged for share certificates once the company had been incorporated. A market developed in these scrip certificates and even in the letters of allotment sent to subscribers.[20] By purchasing ordinary shares in a railway company, the investor became a part-owner of the company. Once the company was in operation and earning revenue from running its services, the shareholder was eligible to receive a share of any profit in the form of a dividend after the expenses and charges of the company had been paid.

Railway companies were required to deposit a proportion of their subscription capital with the government as a form of surety, which was repaid when half of the share capital had been raised and spent or if the company was subsequently wound up. This sum had to be deposited with the Bank of England, a Scottish bank or placed in government stock. From 1837, the parliamentary deposit was set at ten percent, but reduced to five percent in 1842, only to be raised back to ten percent in 1845 as the speculative boom in railway shares reached its peak.[21]

After the promotion was authorised by Parliament and the company was incorporated, the directors raised the railway's share capital by requesting the payment of a number of instalments, or calls, on each issued share over a period of time until the full specified price of the share had been paid. The price of each share was stated in the company's parliamentary act, but it often reflected factors such as the scale of the enterprise, the prospect of future profit, the likelihood of attracting new investors, and the ability and potential willingness of those in the area to be served by the railway to subscribe to the company. Shares in the Caledonian Railway, for example, approved in 1845 to connect Glasgow and Edinburgh with the English west-coast route to London, were priced at £50 each, whereas, ten years later in 1855, the local Inverness and Nairn Railway, like many other railway companies in northern Scotland, offered its shares at £10 each.

Once the railway company had raised at least half of its share capital, it could exercise its parliamentary powers to borrow money to increase its capital receipts. Such authorised borrowing was usually obtained by offering debenture loans for a specified period of time, with a fixed rate of interest paid to lenders. Although these debentures gave the lenders a priority to receive the interest payments due to them before any dividends were paid on ordinary shares, these loans did not confer any ownership of a part of the company on the lenders, unlike that granted to the holder of ordinary shares. From 1863, railway companies were permitted to convert debenture loans into debenture stock without the need to seek parliamentary sanction, provided shareholder approval had been obtained.[22] Debenture stock, like debenture loans, offered lenders a fixed rate of interest, but the stock did not have to be regularly renewed by the company.[23] This practice avoided the difficulties of managing a wide portfolio of debentures at different interest rates and for different lengths of time, and it also obviated the additional expense that could be incurred by the need to renew debenture loans when market interest rates were unfavourable.

Unlike their English counterparts, Scottish railway companies had access to a well-developed system of branch banking in Scotland, the growth of which had been aided by differences between Scottish and English law that were not harmonised until 1856.[24] Scottish law,

for example, allowed a business partnership to sue and be sued in the name of the firm rather than in the names of its individual members, which gave more protection to its partners.[25] An act of 1709, designed to protect the monopoly of the Bank of England, prohibited any English bank from comprising more than six partners and thereby restricted its size to the capital that those partners could provide, whereas in Scotland any number of partners was permitted. The 1709 Act was not repealed until 1826.[26]

The Commercial Bank of Scotland was the first large joint-stock bank in Scotland with a capital of £3 million in shares of £500, 673 shareholders and 14 branches by 1815; the Aberdeen Town and County Bank, established in 1825 with capital of £¾ million also in shares of £500, was the first regional joint-stock bank in Scotland and had 470 partners.[27] Although legislation was passed in 1845 to prevent the creation of any new banks with powers to issue their own notes, nineteen Scottish banks had, by that date, been authorised to circulate notes to a total value of £3.085 million.[28] Six of these banks were based in Edinburgh, five in Glasgow, and eight in the regions. Of these regional banks, three had their headquarters in Aberdeen – the Aberdeen Town and County Bank, the Aberdeen Banking Company and the North of Scotland Bank – and one, the Caledonian Bank, in Inverness. The founder of the North of Scotland Bank was lawyer Alexander Anderson and among the first directors elected in 1836 were Anderson, George Thompson, and Alexander Jopp, all of whom were later to serve on the board of the Great North of Scotland Railway.[29] Promoters of the Caledonian Bank, established in 1838, included engineer Joseph Mitchell, who with the bank's first manager, Charles Waterston, was to become deeply involved in the promotion of the railways centred on Inverness.[30]

Scottish banks pioneered the short-term cash credit, or overdraft, facility and, by 1850, the average number of branches per joint-stock bank in Scotland was 50 but only 5.8 in England and Wales.[31] By 1857, Scottish banks were operating through 607 branches. This branch banking structure assisted the accumulation and channelling of deposits to meet new demands for investment funds, such as those arising from the process of industrialisation and amongst which were the financial needs of new railways. Early Scottish railway acts, such as that approved for the Dundee and Arbroath Railway in 1824, often specifically identified banks as a source of lending.[32]

RAILWAY ACCOUNTS

Railway companies operated two main accounts, a capital account and a revenue account. The capital account recorded the sums of money raised from the sale of shares and the acceptance of loans and also indicated the total amount of share and loan capital that Parliament had authorised the company to issue, although it was not unknown, through error or design, for railway companies to exceed the powers that Parliament had granted. The capital account also recorded the amounts of money spent on capital items, such as construction of the line, the purchase of land, locomotives and rolling stock, the provision of stations, and any subscriptions made to other companies with which the railway might have some alliance. The difference between the amount of capital received and the amount of capital spent produced the capital balance. If more had been spent than received, the company had to find an alternative source of temporary funding to balance its books. This temporary borrowing was usually held outside the main accounts on the general balance sheet so that this short-term debt did not sully the main trading accounts of the company. Consequently, transactions shown on the general balance sheet are sometimes referred to by the term "below the line". Many financial manoeuvres and indiscretions were often buried within the general balance sheets of railway companies, where they remained largely unseen by shareholders.

The revenue account recorded the receipts obtained from various types of traffic, such as passengers, parcels and mail, goods, minerals and livestock. Against these receipts would be set the working expenses of the company including wages, locomotive and operating costs, rates and taxes. If receipts exceeded costs, the interest due on loans and debentures was then deducted and paid, and any remaining surplus became available for a dividend to ordinary shareholders. If, however, the costs exceeded the receipts, the company had to find funds to cover the difference, which usually required the directors to obtain temporary credit.

Railway companies obtained short-term or medium-term credit from a variety of sources to balance their accounts. These might include temporary loans from banks, credit from other financial intermediaries and railway contractors, and the issue of bills of exchange to suppliers of goods instead of paying cash. Bills of exchange were a written commitment to pay a sum due to a creditor by a fixed date, which almost always required the payment of interest on the debt due until it was discharged.

These types of temporary or floating debt, if they were

reported at all to shareholders, usually appeared in the general balance sheet of the company and therefore did not present an immediate charge on the revenue or capital account of the company. Nevertheless, such "hidden" debt still required servicing and ultimate repayment, despite being recorded outside the main accounts.

Unfortunately, there was widespread inconsistency in the way that railway companies maintained and presented their accounts, particularly in the allocation of expenditure between the capital and revenue accounts. Some companies, for example, moved costs out of the revenue account and paid them from capital in order to try to retain sufficient receipts to be able to pay a dividend to their ordinary shareholders. In such cases, these dividends, which were intended as a return on prior investment, were in effect paid using money which had been received from the shareholders themselves rather than from any genuine profits earned from trade. Railway companies were not alone in seeking to preserve revenue to pay dividends. The North of Scotland Bank came close to collapse in February 1848 by trying to sustain dividends after overextending its lending during the great railway mania and, in its aftermath, a run on the bank reduced its capital by more than a half from £380,000 to £115,000.[33]

Parliament issued little regulation on railway company accounts, other than to require that books were to be kept and a balance sheet was to be published for shareholders' meetings.[34] It was not until 1868 that some uniformity in railway accounting was defined in the Regulation of Railways Act, following the financial crisis of 1866 in which railway securities played a central role.[35] Although specific accounts were then required in a prescribed form half-yearly by the Board of Trade, differences persisted in the ways companies constructed and reported their capital and revenue accounts.[36] Some care is therefore required when examining the surviving records and accounts of railway companies.

Aberdeen was the northern limit of the railway network authorised in 1845. Even when the Great North was opened northwards, there was a gap of half a mile until the costly link across the city was built in 1867 and the original Joint Station, seen here about that time, was opened.
(GNSRA collection)

CHAPTER 4

THE GREAT RAILWAY MANIA AND SCOTLAND, 1845-46

The performance of the British economy has for centuries followed a cyclical path, marked by a pattern of peaks and troughs. In the early 1840s, growing prosperity as a result of a cyclical economic upswing generated wealth at a time when new railway schemes were seeking investors. This newly-created wealth naturally sought a home which could produce a good income for its owners. Professor W E Aytoun of Edinburgh University and *Blackwood's Edinburgh Magazine* warned of the 'epidemic' of seeking to grow rich as:

> … a disease which infests the nation whenever capital, in consequence of the success of trade and prosperous harvests, becomes abundant.[37]

Many established railways were paying attractive dividends on their ordinary shares. In 1842, for example, the London and Birmingham and Grand Junction companies in England paid 10% on their ordinary shares, while the newly-opened Edinburgh and Glasgow Railway declared its first dividend at a rate of 5%.[38] The increasing supply of funds created from the economic boom and the prospect of similar, or higher, returns to investors encouraged the formulation of other railway plans, increasingly variable in their economic realism. There was an explosion of interest in subscribing for railway shares and so the great railway mania gathered momentum.[39]

As the English network of trunk lines grew during the early 1840s, the scale of capital required escalated beyond local supply and was increasingly obtained from a capital market that could attract and direct investment funds nationally.[40] Railway shares were now bought, not so much by local residents and entrepreneurs as before, but by "blind" investors, remote from the promotions and promoters, who were seeking the best returns on their money. Decisions on where to place this "blind" investment were informed and influenced by the news and comment given in the railway journals of the period, such as *Railway Times*, *Herapath's Railway Journal* and *Railway Chronicle*.

An offer to buy shares, however, was no guarantee that a short-term subscription would be translated into firm longer-term investment. Even prior to the 1845 mania, the original subscribers in many railway companies in Britain were in a minority within a few years of incorporation.[41] A subscription contract to buy shares only required the initial payment of a deposit and, as growing numbers of new railway projects were advertised to the public through their prospectuses, the prospect of making substantial profits from short-term dealing in shares encouraged speculation.

THE 1845 SPECULATIVE BUBBLE

The consequences of speculation were parodied by Professor Aytoun in *Blackwood's Edinburgh Magazine* in October 1845 as the mania reached its climax.[42] The fictional *Glenmutchkin Railway*, the centrepiece of his satire, was based on the Scottish Grand Junction Railway, which proposed a share capital of £1 million to build a line from Oban to Callander where a junction with the projected Dunblane, Doune and Callander Railway would give onward connection to Stirling and the emerging Scottish railway network. The Scottish Grand Junction also included two branches in its scheme, one to Loch Lomond to connect with the steamer service and a second from Tyndrum to Dalwhinnie where the line was to connect with the projected Perth and Inverness Railway.[43] It had a rival, the Scottish Western, which proposed a line between Oban and Glasgow, but its promoters withdrew in November 1845 in favour of the Scottish Grand Junction. The *Scottish Railway Gazette* may have contributed indirectly to Aytoun's imaginative writing, for it sharply questioned the feasibility of the Scottish Grand Junction and Scottish Western schemes and asked:

> Can human folly or gullibility go further?[44]

The Scottish Grand Junction Railway, the brainchild of the Marquis of Breadalbane, planned to open up the west highlands to rail transport and it was one of the largest schemes promoted in Scotland during the mania period. Yet even a reduced scheme between Oban and Crianlarich, with a branch to Loch Lomond, could not raise the necessary capital of £350,000 and the Scottish Grand Junction was finally abandoned in 1852.[45]

Glenmutchkin was an influential piece of contemporary writing. Over the following two decades at least, there are references to it at public meetings and in contemporary journals where railway promotions in northern Scotland were being considered.[46] Aytoun's short story recounts how a couple of Glaswegian misfits, Augustus Dunshunner and Robert McCorkindale, promote a railway into the wild and remote regions of the highlands during the railway mania. Amid all the schemes coming forward, they ponder where to build a line and decide, fortified by a substantial cask of Oban whisky, that a highland scheme offered good scope to attract greedy speculators, despite the lasting legacy of the highland clearances:

> **McCorkindale:** "Well, then, why not try the Highlands? There must be lots of traffic there in the shape of sheep, grouse, and Cockney tourists, not to mention salmon and other et ceteras. Couldn't we tip them a railway somewhere in the west?"

Dunshunner: "There's Glenmutchkin, for instance –"

McCorkindale: "Capital, my dear fellow! … There may be some bother about the population though. The last laird shipped every mother's son of the aboriginal Celts to America; but, after all, that's not of much consequence".[47]

Although Aytoun astutely used the depressed economic condition of the highlands to parody the naivety of many investors, who were animated by the speculative surge in railway shares to the point of irrationality, railway historians generally agree that Scotland was less affected by the 1845 speculation than other parts of Britain.[48] Many of the Scottish mainline projects were planned, launched and authorised before the frenetic trading in railway shares reached its peak in the late summer of 1845. They were for logical routes, which offered good potential for profit and attractive returns to shareholders, but required large amounts of capital for their construction.

The North British Railway obtained parliamentary approval in 1844 for its line from Edinburgh to Berwick, where it was to connect with the Newcastle and Berwick Railway, a protégé of the Railway King, George Hudson, and form part of the east-coast route to London. The Caledonian Railway, authorised in 1845, provided the cross-border link to Glasgow and Edinburgh for the west-coast alliance of companies that came to be dominated by the London and North Western Railway, formed by amalgamation of the London and Birmingham, Grand Junction, and Manchester and Birmingham Railways in 1846 and managed by the redoubtable Captain Mark Huish. The extension of this west-coast trunk route northwards to Aberdeen, recommended by the Railway Board of the Board of Trade, was also authorised by Parliament in 1845 by incorporating three companies, the Scottish Central, Scottish Midland Junction and Aberdeen Railways, to construct it.

Considerable sums of English money were offered as subscriptions to these infant Scottish companies. The North British attracted 42% of its subscriptions from England, the Caledonian 78%, doubtless because each provided a direct cross-border link into the important English trunk routes controlled by the east-coast and west-coast alliances.[49] Even the more remote Scottish Central Railway, which was to extend the Caledonian line from Greenhill near Falkirk to Stirling and on to Perth, attracted 30% of its subscriptions from England, while the Scottish Midland Junction, which was to push the trunk route north-eastwards beyond Perth to Forfar, obtained 78% of its subscriptions from England, boosted by the enticing, and possibly unsustainable, offer to English subscribers that deposits would be returned if the company's bill was rejected in Parliament.[50]

Unfortunately, these new Scottish railway companies, proposing important, evolutionary, and viable schemes, were caught up in the widespread financial difficulties that arose across Britain in the aftermath of the great railway mania when confidence in railway shares evaporated. It was to be April 1850 before the Aberdeen Railway opened the final section of the authorised northern trunk route to Ferryhill on the outskirts of Aberdeen, linking the north of Scotland to the developing national railway network for the first time.

Railway investment driven by speculation posed a serious problem for the financial health of companies because railway construction

The Route to the North, 1845

Key	
AR	Aberdeen Railway
CR	Caledonian Railway
E&GR	Edinburgh and Glasgow Railway
E&NR	Edinburgh and Northern Railway
GP&GR	Glasgow, Paisley and Greenock Railway
GPK&AR	Glasgow, Paisley, Kilmarnock and Ayr Railway
NBR	North British Railway
SCR	Scottish Central Railway
SMJR	Scottish Midland Junction Railway

was contra-cyclical and capital was usually required after the peak of the economic cycle had passed.[51] As a result, capital shortfalls arose in many railway companies once funds were called from subscribers who had made their commitments in the exhilarating days of the boom period. A poor harvest, the arrival of potato blight and a rise in interest rates prompted a wave of share selling across the nation by the end of 1845. Demand for railway shares dwindled and, in an economy dominated by the free market forces of supply and demand, prices tumbled. In October 1845, *The Spectator* reported falls in the premiums on railway shares 'for the first time in months'; in December, *Bradshaw's Railway Gazette* commented that 'something more than a panic ... has taken place in the sharemarket', by when over five hundred provisionally registered British railway companies had disappeared.[52]

By June 1846, subscribers who had paid £2 10s as deposit for each £25 share in the Scottish Grand Junction Railway, the *Glenmutchkin* of Aytoun's caricature, could sell for only fifteen shillings, seeing their original subscriptions reduced by almost a third.[53] Companies that survived the repercussions of the mania and sought to raise capital by making calls on their shares discovered that many subscribers were unable, or unwilling, to pay. The previous flood of new railway capital was rapidly reduced to a trickle. Many projects were curtailed or stopped and new legislation was passed to permit the dissolution of railway companies.[54] In 1847, *Herapath's Railway Journal* reported the effects of what that journal described as 'The Railway Storm':

> It is most distressing to look into a Railway Share-list. New lines, no matter of what promise, are universally at a discount, £100 being worth about £50.[55]

By the time the speculative bubble burst at the end of 1845, one hundred and fifteen sets of plans for new Scottish railways had been deposited for Parliamentary scrutiny during the 1845-46 session.[56] Amongst these bills were various proposals to extend the railway network further north to Inverness. The rival promoters, already aware of the severe economic difficulties within the northern counties and the potential impact of these on the profitability of their lines, now faced the additional obstacle of trying to raise large amounts of money for their construction from a capital market which was in retrenchment. Moreover, any investment funds that remained available were unlikely to be attracted to new and remote northern railways where the predicted returns on capital, as advertised in their prospectuses, were purely hypothetical.

NORTH TO INVERNESS

The parliamentary approvals of July 1845 had granted powers to four companies to construct the continuous trunk line of railway from the border via Perth to Aberdeen. Beyond these two important trading towns, both of which had relied on sea transport for communication and their prosperity, the feasibility of constructing and operating any railways for profit had already been questioned. When a proposal to link Perth and Inverness by railway was mooted in 1841, *Railway Times* commented:

> ... the comparative scantiness and poverty of the population are such as to render it doubtful whether, as mere pecuniary speculation, any very extensive schemes of Scottish railways would answer.
>
> ... excepting shepherds and sheep, with a few sportsmen and dogs in August, we know of no other living creatures betwixt the two towns whom it would accommodate.[57]

This depressing assessment was also reflected in census data covering the decades when new railways were being promoted to serve the north of Scotland, which suggest the relatively prosperous nature of Aberdeen and its hinterland in contrast to Inverness and the highlands, suffering the continuing effects of famine and the highland clearances (table 1). Aberdeenshire and its surrounding counties maintained a fifth of the increasing Scottish population between 1841 and 1861, but the populations of the six northern counties were in decline.

The highland counties not only contained a scarce and declining population with a significant proportion in poverty, but they also lacked any significant supply of raw materials other than timber. New railways would therefore have to rely substantially on traffic generated by agriculture, fishing and tourists, which inevitably was distinctly seasonal in nature. Aytoun's fictional *Glenmutchkin Railway* embodied these same characteristics, but it was also burdened by the ubiquitous problems encountered by railways across Britain of underestimated costs, unanticipated engineering difficulties and unrealistic timescales.

Yet the dire economic conditions of the northern counties conspired to give an unexpected and indirect financial impetus to railway development in the north. The gradual collapse of the feudal clan structure, the enforced highland clearances and the effects of famine contributed to a major change in the structure of northern society. By the 1840s, over three-quarters of all estates in the famine zone had been acquired by merchants, bankers, lawyers, financiers and industrialists.[58] Joseph Mitchell, surveyor of Highland Road and Bridges and engineer of the Inverness web of railways, later commented:

> Scotland, in fact, does not belong to the people of Scotland. They are permitted to reside in it ... One half of their country is owned by seventy proprietors, while nine-tenths belongs to seventeen hundred persons.[59]

Although the state gave some financial assistance in northern Scotland for the construction of roads and provided the funds to construct the Caledonian Canal as a contribution to alleviating the region's economic difficulties, any requests to support railway development were declined, in contrast to policy in Ireland.[60] The only source of long-term investment for economic progress in northern Scotland, therefore, was likely to come from these new wealthy landowners.[61] It

Table 1: Population by counties in the north of Scotland, 1841–61

	1841		1851		1861	
Population of Scotland	**2,620,184**		**2,888,742**		**3,062,294**	
Growth 1841-61						+ 16.9%
		%		%		%
Aberdeen	192,387	7.34	212,032	7.34	221,569	7.24
Banff	49,679	1.90	54,171	1.88	59,215	1.93
Angus	170,453	6.50	191,264	6.62	204,425	6.68
Perth	137,457	5.25	138,660	4.80	133,500	4.36
		20.99		**20.64**		**20.21**
Inverness	97,799	3.73	96,500	3.34	88,888	2.90
Nairn	9,217	0.35	9,956	0.34	10,065	0.33
Moray	35,012	1.34	38,959	1.35	42,695	1.39
Ross and Cromarty	78,685	3.00	82,707	2.86	81,406	2.66
Sutherland	24,782	0.95	25,793	0.89	25,246	0.82
Caithness	36,443	1.39	38,709	1.34	41,111	1.34
		10.76		**10.12**		**9.44**
Orkney	30,507	1.16	31,455	1.09	32,395	1.06
Zetland (Shetland)	30,558	1.17	31,078	1.08	31,670	1.03
		2.33		**2.17**		**2.09**

Source : National census data, quoted in RH Campell and JBA Dow (eds.) *Source Book of Scottish Economic and Social History* (Oxford, 1968), p.2 and insert 8.

was to be the railway companies centred upon Inverness in particular that were to benefit from the investment provided by several of these new landowners.

A parliamentary select committee met in March 1846 to begin examination of the proposals to build railways to Inverness. The town was known unofficially as the capital of the highlands and was recognised by the rival promoters as the key strategic centre for traffic to and from the highland region. Inverness interests were represented by the bills for the Perth and Inverness Railway, which proposed to construct a line from Nairn to Perth with a share capital of £1.4 million, and the Inverness and Elgin Railway, which sought powers to link the two towns of its title with a share capital of £350,000.[62] Since publishing their prospectuses, these two concerns had each increased their proposed share capital, the Perth and Inverness by £200,000 and the Inverness and Elgin by £50,000, and the companies had agreed an amalgamation.[63] Irrespective of any concerns about the forthcoming parliamentary decision on these two bills, the need to raise share capital of £1.75 million in the immediate aftermath of the great railway mania must have been a daunting prospect to the Inverness promoters as they faced the select committee.

Aberdeen interests were divided, but their proposals were equally expensive. The Great North of Scotland Railway, seeking powers to build a line from Aberdeen via Huntly, Elgin and Forres to Inverness, with four branches to coastal settlements on the Moray Firth, had raised its projected share capital from £1.1 million in its prospectus to £1.5 million in its bill.[64] Dissatisfaction with the route of the Great North of Scotland Railway resulted in the promotion of a rival scheme to link Aberdeen with Banff and Elgin, where an end-on junction with the proposed Inverness and Elgin Railway was planned.[65] The Aberdeen, Banff and Elgin Railway sought powers in its bill for share capital of

£1.2 million, slightly less than the £1.25 million in the prospectus, but *Bradshaw's Railway Gazette* reported In January 1846 that:

> … a serious difference has arisen among the proprietors of this line in regard to money matters, which is now in the Bill Chamber of the Court of Session, in the shape of a suspension.[66]

The Perth and Inverness and Great North had made an attempt to avoid an expensive parliamentary contest, but the tone of the conference between these rivals held at Elgin in October 1845 indicated the depth of division. The Perth and Inverness offered 'the most favourable terms' to the Great North to use their line to Inverness if that company would stop at Elgin: the Great North responded:

> This was wholly out of the question as the Great North of Scotland would on no account surrender this part of the Coast line …[67]

The response of the Perth and Inverness representatives clearly set the parameters for future relationships between Inverness and Aberdeen:

> The line between Elgin and Inverness fell naturally to be under the management of parties interested in the Northern Counties and that the assumption of it by parties in Aberdeen was an Act of aggression …[68]

Inverness wanted control of railways to and from the town and defended that strategic principle resolutely throughout the remainder of the century. The *Inverness Courier* continued to press the case for Elgin to be the limit of any Aberdonian advances towards the highland capital:

> It is clear that the Perth and Inverness Railway should secure the support of every individual

14

interested in the welfare of the northern counties ... we learn that the town council of Elgin have resolved to petition in favour of the Perth and Inverness Company. The town council of Inverness, and almost every parish along the line, have already done so. It is thus quite apparent that the local feeling is against our Aberdeen friends pushing their claims beyond Elgin.[69]

As the parliamentary select committee continued its scrutiny of the bills, it may have noted an observation contained in the 1845 report of the Railway Board of the Board of Trade, which had recommended the northern trunk route to Aberdeen that Parliament had already accepted. The Board, established in August 1844 to provide advice to Parliament on the burgeoning number of railway bills, was widely regarded as interference by the State in matters of private enterprise and it was abolished in July 1845 before it could report on the proposals for lines to Inverness.[70] But, in recommending approval of the Aberdeen Railway's bill in 1845, it had identified the possibility of a logical extension of the trunk route northwards from Aberdeen through an area that offered good potential for traffic:

The importance of this line [the Aberdeen Railway] is increased by the consideration that a cheap and easy line, traversing a district of considerable population and local traffic, is stated to have been surveyed between Aberdeen and Inverness. Should this be the case, it seems not impossible that railway communication to the more northern counties may be extended in this direction.[71]

By April 1846, when the select committee was hearing evidence from the rival promoters of Inverness lines, prices of railway shares had fallen sharply in the wake of the railway mania, but the market appeared to favour Great North shares over those of the rival Perth and Inverness. Great North shares, on which £2 10s deposit had been paid, were standing at £2 7s 6d, although they had reached £4 17s 6d in November 1845, whereas Perth and Inverness shares on which £2 10s had also been paid were quoted at only £1 5s.[72] *Railway Times*, however, pointed to the significance of the direct route proposed by the amalgamated Inverness and Elgin and Perth and Inverness companies to connect the highland capital with the south:

These lines now amalgamated may be regarded in a national point of view as some of the most important before Parliament. They carry on the direct communication from the capital to the shores of the Moray Firth. The occupation of the line from Inverness to Elgin is to be disputed in Parliament by the Great North of Scotland Company for forming a railway from Aberdeen to Inverness. The superior pretensions of the former amalgamated lines rest on the comparative shortness of the line to Perth ... [73]

Given the parliamentary approval of a trunk line from Carlisle via Stirling and Perth to Aberdeen and the observation made by the Railway Board that a continuous route onwards from Aberdeen to Inverness was being planned, the Great North's scheme to reach Inverness might have been expected to hold an advantage in the parliamentary deliberations. In the event, the decisions of the select committee on 12 May 1846 left the Great North as the sole contender. *Railway Times* reported:

A dense crowd was drawn together to hear the decision of the Perth and Inverness, and the Inverness and Elgin lines. Both were thrown overboard; the Perth and Inverness on the grounds of its gradients. The Committee have come to this conclusion, with reference to the proposed altitude and engineering character of the proposed Perth and Inverness line, as compare[d] with those of any other line actually competed and in operation.[74]

Significantly, the Committee emphasised that they were not 'giving any opinion against the formation of the Perth and Inverness line' should later experience of working railways show its feasibility:

Neither is it the intention of the Committee in any way to prejudice the question – whether if a line be constructed from Aberdeen to Inverness, the northern counties of Scotland are not entitled to the benefit of a second line from Perth to Nairn.[75]

The Aberdeen, Banff and Elgin bill was withdrawn the next day after the select committee intimated that 'they could not view it favourably, as it was not a through line', whereupon the Great North's bill was approved unopposed.[76] That decision not only realised the Railway Board's vision of a continuous railway route through Aberdeen to Inverness, but the State, in effect, awarded a new and large transport monopoly to Aberdeen, because the Deeside, the Alford Valley, and the Great North of Scotland (Eastern Extension) Railways, were also authorised in the same parliamentary session as the Great North.

All directors on the first board of the Aberdeen Railway were also board members of the Great North and they held absolute control of these three other companies as well. The close link between the Aberdeen and Great North companies was soon formalised. In March 1845, over a year before the Great North was incorporated, its provisional committee resolved that it 'may ultimately be considered desirable' to amalgamate with the Aberdeen Railway.[77] In May 1846, the Aberdeen Railway chairman James Hadden sought his shareholders' approval for a fusion of interests:

... when the proposed amalgamation of this Line with the Great North of Scotland Railway is carried into effect, the United Company will have the command of a most valuable and extensive field of railway enterprise which cannot fail to realize an ample return on the capital invested at no distant day.[78]

The amalgamation bill passed without opposition in 1847, but a clause in the Act specified that amalgamation could not take effect until half of the capital in

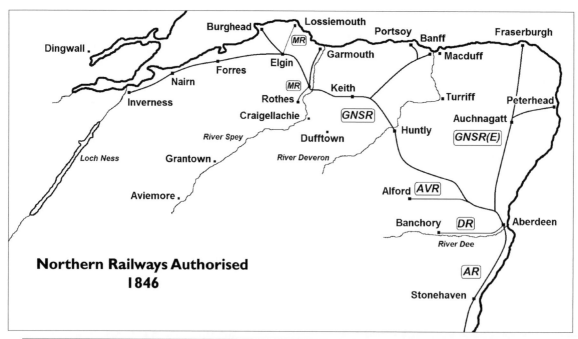

Northern Railways Authorised 1846

Key			
AR	Aberdeen Railway	GNSR(E)	Great North of Scotland (Eastern Extesion) Railway
AVR	Alford Valley Railway	MR	Morayshire Railway
DR	Deeside Railway	I&AJR	Inverness and Aberdeen Junction Railway

each company had been paid up.[79] This restriction inadvertently ensured that the amalgamation would never take place.

The 1846 parliamentary session which approved the Great North scheme also authorised the independent Morayshire Railway to link Lossiemouth harbour on the Moray Firth to Elgin and, by use of the Great North's line from Elgin to Orton, to extend from Orton to Rothes, thereby providing a northerly outlet from the Spey valley to the coast.[80] This little company was to play a significant part in later deliberations within the railway boardrooms of Aberdeen and Inverness.

In July 1846, *Railway Times* reported a meeting of the Perth and Inverness Railway which had voted unanimously to dissolve the company.[81] Deposits had been paid on 46,089 shares, but liabilities of £38,899 had to be met from receipts of £115,539, and so shareholders were to receive 33s 4½d for each of their shares, two thirds of the £2 10s deposit paid on each share. The committee of the Inverness and Elgin Junction Railway advertised the winding up of the company in May 1846, informing shareholders that they 'cannot at present form a correct estimate of the expenses incurred' but giving assurances that 'all amounts will be strictly scrutinized'.[82] The spirit of the Inverness and Elgin survived in the form of some unappropriated funds, which remained held in trust. Seven years later, when the Inverness and Nairn Railway was promoted as the first stage of a rejuvenated Invernessian plan to control the railways and traffic of northern Scotland, a minute of the provisional committee reveals that committee member Charles Waterston, who was manager of the Caledonian Bank and one of two trustees of these funds, had approved their release for the use of the new company.[83] The size of these funds, which probably comprised the remnants of unclaimed shareholder

deposits, is not known.

Although Parliament had rejected the plans of Inverness to establish a main railway route to Perth and the south, its promoters were at least spared the considerable headache of attempting to raise £1.75 million for construction of the Perth and Elgin lines from a capital market deserted by investors and where the direction in railway share prices was firmly downwards. The State had left open the future option of a direct route to the highland capital and the Inverness promoters, relieved of any immediate financial pressure, continued to plan to acquire control of railways in their district. The sharp division now evident in aspirations and policy between Inverness and Aberdeen was to dominate the future strategic planning of railways in the north.

THE GREAT NORTH'S PREDICAMENT

The Great North had won its parliamentary battle for powers to extend the northern trunk route to Inverness and now expected to channel the traffic of northern Scotland down its branches and main line into Aberdeen. The prospectus had forecast a dividend of 7%, although its provisional committee had been advised in March 1845 that 'upwards of 10%' could be expected.[84] Before any revenue could be earned, however, its directors faced the considerable challenge of constructing a main line of some 108 miles and an additional 30 miles of branch lines to Banff, Portsoy, Garmouth and Burghead, financed by capital powers to raise £1.5 million in shares and, once half the share capital was paid up, £0.5 million from debenture loans.

The prospectus had invited subscriptions during the heady days of the great railway mania. A meeting of the Great North's provisional committee on 31st March 1845 was informed that:

> ... exclusive of the London and Glasgow Lists (neither of which have yet been received), the number of applications is beyond 75,000, and the capital stock consisting of 22,000 shares there can be no doubt that a selection of a wealthy, and influential proprietary can be made from among the numerous applicants.[85]

The meeting elected a subcommittee of fifteen members to act as the first directors of the company and to allot the stock.[86] When these provisional directors met later that day, they discovered that the number of applications in fact exceeded 150,000 shares and, after examining the list, they resolved to meet on the following day to agree the allotment.

On 9th April, the *Aberdeen Courier* reported that 200,000 applications had been received for the 22,000 £50 shares, which illustrates the scale of demand for railway shares in this exceptional period.[87] The Great North was closely allied to the Aberdeen Railway at this time and, with a future amalgamation planned, the two boards remained closely inter-twined after incorporation.[88] Drawing upon recent experience of the Aberdeen Railway, where there had been a shortfall of payments on the shares allotted, the Great North's provisional directors allocated 27,776 shares, a quarter more than the 22,000 advertised in the prospectus 'so that deposits produce the sum of money required'.[89] The plan back-fired, and deposits were paid on 27,415 shares, almost all of those allotted. The proposed share capital in the prospectus of £1.1 million was subsequently raised to £1.5 million in the act of incorporation, which provided 8,000 more shares and legitimised the committee's dubious decision.[90]

The speculative frenzy in railway shares encouraged several of the Great North's promoters to participate, which subsequently added to the impending financial difficulties faced by the new company. Using bank loans to finance some of the deposits, a portion of the company's stock was held back by the promoters for themselves. A charitable view of this episode would suggest that the promoters had created a cautionary reserve, given the over-allocation of shares, but their actions left considerable scope for personal gain by selling the shares at a profit before any calls were made on them. Joseph Mitchell, engineer to the Inverness promoters, claimed that this sum amounted to £336,500, which equates to 6,730 £50 shares or almost a third of the shares advertised in the prospectus.[91] Of this amount, eight Great North directors subscribed for 3,400 shares (£170,000) and 2,130 shares (£106,500) were transferred to Adam and Anderson, the company's lawyers who subsequently became Great North directors following incorporation of the company. The remaining shares, according to Mitchell, were taken by the company secretary (500 shares, £25,000) and company agents (700 shares, £35,000).

Mitchell's account is partly supported by the records of one particular bank based in Aberdeen. In 1845, five directors of the North of Scotland Bank held £60,000 of local railway stock between them, although not all of this amount necessarily comprised Great North shares. William Adam held £10,000 of stock, Alexander Anderson £15,000, Thomas Blaikie £15,000, Alexander Jopp £10,000, and George Thompson £10,000, while the bank's manager, Henry Paterson, held a further £22,500.[92] All of these six individuals were also directors of both the Aberdeen and Great North of Scotland Railway and the £82,500 of railway stock held in their names represents over £42 million in current value. In the financial crisis of 1847-48, when the North of Scotland Bank lost over half its capital, it was discovered that bank funds had been drawn by some directors and the manager for individual speculation without giving or obtaining adequate security. Anderson, in particular, was found to have used large sums of bank money for various commercial activities with 'slender security', and Jopp, 'another fairly large debtor' and an associate of Anderson, is recorded as eventually redeeming his advances.[93] Unsurprisingly, Henry Paterson was replaced as manager of the North of Scotland Bank in 1848 by James Westland.

In May 1846, just over a year after the provisional directors had first met to apportion the company's stock, a meeting of holders of Great North scrip was held in Aberdeen. This scrip was about to be converted into shares because the Great North's bill received the Royal Assent the following month in June 1846. The 54 individuals present had paid the required 5% deposit of £2.10s on each of the 22,172 shares they held, and their combined holding represented four-fifths of the 27,766 shares allotted in 1845.[94] Of these 22,172 shares, Aberdeen addresses were given for 21,285 of them, which indicates that, after the great railway mania had subsided, Aberdonians held at least three quarters of the Great North's stock. Twelve of the fifteen provisional directors attended the meeting and their individual holdings totalled 8,420 shares, almost a third of the company's stock. Their deposits alone had cost £21,050, while the face value of these shares, on which they were committed to pay a further £47 10s for each share, amounted to £421,000. These very significant sums represent in current value over £1.2 million in deposits and £23 million in shares.

As the speculative bubble of the mania burst, demand for railway shares plummeted. Prices were quoted, but buyers were scarce and the market in railway capital froze. These Aberdonian shareholders, together with many other investors in railways throughout Britain, not only were unable to realise any profit, they lacked the funds to meet any calls made on their shares, and they could not sell the stock at a price to recoup their outlay. Consequently, the Great North of Scotland Railway was powerless to raise sufficient capital to begin construction of its lines until market circumstances improved. The dire economic conditions to which the highland region had already become accustomed had suddenly and unexpectedly hit the prosperous commercial centre of Aberdeen, presenting the newly constituted board of directors of the Great North of Scotland Railway with their first major financial crisis.

CHAPTER 5

THE ROUTE TO INVERNESS: THE GREAT NORTH'S PERSPECTIVE

The inaugural general meeting of shareholders of the Great North of Scotland Railway was held in Aberdeen in August 1846. The difficulties being experienced by its immediate neighbour, the Aberdeen Railway, in raising the necessary funds to complete its section of the northern trunk route were reported and, with the Great North's accounts showing that the company had already spent £18,436 more than it had received, the directors recommended shareholders 'to pause for a time':

> They have after maturely weighing this important subject come to the resolution that it is their duty to recommend to the shareholders to defer proceeding with the undertaking in the meantime until the works of the Aberdeen Railway, with which it is closely linked, shall have reached a more advanced stage.[95]

The Great North had paid dearly to obtain its parliamentary act. In the accounts for August 1846, four items alone accounted for nearly 10% of the company's expenditure of £161,852: £7,077 had been spent on parliamentary notices, £4,861 paid to parliamentary witnesses, £3,462 spent to meet the cost of deputations to London and almost £2,000 in specific payments to appease certain elements of opposition.[96] Furthermore, as the act had been granted only two months earlier, some costs remained to be paid and were not yet reflected in the accounts.

The company held powers to build a main line and branch system of some 140 miles that was expected to cost £1.5 million, yet when the parliamentary deposit required for railway bills was raised from 5% to 10% of proposed share capital in 1846, the Great North had to resort to borrowing £73,350 from the North of Scotland Bank via their law agents, Adam and Anderson.[97] It considered making a call on its shares to meet the increased cost but, in common with many other railway companies, saw little prospect of raising additional funds from its shareholders; its stock was virtually unsaleable on the depressed post-mania markets.

DISSENTION AND DIVISION IN ABERDEEN

The Great North was not alone in its financial troubles. A letter from 'HS of York', published in *Herapath's Railway Journal* in May 1847, summarised this widespread problem:

> ... if any man will take the trouble of ascertaining from a body of Railway Shareholders their means of paying their liabilities in the shares they hold, I have little doubt but his inquiries will correspond with the result of my own,

that not one in twenty-five are prepared to meet them ...the prospects of future demand is compelling them to send their shares into an already overstocked market at an awfully ruinous loss ...[98]

By the time the second general meeting of Great North shareholders was held in November 1847, the prospect of beginning the construction of the railway had not improved:

> In consequence of the continued embarrassment of mercantile affairs, the Directors were again induced to recommend a postponement of operations for another year ...[99]

Moreover, the development of the network of allied lines in and around Aberdeen that Parliament had approved in 1846 was also moribund. *Herapath's Railway Journal* reported:

> The Great North of Scotland Eastern Extension, Dee-side, and Alford Valley Railway Companies, all of which are immediately connected with the Aberdeen Railway, and chiefly belong to the same proprietors, met ... and resolved to postpone the commencement of their works until better times than the present.[100]

Great North shareholders agreed to take advantage of new parliamentary legislation to extend the period of time permitted for the construction of railway lines by two years, introduced because of national economic conditions.[101]

Financial pressures continued. The capital account showed a deficit of £20,420 in August 1848 and construction was again postponed. The Great North had agreed in 1845 to purchase the Aberdeenshire Canal for £36,000, intending to use part of its route for the new railway, but the board had to negotiate deferment of the payment due in April 1848 at a cost of 5½% annual interest because it had no funds available to complete the purchase.[102] The purchase price of the canal with interest amounting to £39,272 was finally paid almost six years later in February 1854.[103]

In December 1848, internal conflict erupted within the Aberdeen Railway which was to have a significant and long-lasting effect on the development of the railway system of northern Scotland. Three months earlier in September, the Aberdeen Railway had managed to open the first section of its line extending northwards from the Scottish Midland Junction Railway at Forfar as far as Montrose, but almost forty miles of the route remained to be completed to reach the projected terminus at Aberdeen. With the national economic depression and the great distrust of railway equity, it had taken three years to get this far but, during this time, the Aberdeen

Railway had found the calls made on its shares hard to obtain and loans increasingly expensive. Like many other British railway companies in similar predicaments, it attempted to raise new funds by converting unissued ordinary shares into preference stock.

Preference shares held some attraction for investors because the rate of dividend on them was fixed and was to be paid before any dividend was distributed on ordinary shares. This preferential position represented a prior claim on any available funds, but gave no guarantee that the specified dividend would be paid in full on the due date, as both Aberdeen shareholders and Great North shareholders were later to discover. The Aberdeen Railway gained approval in 1848 for a 6% preference stock and then in 1850 for a further stock at 7%.[104] These high rates of preferential return, at a time when bank discount rates fell from 4% in 1848 to 3% in 1850, indicate the desperation of the Aberdeen to obtain capital to complete its line.[105]

Although in serious financial difficulties, the Aberdeen Railway held parliamentary powers to build the important final section of the northern trunk route. The future of the company became the subject of competition between the west-coast and east-cost alliances as a means to establish their influence in northern Scotland. An offer from the London and North Western Railway and its allies was initially approved by the Aberdeen board in August 1848, but then in September the board accepted a more attractive offer from the Edinburgh and Northern Railway, backed by the east-coast companies.[106] The *Aberdeen Journal* wryly compared the Aberdeen's fate to that of a corpse:

> Competition hotted up towards the end of the year between the vultures waiting to seize the dying body of the Aberdeen Railway ... the Edinburgh and Northern backed by the North British and the notorious Hudson made an offer in October that topped the London and North Western Railway's earlier offer ...[107]

Aberdeen Railway shareholders accepted the Edinburgh and Northern's offer in October 1848, but dissatisfaction materialised at the half-yearly general meeting in November.[108] Not only was the validity of the share qualification of some of the directors challenged, the financial probity within the company was also questioned by James Spicer, representing a large group of English shareholders, and the meeting was adjourned until December.[109]

The Aberdeen Railway's board was split between support for the rival west-coast and east-coast offers, but the English shareholders preferred the company to retain its independence, seeing the potential for profit once the railway was finally completed. The large number of proxy votes held on behalf of the English shareholders ensured that the new board of directors proposed by Spicer was elected without a formal vote; only four of the original board were retained.[110] Significantly, all of the rejected Aberdeen directors also held seats on the board of the Great North of Scotland Railway, amongst whom was Sir James Elphinstone who was found to be without the requisite number of

shares to qualify as an Aberdeen director even though he held office as its deputy chairman.[111] *Railway Times* was incredulous at the outcome of the Aberdeen shareholders' meeting, especially as the struggling Aberdeen had been thrown two financial lifelines by the prominent English alliances and accepted neither:

> How a squabble amongst the Directors ... should have occasioned so disastrous a disruption, we can by no means make clear. The line is stopped, and literally "rotting" for want of funds ... The Company is in the most serious difficulties. Indeed, at this moment, we are not aware whether it is solvent or not ...[112]

The factional dissent, previously contained within the Aberdeen Railway boardroom, now flared into open animosity between the board of the Great North of Scotland and the newly-elected board of the Aberdeen. One immediate result was the abandonment of the authorised amalgamation between the two companies. In November 1849, the new board of the Aberdeen Railway advised its shareholders of their intent:

> At the time the Act was obtained, the Directors of both Companies were the same, with one or two exceptions – the circumstances of both Companies were similar, and the arrangement was gone into in the belief that, from the intimate connection of the two Lines, it would be for their mutual advantage were they carried out, and wrought as one undertaking. The circumstances in which the Companies are now placed are very different – nothing has been done towards the formation of the Great North Line, while the Aberdeen Line is nearly finished ... it does not appear to your Directors that there are any advantages secured to you by the Amalgamation Act, which would not equally accrue on the completion of the Great North Line ... your Directors have included in the Parliamentary notice an intimation of the intention to apply for a Repeal of the Act accordingly.[113]

The parliamentary notice to which the Aberdeen's directors referred was for a bill to raise further capital, despite the additional capital powers already granted in the previous year. The Great North board therefore justified the divorce to its shareholders as a means to distance itself from the Aberdeen's persistent financial troubles:

> By the Amalgamation Act the two Companies become consolidated as soon as the one half of the Capital of each is paid up and expended on the respective lines, and hence any increase of Capital of the Aberdeen Company so long as the Amalgamation Act is in force would become a burden on this Company. But as your directors are satisfied that the repeal of this act would facilitate the obtaining [of] funds for the construction of the works, and be otherwise advantageous for this company, they have no hesitation in recommending the shareholders to consent to its repeal.[114]

The act of amalgamation was duly repealed by Parliament in 1850.[115] Relationships between the two companies oscillated thereafter between periods of detached indifference and resolute opposition for almost two decades. This serious division was to prove detrimental to the interests of the people and the economy of northern Scotland.

A HESITANT START

Economic conditions began to improve in 1849, indicated by the fall in bank discount rates to 2½%. The Great North directors saw an opportunity to begin construction of their railway as other lines promoted in the speculation of 1845-46 were completed and contractors began to seek new work:

> … a large amount of the capital, skill, and plant, which had been employed in their construction was, or would shortly be, unemployed and that an opportunity might then be afforded for the formation of this Line on very favourable terms …[116]

The board still faced the difficult task of raising the necessary capital from existing and new shareholders. Only £71,242 had been raised by August 1849, after £73,350 had been paid to the company's law agents, Adam and Anderson, to recover shares issued against the loan negotiated from the North of Scotland Bank in 1846, and the deficit on the capital account was balanced by a bank overdraft of £21,284.[117] The liabilities of the Great North in March 1849 exceeded its assets by £8,275, but the directors decided to seek tenders and begin construction so that the anticipated future revenue to be earned from operating the railway could be used to repay its debts.[118] Significantly, the construction tender included the option of building no further than Keith, just half the distance between Aberdeen and Inverness and, by containing costs, the directors expected to open 54 miles of single line to Keith for £470,000.[119] The contract for construction was finally signed in March 1851.[120]

The majority of the Great North's directors had already experienced the serious consequences of unrealistic estimates made for construction and land costs during their earlier appointments as directors of the Aberdeen Railway. Accordingly, Sir James Elphinstone, who replaced Provost Thomas Blaikie as chairman of the Great North in April 1849, sought the agreement of landowners to accept either a feu duty, an annual sum payable in respect of a grant of land, or the price in company shares for the land required in order to avoid expensive capital expenditure.[121] In December 1851, *Railway Times* reported the expected annual cost of feu duties payable by the Great North to landowners:

> The land is now to be had at a yearly ground rent, by which it will be acquired at the average rate of £2 an acre. The rent per mile will thus be £16 … The rent of the whole 50 miles, taken in this way, amounts to £800 per annum.[122]

Before giving possession of their land, however, landowners sought assurances that the line would be completed and banks refused further advances to the Great North without guarantees of construction.[123] The Duke of Richmond was the largest landowner in the district to be served by the Great North and when he agreed to take £15,000 of stock, other landowners were prompted to provide a further £10,000.[124]

The Great North then gained parliamentary approval in 1851 to re-structure the capital of the company, converting the former £50 shares on which £2 10s deposit had been paid into £10 ordinary shares, creating 83,058 new 5% preference shares at £10 each, and reducing the share capital of the company from £1,500,000 to £1,107,440.[125] This preference dividend was attractive in comparison to the bank discount rate of 2½% prevailing in 1852, yet only 4,000 preference shares had been sold by September of that year although applications for at least a further 3,000 were expected.[126] By August 1853, capital receipts totalled £188,210, of which half had been raised from this new preference stock.

The Great North desperately needed new capital, but a proposal made in 1852 to the Great Northern, the York and North Midland, and the North British Railways for an investment of £150,000 in the Great North in return for a guaranteed dividend and the direction of traffic via the east-coast route was unsuccessful.[127] Despite the antagonism generated in 1848-49, an approach was also made that same year to the Aberdeen Railway, which commissioned two of its directors 'to examine into the position of the affairs of the Great North of Scotland Railway Company'.[128] The Aberdeen was anxious to attract traffic from the north of Scotland onto its own line and it therefore criticised the Great North's proposals to build only to Keith and to defer the construction of a link between the two railways at Aberdeen:

> The want of a junction with the Aberdeen Line would be an entire bar to the interchange of traffic, while Keith, as the Northern terminus, would not, by any means, secure for the Railway the Traffic from the Northern Counties … it should extend, at the outset, from the junction with the Aberdeen Railway to Burghead where, opening upon the sea at a very convenient harbour, it would at once secure the large traffic from the extensive coasts on both sides of the Moray Firth.[129]

The Aberdeen directors suggested that 'the Line from Elgin to Inverness does not appear to be so essential in the meantime, to the success of the undertaking …', a view which was most unlikely to meet with approval from the residents of the highland capital, but they did express their opinion that 'if the necessary funds could be obtained, the continuation to Inverness would be very desirable'. The cost of a line from Aberdeen to Burghead was estimated to be £900,000, but with only £399,000 of the Great North's share capital taken, the Aberdeen directors advised the Great North not to begin construction with less than £750,000 in capital.[130] Any recommendation of financial support for the line from the Aberdeen company was to be conditional upon acceptance by the Great North of the larger scheme.

The 1846 parliamentary powers granted to the Great North had been extended for two years in 1848 and remained valid until 1853. The Great North board approved a new prospectus in November 1852 for a line to run from Aberdeen to Elgin at an amended cost of £750,000, but the directors reported that capital was available to build only half that distance.[131] A northern terminus at Elgin would at least provide the Great North with a link to the Moray Firth coast over the independent Morayshire Railway, which opened its short line between Elgin and the port of Lossiemouth in August 1852. But the Great North's directors had to advise their shareholders that, while they might wish to build to Elgin, resources were only sufficient for 'construction of a line from Kittybrewster to Huntly with the prospect of a speedy connection to Keith'.[132]

The Aberdeen board made their response in an open letter to the press, stating that they could not recommend the proposed Great North scheme.[133] The divorce between the Aberdeen and Great North thus became absolute, but Great North chairman Sir James Elphinstone re-assured his shareholders and anticipated a return of 7% on the capital outlay:

> ... this is almost the only Railway in Great Britain on which there is a monopoly of the traffic of the district through which it passes. We can have no sea competition, and must carry the whole of the traffic of the country ...[134]

Construction of the line between Kittybrewster and Huntly finally began in the summer of 1852. In November 1853, when the directors reported that the line was almost complete, Great North shareholders approved a recommendation from the board to seek powers to divert the route of their authorised, but unconstructed, line southwards from Kittybrewster, instead to follow the path of the Aberdeenshire Canal for just under two

miles to Victoria docks at Aberdeen.[135] The resulting act of Parliament for this 'short branch' indicated an estimated cost of £40,000, much more than the £10,000 that was suggested to shareholders.[136] From the time of the parliamentary contest in 1846, the Great North had been expected to construct a continuous line across Aberdeen to make a connection with the Aberdeen Railway and the trunk route southwards, but divisions of opinion between the Great North and Aberdeen over a junction had remained unresolved.[137] The Great North board justified its decision to construct the line to what became known as the Waterloo terminus by explaining that 'construction of the line through Aberdeen ... must take some time to complete'.[138]

By the time the line opened to Huntly in September 1854, the Great North had raised £485,946 from the sale of shares, but had spent £518,232, leaving a deficit on the capital account of £32,286. Its powers to construct the line to Inverness had expired and rival promoters in Inverness were preparing a parliamentary bill to build a fifteen mile line from Inverness eastwards to Nairn.[139] This new incursion from Inverness into its perceived territory did not arouse major concern in Aberdeen. The Nairn line and a projected extension eastwards was intended to connect to the Great North to complete the through route between Aberdeen and Inverness and so any traffic from the northern counties would still flow down the railway into Aberdeen, but without the need for the impecunious Great North to find new capital. To protect its future interests, the Great North made a draft agreement for running rights over the Inverness and Nairn Railway in 1854 in return for withdrawing its opposition to the Inverness company's bill in Parliament.[140] Through oversight, intrigue or naivety on both sides, that agreement was never formally completed with the result that the Great

OPENING OF THE GREAT NORTH OF SCOTLAND RAILWAY.—THE HUNTLY STATION.

The opening of the Great North of Scotland Railway to Huntly in 1854, as seen through the eyes of the Illustrated London News.
(Keith Fenwick collection)

North was denied its own access into Inverness for the rest of the century.[141]

When the Inverness and Aberdeen Junction Railway was promoted in 1855 to extend the newly-authorised Nairn line eastwards, the Great North agreed that the new company might extend from Nairn as far east as Keith, rather than to Elgin as originally projected in 1854. It saw advantage in investing £40,000 in the new company, primarily to fund the section of the line between Keith and the Spey viaduct, but, by the appointment of two representatives to the board of the Inverness and Aberdeen Junction, the Great North ensured that its interests were represented in Inverness.[142] Great North chairman, Sir James Elphinstone, explained to his shareholders:

> '... I am happy to say that the Inverness company had, within the last few days, definitively proposed to construct the line to Keith from Inverness, provided the Great North company agreed to hold stock to the extent of £40,000 in their undertaking. This arrangement ... will relieve us of having anything to do with crossing the Spey, a matter of vast importance ...[143]

That 'matter of vast importance' was the absence of any resources within the Great North for immediate and expensive expansion. In May 1854, four months before its line opened to Huntly, the company had assets of £434,453 but liabilities of £573,856.[144] That same month, the North of Scotland Bank made a temporary loan of £64,000 to the Great North conditional upon the company's assurance that no extension would be made beyond Huntly without the consent of the bank whilst any of that loan was outstanding.[145] The bank also required a deposit of 10,000 £10 preference shares as

security, the face value of which exceeded the amount of the loan by over fifty percent. Just three months later, the Great North sought a further loan from the North of Scotland Bank for £50,000, using the company's rolling stock as security.[146] Such were the financial constraints on the Great North prior to opening that director John Stewart revealed to shareholders that the board had been prepared to allow the Inverness promoters to push even further eastwards:

> Had the gentlemen who were proposing the line from Nairn to Elgin given any indication that they would meet the Great North Railway at Huntly, the Directors of that line would not have offered the smallest opposition to the Inverness company.[147]

TOWARDS PROSPERITY

Once the line opened to Huntly, the financial prospects of the Great North improved. Although the company reported a deficit of £32,286 on its capital account to August 1854, it was now able to generate revenue from transporting passengers and goods over the new line. After the first year of operation, the company produced a reassuring revenue surplus of £15,102 and paid 1½% dividend on its ordinary shares.[148]

The Great North obtained powers in 1855 to extend its line by just over twelve miles from Huntly to Keith, where it was to connect with the newly-authorised Inverness and Aberdeen Junction Railway.[149] The estimated cost of the extension was £80,000, but new capital powers were not required because those contained in the company's parliamentary acts of 1846 and 1851 had anticipated construction of the complete

Keith Station around 1912, looking along the Highland Railway platform towards the Great North side of the station. It had originally been designed to accommodate extension of the line towards Elgin, with the main roof over what would have been two through platforms. However, by the time the Inverness & Aberdeen Junction Railway was built, it was provided with just a single platform, seen on the left, which was built in place of the original carriage shed. This arrangement survived until the late 1960s. Since then, the station has been completely rebuilt and only the former through platform survives.   (L&GRP)

line from Aberdeen to Inverness. When the Great North opened to Keith in October 1856, it had built just half of the main line and none of the branches that it was originally authorised to construct, but the cost had reached £846,318 by August 1857, sixty percent of the revised share and loan capital of £1.4 million authorised in the 1851 Act. Although this figure was eighty percent above the directors' estimate of £470,000 given in 1849 for a line between Aberdeen and Keith, it indicates a capital cost of just under £16,000 per mile, including operating plant and the cost of purchasing the Aberdeenshire Canal, much less than the average cost of Scottish lines which, six years earlier in 1851, had been £32,113 per mile.[150]

The Great North had failed to realise its ambitious railway scheme approved in 1846, but, as a consequence, it had retained unused capital powers which remained available for the further development of the company. At the general meeting of shareholders held in October 1855, chairman Sir James Elphinstone announced the commencement of services to the new terminus alongside the docks in Aberdeen:

> Within the last month they had opened their canal branch for goods traffic, and the goods of the district connected with the Great North of Scotland were now carried down to the quay at Aberdeen.[151]

The Great North commenced passenger services from its new Aberdeen terminus at Waterloo in April 1856 following an inspection of the line by the Board of Trade.[152] Its former ally, the Aberdeen Railway, had extended its line from Ferryhill into the town to a new terminus at Guild Street in 1854, but a physical gap of half-a-mile existed between the two stations and only a very basic connection for goods was eventually provided via a horse-drawn tramway along the dock quays.[153] With these difficulties in the transhipment of goods between the two railway companies, the commencement of Great North services to Waterloo provided some stimulus to steam shipping from Aberdeen to the south.[154] In 1859-60, the Great North also resorted to subsidising steamships of the Inverness

and Edinburgh Steam Packet Company to run to ports on the south and north coasts of the Moray Firth, but a loss of £4,910 was sustained by June 1860 and the support was withdrawn.[155]

The increasing flow of northern traffic steadily strengthened the Great North's finances. Gross annual revenue of £46,368 was reported in August 1856, two months before the extended line opened to Keith, which rose to £69,468 in 1859 after the Inverness link was completed, a rise of fifty percent (table 2). By 1861, gross annual revenue reached £89,895, a further rise of almost thirty percent. As a result, dividend on ordinary shares rose from 2¼% in 1856 to 5% in 1859 and 6¾% in 1861.

After ten years of financial tribulation, the shareholders of the Great North had entered a period of considerable prosperity. In April 1862, *Herapath's Railway Journal* commended the progress that the Great North had made:

> … this high rate of dividend does not arise from any great stream of traffic. It arises from great economy in the management, particularly the capital account.[156]

There was no significant competition by land transport to the Great North, but its new-found prosperity was fragile. A projected trunk route of over one hundred miles authorised in 1846 had shrunk to an isolated rural line of some fifty miles. Its rising revenue was largely dependent on the flow of traffic to and from the north of Scotland, but which also had to pass over the metals of two Inverness-based railway companies. With no continuous railway link across Aberdeen and a terminus established at the docks, the use of sea transport for much of the Great North's traffic to the south progressively fuelled resentment within the Aberdeen Railway and its southern allies. These companies had expected to benefit from this new flow of northern trade, only to see it captured by their seafaring rivals. These fateful circumstances were to make a decisive contribution to the future financial collapse of the Great North of Scotland Railway.

Table 2: Capital and revenue data, Great North of Scotland Railway, 1854–61

Capital (£)	August 1854	August 1855	August 1856	August 1857	August 1858	July 1859	July 1860	July 1861
Capital raised	485,946	582,742	733,765	816,652	865,145	947,928	1,127,929	1,128,804
Balance	- 32,285	- 42,569	- 14,558	- 29,665	- 42,077	- 38,296	+ 86,784	+ 49,258
Capital spent	518,232	625,312	748,323	846,318	907,223	986,225	1,041,144	1,079,546
General Balance Sheet								
Due to bankers		41,244	5,983	13,840	50,837	33,652	34,703	70,985
Revenue (annual) (£)								
Gross revenue		34,123	46,368	59,751	63,201	69,468	84,603	89,895
Gross expenditure		19,021	21,500	27,083	27,253	40,976	40,502	37,557
Surplus		15,102	24,868	32,668	35,948	28,492	44,101	52,338
Dividend								
Half year to January							6%	6½%
Half year to July							7%	7%
Annual dividend		1½%	2¼%	4½%	4½%	5%	6½%	6¾%

Source: National Archives of Scotland, BR/GNS/1/1-9 and BR/RAC(S)/1/14).
Notes: (1): In 1859; the reporting period was adjusted to July rather than August; half-year reports began in 1860.
(2): Shillings and pence have been rounded down and so totals may not match precisely the sum of component items.

CHAPTER 6

THE ROUTE FROM ABERDEEN: THE INVERNESS PERSPECTIVE

A pocket-sized guide book to the new Great North of Scotland Railway was published in 1854 by the Provost of Banff. In its introduction, Provost Ramsey reminded his readers of the financial difficulties the Great North had faced:

> The Great North of Scotland line was projected during the period of the great railway agitation, and after competition with the Aberdeen, Banff and Elgin Company, an Act was, at considerable expense, obtained in 1846 ... prudential considerations have induced the Directors, with the approval of the Shareholders, to construct, in the first instance, only the portion from Aberdeen to Huntly.[157]

Reactions in Inverness were less sympathetic. The 'prudential considerations' in Aberdeen, to which Provost Ramsey tactfully referred, had left the highland capital almost 70 miles distant from the new railhead at Huntly, eight years after Parliament had approved powers for the Great North to connect Aberdeen with Inverness. Joseph Mitchell, who had seen his plans for a direct line from Inverness to Perth rejected in Parliament in 1846, later wrote that the slow progress of the Great North was seen as 'giving little hope to the northern counties of obtaining railway communication even by Aberdeen'.[158] With the prospect of opposition from the Great North to the Inverness and Nairn Railway's bill in Parliament, the Inverness newspapers were scathing of the Great North's inability to build the full line:

> These parties have for eight years had an act for giving the public railway accommodation to Inverness. They had not used their powers. They have kept others, by pre-occupation, out of the field. (*Inverness Advertiser*, 7 February 1854)

> They [the Great North] have proved an incubus on social progress in this quarter ... They can qualify for no right of interference with the internal concerns of the northern counties ... (*Inverness Courier*, 19 February 1854)

OLD AND NEW HIGHLAND CAPITAL

Ironically, the growing prosperity of the Great North from the mid 1850s was due in part to the long-held ambition of the railway promoters in Inverness to develop their own system of lines for the benefit of the highland region, for it was their enterprise which provided the railway link between Inverness and the Great North's terminus at Keith. Supporters of the rejected Perth and Inverness Railway in 1846 had already recognised the scope to improve the economy of the whole of northern Scotland by constructing railways:

> It is not Inverness, or Nairn, or Elgin, which is to be regarded as its terminus. The northern terminus ... is the whole of those vast districts to the north and west of the Spey.[159]

The difficulties of capital supply which had caused severe delays in the construction of the Great North's line from Aberdeen did not pass unnoticed in Inverness, despite the outward criticism of that company's dilatory progress. New northern lines would require substantial local finance and strict economy in construction. As plans for the short local line between Inverness and Nairn were outlined to the public, engineer Joseph Mitchell explained the intent and urged highlanders not to miss the present opportunity to shape and direct the future railway network of northern Scotland:

> I do not mean to say that the works on the Inverness and Nairn will not be perfect, but we are not to have a railway with the expensive works and appurtenances of the London and Birmingham for carrying the Nairn traffic.

> I know there is ample means in the country to make the line, and I should be sorry if one farthing of the stock was taken out of the district, because I believe shares in this line will ultimately be of great value.

> I am anxious that they should have the management of their own line of communication to and from Inverness, as it is the first step for extending our commerce ... You have the chance now of securing the management of the whole railway communication of the north. If you lose it this year, you may never have such an opportunity again.[160]

Mitchell cogently advocated the principles of the cheap railway, already successfully adopted in America and Canada. These 'cheap railway' principles might include a less direct route following the natural topography of the district, the lease of land rather than its outright purchase, single line operation and a scale of construction matched to the anticipated traffic. He maintained that Scotland could learn from the American experience:

> The extent of railway enterprise in America does not appear to be fully understood in this country otherwise the north of Scotland would not be at this day unprovided with railway communication.[161]

Mitchell quoted statistics to show that 10,921 miles of railway were in operation in America in 1851 with a further 7,560 miles under construction, but achieved at an average cost of £5,500 per mile including operating plant. He suggested that, using similar principles, the direct line from Inverness to Perth could be constructed for £7,000 per mile and yield a 5% return on the capital invested. This projected figure was a mere fraction of the average cost of Scottish railways, which in 1851 was £32,113 per mile, albeit slightly less than the £38,258 per mile expended in England.[162] The economical ambitions of the Inverness promoters were commended by *Railway Times*:

> ... they arrive at the conclusion that it would be profitless to construct a line at £35,000 per mile, when one at £5,500 is sufficient ... More inquiry, closer investigation, reduced estimates, new allies, avoidance of offence with existing interest – these are the means of progress which they use ...[163]

With a sparse population living and working in a largely agricultural economy throughout the northern counties of Scotland, large landowners afforded the most likely source for the substantial amounts of local capital needed for new northern lines. The benefits that railways had brought to landowners elsewhere in Britain were identified by *Herapath's Railway Journal*:

> We are satisfied that there is not a landed estate traversed by a railway which is not greatly enhanced in value by being placed in the course of a great public thoroughfare.[164]

Established landowners were well represented on northern railway boards from the 1850s, often by their commissioners, in particular the Hon Thomas Charles Bruce for the Earl of Seafield, William James Tayler for the Earl of Fife and George Loch for the Duke of Sutherland, but not all highland railway investment came from aristocratic roots. Two notable supporters of highland lines, for example, had earned their wealth elsewhere and were symbolic of the new type of landowner buying property in the highlands.[165]

James Merry was a wealthy coal and ironmaster from central Scotland who had helped to finance the Monkland and Kirkintilloch Railway, the first railway north of the border to use locomotives and which opened in 1826. He bought the Belladrum estate near Beauly to the west of Inverness in 1857 and was the Member of Parliament for Falkirk.[166] Merry became a substantial investor in Inverness railway companies and joined the board of the Inverness and Perth Junction Railway in 1864, subsequently serving on the board of the Highland Railway.

Alexander Matheson, who became chairman of the Inverness and Aberdeen Junction and Inverness and Ross-shire companies and later chairman of the Highland Railway, was the senior partner in the international trading firm of Jardine-Matheson from 1842. From 1847 to 1884, he was both a director of the Bank of England and a Member of Parliament, first for Inverness Burghs from 1847 until 1868 and then for Ross-shire until 1884.[167] He acquired considerable wealth from far-eastern trade and bought the Ardross estate near Invergordon in 1846 and the Lochalsh estate

Alexander Matheson, later baronet of Lochalsh, from a photograph in 'The Iron Track through the Highlands' by JE Campbell.

in the north-west highlands in 1851. Matheson spent over £1,460,000 in the purchase and improvement of his 220,000 acres of land in Ross-shire, a sum equivalent to at least £73 million in current value, and has been aptly described as:

> ... an individual of colossal wealth who lavished expenditure on his estates and in the process helped to subsidise the local economy from the profits of trade earned in distant and exotic parts of the world.[168]

Ten individuals alone ultimately provided £761,118 for highland railway schemes, over £38 million in current value, ninety-four percent of which came from just five northern landowning sources: £355,545 from the Duke of Sutherland and a further £100,000 from three members of his family, £73,370 from the Earl of Seafield, £73,623 from Alexander Matheson, £85,000 from James Merry and £26,500 from Eneas W Mackintosh of Raigmore, Inverness.[169] Mackintosh was a particularly long serving director of the Inverness railway companies: he was named as a first director of the Inverness and Nairn Railway in the parliamentary act of 1854, held seats on the boards of all four of the Inverness railway web companies prior to the formation of the Highland Railway in 1865, on which he then served as a director until 1897, including a period between 1891 and 1896 as its chairman. Without the very substantial local investment, exemplified by these large sums supplied by both old and new landowners, it is doubtful whether many of the railways in northern Scotland would ever have been built.

Tentative Steps: The Inverness and Nairn Railway

By 1853, trade and economic conditions in Britain had improved. With the Great North's line still to open to Huntly and the lapse in their powers to build the railway through to Inverness, the Inverness promoters resurrected their scheme for a network of lines centred on Inverness. A delegation was appointed to canvass major English companies, reviving the 1846 plans for a direct line south via Nairn to Perth, an eastern extension to Elgin and a branch to Burghead. Drawing upon data compiled for the unsuccessful 1846 parliamentary bill, engineer Joseph Mitchell and Inverness solicitor Peter Anderson produced a new estimate of £1,735,979 for a scheme encompassing 156 miles of single line railway but including sufficient land to allow for a future double track, although they anticipated that 'the above stated cost may be considerably reduced' as a result of economy in construction and the 'better feeling that exists on the part of landed proprietors'.[170] Mitchell and Anderson's report emphasised that the success of the scheme depended upon landowners 'doing all in their power to bring the cost within a reasonable compass':

> ... the great majority of them are most favourable, and are disposed to give their moor land gratis, the arable land for its bare agricultural value, without any allowance for severance and generally, if wished, to commute the price into a moderate fixed [feu] duty.[171]

The delegation, comprising Mitchell, Anderson and Mackintosh, met the eminent engineer Joseph Locke and contractor Thomas Brassey, and representatives of the London and North Western, York, Newcastle and Berwick and Great Northern Railways.[172] Mitchell recalled that Locke and Brassey had 'urged us to get the proprietors along the line to show practical evidence of their willingness to give the land required on advantageous terms'.[173] Anderson later confirmed in a letter to the Great Northern Railway the promoters' intention to secure landowner agreements in advance of seeking parliamentary powers and to pursue the 'utmost practicable economy' in a re-survey of the route, but the advice of the English companies to the delegation was unequivocal: '... the present was not the proper moment to bring a great measure of this sort before the public ...'.[174]

Despite this apparent set-back, the *Inverness Advertiser* re-iterated the Inverness ambition for a railway to Perth, whilst keeping the Great North at a distance from the highland capital:

> We are glad to hear that the formation of the Aberdeen line proceeds apace; but Elgin is its proper and natural terminus ... To run a direct line of railway betwixt Inverness and Perth, and thus beget the necessity of an extension northwards would be like infusing the breath of new life into the Highlands.[175]

The delegation reported to a public meeting in Inverness in April 1853, called to support plans for a direct line to the south. Provost Sutherland cautioned the

Peter Anderson, as portrayed in 'An Inverness Lawyer and his Sons, 1796-1878', by Isabel Harriet Anderson.

audience about extravagance in railway construction, quoting Aytoun's *Glenmutchkin* parody of 1845, but he pointed to the advantage of the Perth route:

> The direct line was decidedly the line which was most wanted ... and there was no other line by which a man could breakfast in London, dine in Edinburgh and go to bed in Inverness.[176]

Without southern capital, however, the promoters accepted the English advice against promoting the Perth route immediately. Instead, Inverness converted its broad aspiration into practical action by promoting the short fifteen mile line from Inverness to Nairn, ostensibly as a contribution towards a connection with the Great North, but in reality the first stage towards securing control of railway development in the highlands and an independent route to the south. Inverness was to be the hub of a web of railways serving the highland region. An early guide book to the Inverness and Nairn Railway by George and Peter Anderson explained the place of the line in the greater plans of the promoters:

> ... it remained for those who were still persuaded of the capabilities of the Northern Highlands for railway enterprise to depart from their original design as a whole, and to endeavour to get it carried out piecemeal, and from stage to stage, as circumstances would permit. For this purpose, and with the view of securing the west end of the line next Inverness as a common centre and connecting link in the future development of the railway system throughout the northern counties, an independent company was formed for the construction of a line from Inverness to Nairn ...[177]

The promoters of the Inverness and Nairn Railway suggested that the next priority was to extend eastwards from Nairn to Elgin and Huntly to provide a link to Aberdeen, although a northern extension to Dingwall and Tain was also anticipated.[178] The *Inverness Advertiser* supported this policy of gradual extension:

> A bit by bit advance is the safest and most certain method ... Short lines, a resident proprietary, and a local management, are the noticeable elements of any plan for giving us railway profits and railway extension ...[179]

The prospectus for the Nairn line proposed capital of £85,000 and estimated the cost at £5,500 per mile, although authorised share capital in the parliamentary bill was set slightly lower at £80,000.[180] A subscription list for January 1854 shows the distinctly local and small-scale nature of individual investment in the railway. One fifth of the subscribers held only one or two £10 shares each and just over one half held five shares or fewer. Over three-fifths of the 213 subscribers listed gave addresses in Inverness or Nairn, but only fourteen were registered in England.[181] Alexander Matheson joined the provisional committee in November 1853, initially subscribing £1,000, although at the shareholders' meeting held in April 1857 Inverness and Nairn chairman Eneas Mackintosh referred to him as the largest shareholder in the Nairn company.[182]

This pattern of local shareholding was maintained after the Inverness and Nairn Railway was amalgamated with the Inverness and Aberdeen Junction Railway, when its ordinary shares were converted into a preference stock at an attractive dividend of 6%.[183] In July 1864, just one year before the formation of the Highland Railway, £59,242 of this former Inverness and Nairn ordinary stock remained extant. Of the 147 registered holders, sixteen (11%) held just one or two shares and forty-eight (33%) held five shares or fewer, while in contrast ten shareholders (7%) held one hundred shares or more.

The Inverness and Nairn Railway opened to traffic in November 1855 and later that month *Herapath's Railway Journal* commented on the promising amount of passenger traffic that had been carried:

> This line has been open for only passenger traffic, but in that capacity had been far more successful than the most sanguine supporter of the scheme could have anticipated ... Every train has been crowded ... and on Thursday last the Company were obliged to press all the carriages in their possession into the service, and still could not fully accommodate all who wanted seats.[184]

The Inverness and Nairn existed as an independent company for only six years, but it produced increasing returns for its shareholders (table 3). Annual gross revenue grew steadily from £6,541 in September 1856 to reach £10,471 in August 1859 after the through line to Aberdeen had been in operation for a year, and then rose further to £12,652 in August 1860 prior to amalgamation with its partner, the Inverness and Aberdeen Junction

Railway, in May 1861. The first dividend of 2% paid for the half year to February 1856 reached 5% for the same half year of 1860.[185]

The seasonal nature of northern traffic was immediately evident. In January 1856, for example, the average gross traffic receipts were £120 per week, but these almost doubled in August, yielding £226 per week.[186] Similar variations between winter and summer traffic were experienced by railway companies throughout northern Scotland; this had a marked effect on the level of dividend that could be paid in each half year and, in some cases, resulted in dividends being paid annually rather than half-yearly.

The economic success of this short, isolated line, reflected in its consistent payment of dividends, was attributed by *Railway Times* to:

> ... careful and energetic management – careful alike in keeping down expenditure, and in abstaining from exclusive arrangements, and energetic in so far as speedy completion of works and rapid development of local resources can be controlled by directorial supervision.[187]

Herapath's Railway Journal also emphasised importance of economical construction, but openly assigned the designation of a trunk railway to this short, local line, recognising that it represented the first stage of a more grandiose scheme for railways in northern Scotland:

> From the working of the first few months since its opening ... this cheap Scottish trunk railway pays (beyond the interest on the borrowed capital) as dividend on the ordinary stock of the Company and at the rate of 2% per annum. This is another and important instance of the economical construction of railways. Made at the usual rate of cost, the Inverness and Nairn would have been as to dividend a dead failure.[188]

Nevertheless, in common with earlier lines in Scotland and England, the Inverness and Nairn Railway encountered substantial increases in its expected costs and, by September 1857, the actual cost of the line including rolling stock had reached £8,003 per mile, almost fifty percent above the estimate of £5,500 advertised in the prospectus, but still a fraction of the costs of earlier Scottish railways.[189] The provisional

Table 3: Capital and revenue data, Inverness and Nairn Railway, 1854–61

Capital (£)	September 1856	September 1857	August 1858	August 1859	August 1860	February 1861 (half year)
Capital raised	79,525	93,133	113,173	119,467	121,649	126,271
Balance	- 36,543	- 26,907	+ 5,175	+ 5,721	+ 1,992	+ 1,359
Capital spent	116,068	120,041	107,997	113,745	119,657	124,912
Interest on temporary loans				113	112	31
Revenue (annual) (£)						
Gross revenue	6,541	8,,964	8,784	10,471	12,652	5,509
Gross expenditure	4,890	8,025	6,936	7,895	9,259	Amalgamated
Surplus	1,651	939	1,848	2,576	3,393	May, 1861
Dividend						
Half year to February	2%	0%	-	3½%	5%	5%
Half year to August	2½%	4%	4%	4½%	5½%	(6% preference)

Sources: National Archives of Scotland, BR/INR/1/1-2; *Herapath's Railway Journal*, 1856-58.
Note: Shillings and pence have been rounded down and so totals may not match precisely the sum of component items.

committee had been assured of landowner support by the widespread acceptance of a feu-duty for the land required:

> All the Proprietors along the Line are favourable, and, in almost every instance, have expressed their readiness to accept a Feu duty, if desired, based on the agricultural value of the land required for the works.[190]

Yet, despite these efforts to obtain land cheaply, land had cost £14,893 by August 1857, which represented 12.4% of the company's capital expenditure, more than the 11.8% incurred by the same date for the Great North's main line to Keith, which also included the expensive purchase of the Aberdeenshire Canal.[191] Two years later in August 1859, Inverness and Nairn records show that £6,240 was still held in a bank account principally to meet outstanding land claims.[192] The increasing cost of the line and the inability to raise its full ordinary share capital forced the company to seek powers to issue a new 5% preference stock and increase its authorised borrowing, which rectified the deficit on the capital account.[193]

The Inverness and Nairn Railway illustrated that a remote, local line could be constructed and operated to yield a satisfactory return to its investors. Moreover, the line effectively blocked the western end of the Aberdeen-Inverness route from an Aberdonian advance and preserved future options for extensions to the east, south and north to form the strands of the Inverness railway web.

THE ROUTE COMPLETED: THE INVERNESS AND ABERDEEN JUNCTION RAILWAY

Before either the Great North or Nairn lines opened, the erstwhile Inverness and Elgin Railway had been resurrected and a deputation comprising its deputy chairman and Nairn director, Captain William Fraser-Tytler, EW Mackintosh, also a Nairn director, and the Hon TC Bruce, commissioner to the Earl of Seafield, sought an agreement with the Great North.[194] The Earl of Seafield owned extensive timber interests and land in the area to be served by the proposed link line and was therefore a key potential source both of traffic and capital. The widespread support of landowners for the Inverness and Elgin company was reported by *Railway Times*:

> The landed proprietors, without exception, have not only expressed themselves favourable to the undertaking, but are prepared to accord every possible facility to the construction.[195]

The Great North was embroiled in its own capital difficulties at this time and, expecting to obtain access to Inverness using running rights over the Inverness and Nairn line, its board was anxious to avoid further expense. In particular, the company wished to agree 'an acceptable division between the two companies of the expensive works connected with the Spey crossing'.[196] In February 1855, however, the Great North's board minuted that the Inverness and Elgin 'are not in a position to carry out their undertaking', but decided to press ahead and seek parliamentary approval to extend their own line from Huntly to Keith.[197]

The Inverness and Elgin Railway was re-constituted as the Inverness and Aberdeen Junction Railway in 1855. The Great North agreed that the Inverness and Aberdeen Junction 'shall have the line up to Keith', obviating any need to spend Great North capital on bridging the River Spey, but the company offered a subscription of £40,000 in the Inverness and Aberdeen Junction in return for two seats on its board.[198] The Inverness and Aberdeen Junction prospectus explained the reason for extending the proposed line beyond Elgin at an estimated cost of £8,000 per mile, including land:

> ... it has been thought preferable that the whole line from Keith to Nairn should be in the hands of one Company, and accordingly the scheme of last year has been extended, so as at once to complete the chain of Railway communication from Aberdeen to Inverness ... in order fully to accommodate the great counties of Ross, Sutherland and Caithness, it has been considered essential to carry a Line to the Harbour at Burghead.[199]

Once authorised in 1856, the Inverness and Aberdeen Junction Railway formed an effective barrier between the Great North and its anticipated running rights between Nairn and Inverness that had been the subject of negotiation in 1854.[200] But even with the Great North's subscription and the support of wealthy landowners, the Inverness and Aberdeen Junction experienced immediate problems in raising sufficient share capital.

By May 1857, the Inverness and Aberdeen Junction had raised £80,828, just a quarter of its authorised share capital of £325,000.[201] Furthermore, the company's assets were valued at £135,543, but liabilities were £203,420. Chairman Alexander Matheson told his board that £70,000 above the resources currently expected by the company would be required to complete the line. With £95,000 of ordinary shares remaining unsold and calls still to be made on existing shareholders, the company had raised insufficient capital to be able to exercise its borrowing powers. As a result, the board decided to seek the approval of shareholders to convert unsold stock into a preference stock to attract new investment.[202] To meet immediate financial needs, the board agreed that its directors would accept personal liability for any temporary loans raised, but this decision was rescinded the following day when director George Loch, commissioner to the Duke of Sutherland, convened a further board meeting to express concern at this universal commitment. Not all Inverness directors were very wealthy individuals like Matheson, although Loch's employer, the Duke of Sutherland, owned very substantial assets and his reluctance to provide guarantees was later quoted against him when he sought a promised subscription from the Highland Railway for the construction of the Sutherland Railway in 1866.[203] Nevertheless, temporary

The Inverness and Aberdeen Junction Railway directors commemorated themselves on plaques on the original bridge over the River Spey at Orton. When the bridge was rebuilt in 1906, the plaques were removed and eventually put on display in Inverness station, where they can still be seen. A separate plaque recorded the names of the engineers and builders.

The names include the two GNSR directors, Sir James Elphinstone and John Blaikie. The spelling of WJ Taylor is at variance with the company records, which show it as Tayler.

(Keith Fenwick)

DIRECTORS

ALEX.MATHESON,ESQ.OF ARDROSS. M.P.CHAIRMAN.
THE RIGHT HON.THE EARL OF SEAFIELD.
CEO.LOCH,ESQ. LONDON.
ENEAS W. MACKINTOSH. ESQ. OF RAICMORE.
SIR JAMES. D.H. ELPHINSTONE. BART. M.P.
WM. JAS. TAYLOR. ESQ. OF ROTHIEMAY.
SIR ALEX. P. GORDON CUMMINC. BART.OF ALTYRE.

DIRECTORS

THE HON.THOS.CHAS.BRUCE.DEPUTY-CHAIRMAN.
ALEX.INCLIS. ROBERTSON. ESQ. OF AULTNASKIACH
THE RICHT HON. THE EARL OF CAITHNESS.
CAPTAIN WM.FRASER-TYTLER OF ALDOURIE.
THE MOST NOBLE THE MARQUIS OF STAFFORD. MP.
JOHN BLAIKIE.ESQ. ABERDEEN.
THE HON.GEORGE SKENE DUFF OF MILTONDUFF.

loans were used as a short-term measure: a £15,000 loan from the Scottish Union Insurance Company in October 1857 was personally guaranteed by eight directors, followed by a loan of £20,000 from the local Caledonian Bank in August 1858, guaranteed by five directors and engineer Joseph Mitchell.[204]

The proposal to issue preference stock aroused opposition, because holders of this new stock would have a priority in the payment of their dividend over existing ordinary shareholders. As large shareholders, the Great North and contractor David Mitchell objected strongly:

> … such a proceeding would be disastrous in the highest degree to the interests of the present shareholders and particularly unjust to the contractors who would never have taken the large amount of shares held by them had such a step been foreseen …[205]

David Mitchell and two other contractors, Charles Brand and the trustees of John Brebner, each held ordinary shares with a par value of £9,250, which in 1857 represented almost nine percent of the company's authorised share capital.

Great North chairman Sir James Elphinstone, in a carefully argued letter to Matheson, suggested that £70,000 of new stock would be insufficient to complete the line, with the danger that more and more preference stock would need to be issued until the original shares became worthless.[206] The letter, which contained a further suggestion that the Great North might work the line to Elgin 'until the Traffic shall be developed when it will be much more easy to issue the remaining stock', received no response from Inverness.[207]

The pattern of shareholding, comprising many small local shareholders and a few large contributors, was similar to that of its neighbour, the Inverness and Nairn Railway. Of the £243,900 of subscriptions made by 1857, £165,900 was to be supplied by 312 local shareholders and £78,000 by eight individuals.[208] The support of small shareholders continued and, by July 1864, 139 (27%) of the 510 registered holders of ordinary shares held just one or two shares each, while seven shareholders held £113,300 of ordinary stock, just over one third of the £330,857 of ordinary stock registered at that date.[209]

Relationships worsened when the Inverness and Aberdeen Junction board convened a shareholders' meeting in July 1857 to seek approval to exercise its borrowing powers. The meeting was adjourned when questions were raised over the validity of the company's claim that half its share capital had been paid up.[210] Elphinstone, a Great North representative on the Inverness and Aberdeen Junction board, had discovered from fellow director Eneas Mackintosh that the general manager, Andrew Dougall, had subscribed for 9,546 ordinary shares, but that company chairman Alexander Matheson and deputy chairman Thomas Bruce had each provided £25,000 to meet the deposit and the calls due on those shares.[211] Dougall was in effect holding these shares in trust for others who had undertaken to meet future calls on the shares, but the purchase allowed the company to declare that over half the company's capital had now been paid up. As a result, borrowing powers could be released and funds obtained which would then be available to buy these shares back, returning the company's share register to its previous position.

This neat, but somewhat Machiavellian, financial practice to release borrowing powers was unsuccessfully opposed by the Great North at the reconvened shareholders' meeting held in August 1857. Great North minutes record Matheson's declaration at this meeting that the Great North 'wished to grasp at the management of the line' and that, while the present board remained elected, 'the Great North should never have the control of a single line north of Keith …'.[212] At the half-yearly meeting of Inverness and Aberdeen Junction shareholders held two months later, shareholder Mr Gentle of Dell stated that he wished to see just one company operating between Inverness and Aberdeen, to which Matheson responded:

> It was for the interest of this part of the country that the management of the line to Keith should remain in the hands of the Inverness board, and as long as he was a member of that board,

he would oppose any amalgamation that would have the effect of taking away our interest in it.[213]

In 1859, a further dispute between the companies arose when the Inverness and Aberdeen Junction board reported that 'the Capital of the Company has been exceeded to some extent'.[214] The company had, in fact, spent £501,421, significantly above the limit of £433,300 authorised by Parliament to be raised in share and loan capital, and it proposed to seek new powers to increase its capital limits, including raising £150,000 in preference stock. With no prospect of gaining concessions from Inverness to extend its own services westwards from Keith, the Great North offered to sell its £40,000 of stock back to the Inverness and Aberdeen Junction and withdraw from the board. Matheson and Bruce recognised the advantage in acceptance:

> ... after careful consideration of all the circumstances, and in particular the importance to this Company of being relieved from all future obstructions and interference ... and also taking into account the steady increase in the traffic of the Company, they had resolved to submit a proposal to the Great North for the purchase of their shares.[215]

In January 1860, the Great North agreed to sell its shares at par, paid by one bill of £20,000 in January 1861 and a second bill of the same amount in January 1862. Until redemption, interest was to be paid on these bills equivalent to the dividend paid on Inverness and Aberdeen Junction ordinary shares.[216] Director John Stewart, deputising for his chairman Sir James Elphinstone, reassured Great North shareholders that the £40,000 now released could yield five percent to their company, rather than the lower rate which had been paid as dividend in previous years by Inverness.[217]

Despite the public disagreement, the Inverness and Aberdeen companies shared a profitable monopoly over the line between Inverness and Aberdeen, but a clear territorial border had been established at Keith. Once the line opened, the Inverness and Aberdeen Junction

paid steady dividends to its ordinary shareholders; the average annual rate never fell below 4% between 1860 and its assimilation into the new Highland Railway in 1865. Nevertheless, the apparent prosperity suggested by shareholder dividends masked the continual financial difficulties that the company faced on its capital account.

FINANCIAL STRAIN IN INVERNESS

Although there was little overt overlap between the first boards of the Inverness and Nairn and Inverness and Aberdeen Junction companies, the two railways were operated almost as one and shared Andrew Dougall as their General Manager. Over a year before its opening, the Aberdeen Junction proposed joint working with the Inverness and Nairn, which developed into a proposal for amalgamation.[218]

Consolidation of these nominally independent companies into a unified concern was always a prime objective for the Inverness promoters and so the Inverness and Aberdeen Junction began to assume the pivotal role of the 'host' company for the developing web of railways centred on Inverness. Subsequent promotions to the north via the Inverness and Ross-shire Railway and to the south via the Inverness and Perth Junction Railway included clauses from the outset for future amalgamation of the new companies with their host.[219] The Inverness and Nairn was amalgamated in May 1861 and the Inverness and Ross-shire in June 1862.[220]

In August 1859, one year after the line opened, the Inverness and Aberdeen Junction company reported a deficit of £75,007 on its capital account (table 4). A financial statement made to the board showed that the line had cost £513,426, £80,126 more than the authorised share and loan capital of the company, and a committee was established to investigate the causes.[221] Unsurprisingly, company accounts show that construction costs and plant were the main items of increased expenditure. The capital deficit was reduced

Table 4: Capital and revenue data, Inverness and Aberdeen Junction Railway, 1859–64

Capital (£)	August 1859	August 1860	August 1861	August 1862	August 1863	July 1864
Capital raised	426,413	483,054	709,844	953,738	1,116,129	1,203,186
Balance	- 75,007	- 49,380	+ 28,485	+ 14,552	- 4,308	- 190,585
Capital spent	501,421	532,435	681,359	939,186	1,120,437	1,393,772
General Balance Sheet						
Sundries due	86,679	112,562	36,161	47,847	26,937	220,352
Revenue (annual) (£)	(1)					(2)
Gross Revenue		44,616	45,251	50,676	63,607	85,957
Less receipts due to the Inverness & Nairn and Morayshire Railways		6,199	2,530			
Gross Expenditure		25,828	23,393	25,374	33,065	53,138
Surplus		12,589	19,328	25,302	30,542	32,819
Dividend						
Half year – January/February	-	4%	3½%	3½%	4%	4%
Half year – July/August	2½%	4%	4½%	5%	5¼%	4%

Source: National Archives of Scotland, BR/IAJ/1/1-3.

Notes: (1):The first printed report to shareholders relates to the half year ending August 1859; earlier data is collated from entries in the company's minute book.

(2):The reporting dates for accounts were amended from February/August to January/July in 1864.

(3): Shillings and pence have been rounded down and so totals may not match precisely the sum of component items.

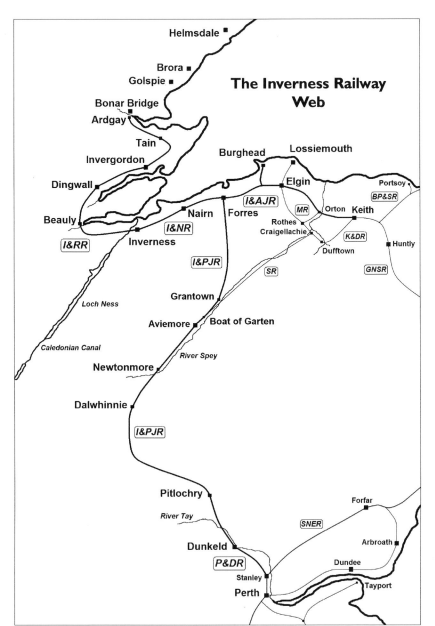

The Inverness Railway Web

Key	
Inverness Lines	
I&AJR	Inverness and Aberdeen Junction Railway
I&NR	Inverness and Nairn Railway
I&PJR	Inverness and Perth Junction Railway
I&RR	Inverness and Ross-shire Railway
P&D	Perth and Dunkeld Railway
Other Lines	
BP&S	Banff, Portsoy and Strathisla
GNSR	Great North of Scotland Railway
K&DR	Keith and Dufftown Railway
MR	Morayshire Railway
SNER	Scottish North Eastern Railway
SR	Strathspey Railway

to £49,380 by August 1860, but thereafter the Inverness and Aberdeen Junction accounts began to incorporate the capital receipts and expenditure of its amalgamated neighbours and so cannot reveal the precise financial position of the original company.

With the widespread acceptance of feu duties by landowners, 7.2% of the capital of the Inverness and Aberdeen Junction had been absorbed by land costs in 1860, less than the proportion spent on the Nairn line, but the capital cost of the line, including rolling stock, had reached £13,395 per mile, almost two-thirds above the parliamentary estimate.[222] When Alexander Matheson addressed the first shareholders' meeting of the Highland Railway in October 1865, following the final consolidation of the Inverness web companies, he announced that the Inverness and Aberdeen Junction line had cost £578,000, just over three-quarters more than its estimate.[223]

It was usual for railway companies to record some financial transactions of a temporary nature on the general balance sheet, separate from the data of capital and revenue in order to avoid any distortion of the main accounts of the company; in particular, temporary loans were usually recorded in this way. Since 1855, the Great North had specifically identified the advances made by its bankers on its general balance sheet (table 2), but the Inverness and Aberdeen Junction preferred to wrap its temporary loans with any other outstanding debts under a single line entry entitled "sundries due" (table 4). These "sundries" amounted to £112,562 in August 1860, over £5.6 million in current value, a very large sum for which no detailed explanation was provided to shareholders. As well as any amounts due to be paid to contractors and suppliers of goods, this figure of sundries included temporary loans and bills of exchange, both of which would require the payment of interest until they were redeemed. Great North accounts began to record expenditure for sundries and other debit balances on its general balance sheet from 1861 as its financial position began to worsen, but it continued to show the balance due to its bankers as a discrete accounting item in contrast to practice in Inverness.

Inverness railway companies had, for many years,

paid some interest charges from their capital accounts rather than from revenue; this allowed the retention of some of their receipts to support the payment of dividends, but this questionable practice in effect paid existing shareholders using funds provided by the shareholders themselves rather than from any profits earned from the business. By paying regular dividends, railway companies aimed to keep their shares attractive to existing and new investors. In 1866, Thomas Bruce, formerly deputy chairman of the Inverness and Aberdeen Junction and by then deputy chairman of the Highland Railway, told shareholders that about £60,000 of interest had been charged to capital since the early days of the Inverness and Nairn Railway, primarily for capital works that were in progress during each accounting period, but that this long-standing practice was to be ended and all interest would in future be charged to revenue.[224] The implication of his announcement, however, was that either more revenue would have to be earned to maintain the previous pattern of dividend payments, or that the level of dividend would be reduced.

A small surplus was recorded on the capital account of the Inverness and Aberdeen Junction company in 1861 and 1862, but the impact of the expansion of the Inverness web via the Ross-shire line to Dingwall, Invergordon and Bonar Bridge and the financial contribution made to the newly-promoted Inverness and Perth Junction Railway sent the capital account of the Inverness and Aberdeen Junction into sharp decline. By July 1864, one year before the Inverness web was finally consolidated as the Highland Railway, the capital account showed a deficit of £190,585, over £9.5 million in current value, which was financed by loans hidden within the one-line entry of £220,352 recorded as "sundries due" on the general balance sheet. The seeds of the approaching financial crisis in Inverness had been deeply sown and were about to be inherited by the newly formed Highland company.

INTO ROSS-SHIRE

The steady growth of traffic over the Nairn and Aberdeen Junction lines between Inverness and Keith allowed both companies to pay dividends consistently to their shareholders. The financial difficulties caused by the increased costs of constructing the lines had been resolved by authorised and temporary borrowing in the expectation that, while the increasing revenue was sufficient to service the capital debt, the evident prosperity of the companies would in time ensure that all the authorised share capital was sold. As long as shareholders received their dividends, they were unlikely to demand explanations of the mysterious contents of the line recorded as "sundries" on the general balance sheet.

The Inverness promoters also anticipated further increases in traffic by extending the network of lines to the west and north of Inverness and, ultimately, by a direct line south to Perth, which would not only capture the bulk of traffic to and from northern Scotland for Inverness coffers, but obviate the expensive and time-consuming diversion via Aberdeen, a route still hampered by the absence of a connection between the Great North's line and the trunk route southwards.

The progress of the Nairn and Aberdeen Junction companies was commended by *Railway Times* in October 1859 and again in April 1860, when the journal reported the promotion of the Inverness and Ross-shire Railway to extend the network to the west and north of Inverness:

> These locally promoted single lines continue to prove of what value a well-regulated system of communication may be to its originators, as well as to the district in which it is placed … This line [The Inverness and Aberdeen Junction Railway], therefore, during its first year of operation, had paid 3% on the whole of its share capital, in addition to improving the estates and increasing the value of the agricultural produce of its shareholders. The Nairn line … is to declare a 4½% dividend compared to 4% in the same period in 1858.
>
> It is not surprising, therefore, with these results before the gentry of Ross-shire, that an extension further north should be in the contemplation … The great secret of success in these districts is to be traced to the fact that moderate charges have been made for the land and difficulty and delay avoided in its transfer. (*Railway Times,* 20ᵗʰ October 1859)
>
> We again have to record out approbation of the manner in which the affairs of these companies are conducted, as well as to express our satisfaction at the results they produce … It is these practical evidences of good results that promote extension further north and which have led to the formation of the Inverness and Ross-shire, a scheme which has already passed the Lords, and will proceed through its stages in the Commons unopposed. (*Railway Times,* 28ᵗʰ April 1860)

Other than the direct route over the Grampian Mountains to Perth surveyed by Mitchell for the 1846 Perth and Inverness scheme, the only realistic southern access to Inverness was available via the Great Glen, already traversed by the Caledonian Canal. Seeking to protect Inverness from this direction, deputy chairman Thomas Bruce informed the Inverness and Aberdeen Junction directors in 1860 'that the Government were most anxious to be relieved of the annual expense attendant on keeping up and working the Canal …' and he suggested a lease of the Canal by the Aberdeen Junction, Nairn and Ross-shire companies 'provided that no expense or liability was incurred beyond wear and tear'.[225] The Aberdeen Junction directors decided that any lease should also include the Crinan Canal, which was an integral part of the established sea route to Glasgow.[226] The Commissioners were reported to have 'generally approved' of the Aberdeen Junction proposals, but they decided to advertise a lease; both canals were heavily in debt and, by 1863, the Caledonian Canal was losing £1,000 per year.[227] A lease of the canal was not pursued further in the Inverness boardroom and the prospect of adding significantly to the company's financial burden was thus avoided. The direct line to Perth retained its priority in the plans for the development of the Inverness railway web, although its capital requirements were about to add considerably to the financial pressures in Inverness.

Ross-shire had attracted interest from railway promoters in 1845 when an 'Inverness and Ross' line was mooted, but no bill was submitted to Parliament.[228] In November 1858, Joseph Mitchell presented details of a proposed extension from Inverness to Dingwall to the board of the Inverness and Aberdeen Junction Railway and a meeting 'to consider the practicality and expediency of constructing a Railway from Inverness to Dingwall by Beauly' was held at the Union Hotel, Inverness, in January 1859.[229] It was acknowledged at this meeting that the traditional returns expected from railway capital were most unlikely from this line, and, unsurprisingly, the press reported that there was:

> ... a good deal of eagerness to know what prospect there was of accomplishing the work without any hope of a dividend.[230]

The Nairn and Aberdeen Junction companies had already encountered a shortage of share capital, although both these lines were returning a steady dividend to their shareholders. The prospect of attracting investment for a new and more remote line without expectation of any dividend therefore appeared bleak. The public was urged to consider:

> ... estimating their profit on investments, not more by the actual dividend to be realised, than by the comfort, public advantage, and improved commercial and agricultural position, which a railway cannot fail to produce.[231]

Alexander Matheson later justified the Inverness and Ross-shire Railway as an essential strand of the Inverness web of railways. Like the short Inverness and Nairn line before, the Ross-shire line was not seen as a branch but part of a future main route into the far north, able to capture traffic previously conveyed by sea:

> ... a line from Inverness to Keith occupied by no means a safe position ... the next step taken by the Directors was to promote the Inverness and Ross-shire line as far as Invergordon and ultimately on to the confines of Sutherland at Bonar Bridge, thus completely securing the traffic of the whole country north of Inverness to the Junction line, and greatly strengthening the position of the Company. Without the extension to Bonar Bridge, we would not have succeeded in driving the steamers from the Moray Firth and the coast of Sutherland.[232]

Subscriptions to the Inverness and Ross-shire from the two existing Inverness railway companies were made conditional upon 'the undertaking being extended beyond Dingwall as far as Alness' in order to capture 'the greater part of the Sutherlandshire and Easter Ross traffic'.[233] Alness was, perhaps coincidentally, very close to Matheson's estate at Ardross, and he became the largest shareholder in the Ross-shire company, holding £11,000 of the £58,318 of the ordinary stock on which dividend was paid in July 1864.[234] Thomas Bruce, deputy chairman of the Inverness and Aberdeen Junction and later of the Highland, supported Matheson's view of the importance of the Ross-shire line:

> Had we not pushed into Ross-shire we would have been liable, at any moment to the threat, if not the performance, of a line which would render our property comparatively valueless ... But having these lines north, we have command of the traffic that concentrates at this town, and no other company can pass over it beyond Inverness; therefore they cannot touch the main source of our traffic'.[235]

The Inverness and Aberdeen Junction offered to work the Ross-shire for fifty percent of receipts and subscribe £15,000 for two seats on the board, but required that £55,000 was raised by local subscription exclusive of any railway contractor or railway company subscriptions. Significantly, it was also specified that amalgamation should be sought within three years of the opening of the Ross-shire line, thereby signalling the consistent intent of the Inverness directors to consolidate the railway companies of the railway web into one concern.[236]

Although the Inverness and Ross-shire minutes omitted the conditions set by Inverness for local subscriptions and amalgamation, the purpose of the Ross-shire as forming the northern arm of the Inverness web was nonetheless explicit.[237] The Inverness and Nairn Railway, already negotiating an amalgamation with the Inverness and Aberdeen Junction, advised its shareholders that the Ross-shire 'cannot fail, when opened, to throw additional traffic on your Line' and offered £10,000 on the same terms as the Aberdeen Junction.[238] The Ross-shire promoters agreed to extend the line from Dingwall beyond Alness to 'the west end' of Invergordon and guaranteed an additional £6,000 of capital for the purpose.[239] The complete interweaving of the Inverness companies, whose directors met in the same Inverness boardroom and were served by the same secretary, Andrew Dougall, is illustrated by the minute of the Aberdeen Junction board, of which Matheson was chairman, recording 'their gratification' to the Ross-shire for agreeing to extend their line; the Ross-shire sub-committee that had agreed to do so was also chaired by Matheson, and Matheson was subsequently appointed the first chairman of the Ross-shire board in 1860.[240]

In December 1859, Mitchell estimated the cost of the extended line to Invergordon as £214,418 and, in the following June, advised that the cost per mile would be £6,852.[241] Authorised capital of the company was set at £215,000, giving a projected capital cost per mile of £6,880.[242] The *Inverness* Courier was enthusiastic, but somewhat over-optimistic about future returns:

> This line, we may remind our readers, is the next great step in the progress of railway communication northwards ... favourable arrangements have been made with

landowners, the contract price is moderate, and the shareholders are sanguine that this will be one of the best paying railway undertakings in the North.[243]

Even with the application of 'cheap railway' principles, financial difficulties were immediately encountered. The directors endeavoured to keep tight control of costs and pressed for an early opening of the line to generate revenue:

> The Board being desirous of ensuring the strictest economy in the construction of the Line and being strongly of opinion that the ultimate success of the Lines in the North, where the Country is thinly populated and great competition for the traffic exists by sea, depend very much on the amount of the original cost, it was resolved that … no deviation from Plans or Contracts involving extra expenditure of money, however small, be entered into without obtaining the express sanction of the Board by a minute … all the stations on the line to constructed of timber and in the most economical manner…[244]

The Inverness and Ross-shire opened to Dingwall in June 1862 and the company was amalgamated with the Inverness and Aberdeen Junction that month, although the full line to Invergordon did not open until March 1863.[245] The terms of the amalgamation placed an additional financial burden on the host company, because a modest guaranteed dividend was offered on Ross-shire ordinary shares, even though the line was yet to open and future revenue patterns were very uncertain.[246] This guarantee was fixed at 3% per annum, rising by one half of one percentage point per year until it reached the level of the dividend paid on Aberdeen Junction shares, when the two stocks were to be merged. For a line that was promoted with little expectation of any dividend, these terms were attractive to its shareholders, but the terms of amalgamation sowed a further seed in the future financial difficulties to be reaped by the Inverness railway web.

Detailed capital accounts for the early years of Ross-shire have not survived and its early absorption into the Inverness and Aberdeen Junction masks its financial fortunes. The accounts of the Inverness and Aberdeen Junction for the half year to 31st August 1862 show that £129,751 of Ross-shire stock had been issued, representing sixty percent of authorised share capital, but an unspecified proportion of this sum had been issued as security for loans.[247] The Caledonian Bank, for example, had granted a £20,000 loan in May 1861 against security of company stock and the personal guarantee of the directors.[248]

The shortage of funds prompted the directors to appeal to shareholders in April 1861 to pay the remaining calls on their shares in advance of the due date, in return for which they would be paid 5% interest.[249] With difficulties in raising capital from the sale of ordinary shares, Matheson informed the Ross-shire board that £150,000 was required to complete the line, but their parliamentary agent, Theodore Martin, had advised that Parliament would not agree to the conversion of unissued ordinary stock as preference stock unless the company refrained from exercising their borrowing powers.[250] The prospect of raising this sum from the sale of a new preference stock was not encouraging and so the Ross-shire board obtained shareholder approval in October 1861 to use the borrowing powers authorised in the parliamentary act.[251]

Half of a railway company's share capital had to be paid up before the borrowing powers specified in its act of incorporation could be exercised.[252] Andrew Dougall, secretary to the Ross-shire and Aberdeen Junction companies, reported to the Ross-shire board in October 1861 'that one half of company capital was expended and that the Sheriff had granted the certificate for the company to borrow on its powers', which implies that the Ross-shire had received £107,500 of its ordinary share capital.[253] The records of the Aberdeen Junction, however, show that only £83,000 had been subscribed to the Ross-shire by that date and so similar creative financial techniques that had caused the dispute with the Great North in 1857 must have been applied again to secure this result.[254]

The release of borrowing powers produced a rapid stream of funds from debenture loans. Within four months of receiving shareholder approval to exercise borrowing powers, the company had obtained £62,770 of the authorised £71.600, but at an interest rate of 4½% at a time when bank discount rates had fallen from 3% in November 1861 to 2½% in January 1862.[255] The company had therefore obtained necessary new funds, but at a premium. This flow of money produced an unexpected short term surplus. When the Ross-shire found itself holding £25,000 in cash at the Caledonian Bank on which it was receiving 2% interest, chairman Matheson reported that the Aberdeen Junction 'would take the temporary use of any sum that this Company could conveniently spare'.[256] The Ross-shire board agreed to transfer £20,000 to the Aberdeen Junction at a rate of interest to be agreed. The integration of management was once again apparent; both board meetings were held on the same day, in the same location, and chaired by the same person.

Like the local Inverness and Nairn line, the Inverness and Ross-shire relied on the investment of a few large landowners and many small local subscribers. By July 1864, two years after amalgamation, £58,318 of ordinary £10 Ross-shire shares remained extant on which guaranteed dividend was paid to 206 registered shareholders. Of these, 27 shareholders held just one £10 share, while 128 shareholders, three-fifths of the total, held five shares or fewer. The largest shareholders were Alexander Matheson with £11,000 of ordinary shares and the Duke of Sutherland with £5,000. These two individuals alone held over a quarter of the issued shares.[257]

The Ross-shire line was estimated to cost £215,000, although Matheson later stated the actual cost to be £285,000.[258] Like earlier Inverness railways, the company was forced to rely on authorised and temporary borrowing to complete its line. The National Bank of Scotland, for example, held £6,000 of ordinary shares in

July 1864 and was paid the due guaranteed dividend. However, other ordinary shares had been issued for which no dividend is recorded. Aberdeen Junction accounts reveal that £136,671 of Ross-shire stock had been issued by July 1864, but dividend was paid on just £58,318 of ordinary shares. The unaccounted difference of £78,353 almost certainly represents shares held by banks as security for temporary loans, a significant sum which represents almost three-fifths of the whole of the issued stock.[259] The scale of temporary loans used for the Ross-shire line to Invergordon, however, cannot be identified precisely because, after amalgamation in 1862, the Aberdeen Junction used Ross-shire stock as security to raise loans for the use of the amalgamated company and the specific application of those funds cannot be determined.[260] Nevertheless, the heavy reliance on bank advances to complete the Ross-shire line and, indeed, the whole of the Inverness railway web is certain. Bank loans required the payment of interest, which placed a prior commitment on the use of revenue generated by the railways once in operation, and, until the loans were repaid, the ability of the companies to pay attractive dividends to investors was constrained. The Inverness web was steadily accumulating substantial capital debt, which demanded future redemption.

THE ROSS-SHIRE EXTENSION

The Inverness directors had intended that Invergordon would be the northern terminus of the Ross-shire line, but a substantial offer of £30,000 from the Duke of Sutherland made in 1862 stimulated an extension of the railway to Bonar Bridge on the southern border of Sutherland-shire.[261] The third Duke, who succeeded to the title in 1861, owned 1.326 million acres of Sutherland by 1872, almost three-quarters of the entire county, and he was anxious to connect his vast northern estates with the evolving railway network.[262] In 1865, Sutherland's gross annual income from his English and Scottish estates was £100,853, over £5 million in current value, and he eventually invested over £322,000 in the Highland Railway and its allied lines to the north of Inverness.[263]

One of the results of the highland clearances had been to relocate much of the remaining population on the eastern seaboard of Sutherland and Caithness. Successive Dukes of Sutherland invested heavily in projects for economic improvement of the area. Between 1803 and 1815, income from the highland estates owned by the then Marquis of Stafford, created first Duke of Sutherland in 1833, trebled, but expenditure on them increased nine-fold:[264] This was investment intended to increase the value of the estates with the potential to yield higher rents in the future. Investment in railways by the successors of the first Duke was intended to bring similar indirect returns to the estates and the region.

In 1862, the State gave notice of the abolition of the Commission for Highland Roads and Bridges and, with it, the cessation of its annual £5,000 grant towards road maintenance,[265] Responsibility for roads passed entirely to the heritors of the district, those individuals owning land valued at over £100 Scots annual valued rent and who held the right to vote at Scottish county meetings where county administrative matters were decided. By 1851, there were only five heritors remaining in the entire county of Sutherland-shire compared to thirteen in 1800, so the responsibilities of road trustees fell on the shoulders of a very few individuals in the far north. Railway companies were themselves substantial landowners and so were routinely added to the list of those liable for local rates.

Although the great wealth of the third Duke of Sutherland could absorb the additional costs that passed from the State to heritor, the change in State policy may have strengthened the Duke's decision to offer funds towards a northerly extension of the Inverness and Ross-shire Railway as a means of securing a more reliable and speedier connection of the extensive Sutherland lands with the south than existing roads or sea transport could provide.[266] As the line was pushed

This view of Inverness station in Edwardian days illustrates the triangular layout created when the line was extended northwards. The original terminal platforms were in the distance with the station to the right. The platforms built for the Ross-shire line are in the foreground. Out of sight on the left is the avoiding line which enabled trains such as the recently arrived overnight train from London on the left to back into the north line platforms and give easy connection for passengers continuing further. The number of passengers and the long trains suggest that this was at the height of the summer tourist season. (HRS collection)

further north, the capital difficulties became more acute. The Inverness web lines had been supported by a cadre of wealthy landowners, but in Sutherland, there was but one. Population was sparse and unlikely to yield either substantial subscriptions or traffic for the new line. In 1861, Sutherland-shire contained 25,246 people, just 0.82% of the Scottish population, while 41,111 were resident in Caithness to the north.

Against this discouraging backdrop, Matheson had informed Aberdeen Junction directors three months before the Ross-shire line had opened its first section to Dingwall that an extension beyond Invergordon to Bonar Bridge had been proposed for which the Duke of Sutherland had offered £30,000, although at a public meeting in Tain he had also stated that the Inverness directors expected £70,000 to be subscribed locally to demonstrate support for the scheme.[267] With £50,000 identified for the extension by March 1862, which included the Duke's contribution, the Ross-shire board recorded that an additional £20,000 was still required to obtain support from Inverness.[268] The Ross-shire, however, was already in the throes of amalgamation with the Inverness and Aberdeen Junction Railway and so the legislation for the Ross-shire extension was obtained and enacted by the Aberdeen Junction without confirmation of the stipulated local subscriptions.[269] The terminus of the line was sited at Ardgay on the Ross-shire side of the Kyle of Sutherland, where an existing road bridge gave access to Bonar Bridge and routes into the counties of Sutherland and Caithness. The name of the station was changed from Bonar Bridge to Ardgay in 1977.

The parliamentary act for the extension was obtained in 1863, but further seeds of financial strain for the Inverness railway web were sown within it. Despite the distinctly uncertain outlook for the revenue that might be generated from the extension line, the ordinary share capital of £160,000 approved to finance its construction was guaranteed a dividend of 3% in the year following the opening of the line to Bonar Bridge, which was then to rise by one half of one percentage point each year thereafter until the dividend matched that paid on the ordinary shares of the Inverness and Aberdeen Junction company.

This guaranteed dividend, although relatively modest, was intended to try to attract capital to this remote railway project. The extension line opened to Bonar Bridge in October 1864 but, by January 1865, only £44,573 of Ross-shire extension share capital had been paid up, just over a quarter of that estimated to be required. The Duke had provided £30,000 and Alexander Matheson £2,500, with a further £2,500 from Matheson's uncle, Sir James Matheson.[270] These three highland landowners had supplied over three-quarters of the capital raised.

The first guaranteed dividends were paid in January 1865 to ninety-four shareholders to reflect the first four months of operation. Thirty of these shareholders, almost one third, held only one or two shares and fifty-three, just over a half, held five shares or less, repeating yet more starkly the local investment patterns of earlier Inverness railway companies.[271] Nevertheless,

Inverness and Ross-shire Railway lamp-post, now at Birnie Kirk near Elgin. (Harry Clye)

the accounts of the Inverness and Aberdeen Junction company show that £144,454 of Ross-shire extension stock had been issued by January 1865, which suggests that £99,881 of stock, almost seventy percent of that issued, was held by banks as security for loans negotiated by the Inverness and Aberdeen Junction company.[272] The Ross-shire extension, like its Ross-shire parent, was thus heavily indebted to banks, a financial burden which was about to be transferred from the accounts of the Inverness and Aberdeen Junction Railway to those of the new Inverness company, the Highland Railway.

As the Inverness and Ross-shire Railway was absorbed into the Inverness and Aberdeen Junction Railway from the opening of the first section of the line to Dingwall in 1862, the revenue generated by the Ross-shire and its extension and their financial contribution to the Inverness railway web cannot be determined. Although Matheson acknowledged that the Ross-shire line to Invergordon had cost £285,000, £70,000 more than anticipated, he claimed that the extension line to Bonar Bridge had cost £160,000, exactly the amount of its parliamentary estimate, but no detailed records survive to confirm or deny that assertion.[273] If indeed it was constructed to the estimated cost, it held the distinction of being the first line of the Inverness railway web to do so.

The Ross-shire lines presented the opportunity for the Inverness web to capture the relatively sparse traffic in the far north of Scotland from the established coastal shipping routes and to channel it over their lines, but the promoters had been unable to raise sufficient share capital to construct the route. The increasing reliance upon temporary bank funding as the line was pushed northwards merely added to the financial pressures faced by the Inverness and Aberdeen Junction company, which by now was also committed to the expensive scheme launched to construct a direct line from Inverness to Perth under the auspices of the Inverness and Perth Junction Railway. These capital difficulties were to be transferred to the newly consolidated Highland Railway in 1865, less than one year after the Inverness and Aberdeen Junction Railway began to operate services to the latest northerly terminus of the Inverness railway web at Bonar Bridge.

CHAPTER 7

AN UNEASY ALLIANCE

The formal alliance made financially between Aberdeen and Inverness in 1855 had been broken in January 1860 when the Great North of Scotland Railway resolved to sell its £40,000 shareholding in the Inverness and Aberdeen Junction Railway and thereby relinquish the two seats held on the board of that company. Nevertheless, the two companies remained inter-dependent, relying on the revenue generated from the flow of through traffic to and from northern Scotland and exchanged at Keith, but relations between Aberdeen and Inverness remained fragile.

Once the through line had opened in 1858, both companies began to benefit from a steady growth in revenue, which was reflected in the consistent payment of dividends to their respective shareholders. The rates of dividend compared favourably to those paid by the well-established railway companies to the south (table 5).

Both companies had experienced serious difficulties in raising share capital and had resorted to the use of bank advances extensively to fund the construction of their lines. Nevertheless, the increasing level of dividend paid by the Great North made investment in the company attractive and, by 1860, the company had reversed the deficit on its capital account. The capital account of the Inverness and Aberdeen Junction moved into surplus by 1861, but both companies continued to owe significant sums to their bankers throughout this period. These loans, which were held on the general balance sheet of the companies and outside the main capital and revenue accounts, offset substantially the apparent financial progress being made (table 6).

The fragile relationship between the Great North and the Inverness and Aberdeen Junction was revealed by numerous disputes that arose between the two companies over the interchange of traffic at Keith and the apportionment of revenue.[274] These visible indications of rivalry were supplemented by growing dissatisfaction with the continued absence of a continuous railway route across Aberdeen to connect into the southern railway network.

The Great North was seen by many as exhibiting the traits of a complacent monopolist. Complaints over the goods rates charged were received soon after the line

Table 5: Comparative dividends, 1856–62

Dividends (%)		1856	1857	1858	1859	1860	1861	1862
Great North of Scotland								
Annual dividend		2¼	4½	4½	5			
January half-year dividend	(1)					6	6½	7½
July half-year dividend	(1)					7	7	7
Inverness & Aberdeen Junction								
February half-year dividend					-	4	3½	3½
August half-year dividend					2½	4	4½	5
Annual dividend to July/August								
Aberdeen Railway	(2)	0	0	0	0	0	½	1³/₈
Caledonian Railway		1½	3½	4¼	3⁷/₈	4⁵/₈	5¼	5¼
Scottish Central Railway		5	5½	5½	5¹/₈	5½	5¾	5¾
Scottish Midland Junction Railway	(2)	3½	3½	4	4	4¹/₈	4¾	5¾
North British Railway		1¼	2⁵/₈	2¾	2⁷/₈	3	3¹/₈	2
Average bank discount rate		5¾	7¼	4¼	3½	4½	5½	2½

Sources: National Archives of Scotland, BR/RAC(S)/1/14 and BR/IAJ/1-3; *Railway Times*, 1856-1862; *Bradshaw's Railway Almanac*, 1875.
Notes: (1): Great North accounting periods were adjusted in 1859 from February/August to January/July.
(2): The Aberdeen Railway and Scottish Midland Junction Railway were amalgamated as the Scottish North Eastern Railway in 1856, but their ordinary dividends were kept discrete.

Table 6: Comparative balances, 1858–62

Great North of Scotland (£)	(1)	August 1858	July 1859	July 1860	July 1861	July 1862
Capital account balance		- 42,077	- 38,296	+ 86,784	+ 49,258	- 40,064
Owed to bankers (general balance sheet)		50,837	33,652	34,703	70,985	50,663
Sundries and debit balances owed		-	-	-	17,017	23,289
Inverness and Aberdeen Junction (£)		**August 1858**	**August 1859**	**August 1860**	**August 1861**	**August 1862**
Capital account balance			- 75,007	- 49,380	+ 28,485	+ 14,552
Sundries due (general balance sheet)	(2)		86,679	112,562	36,161	47,847

Sources: National Archives of Scotland, BR/RAC(S)/1/14 and BR/IAJ/1-3.
Notes: (1): Great North accounting periods were adjusted in 1859 from February/August to January/July.
(2): The Inverness and Aberdeen Junction included temporary bank loans with any other temporary debt on one line of the general balance sheet, marked as "sundries due".

to Huntly opened in 1854 and, to avoid local carriers undercutting the railway's rates, the Great North was obliged to make some reductions.[275] So long as traffic to and from the northern counties had to cross the Great North's main line, the company preserved its land-based monopoly, but northern traffic remained subject to competition from sea transport, a situation that caused natural concern in Inverness which had provided the bulk of the finance for the rail link between that town and the Great North's terminus at Keith.

Only one year after the full line opened between Inverness and Aberdeen, the Inverness and Aberdeen Junction board notified the Great North that they were no longer prepared to agree the differential rates that had been set in favour of steamers sailing south from Aberdeen compared to those set for 'the Southern Railway Companies from stations on this line', and that these rates would be discontinued from 1st August 1859.[276] The unsuccessful subsidisation of the Inverness and Edinburgh Steam Packet Company by the Great North in 1859-60 to capture northern trade, soon after the opening of the Inverness to Keith railway line, did

not deter the company from offering a £1,500 subsidy to the newly-formed Northern Steam Company in 1861 to secure more favourable rates for sea traffic after a dispute with the Aberdeen Steam Navigation Company.[277] John Stewart, a director of the Great North of Scotland Railway and to become its deputy chairman, had been ousted from the board of the Aberdeen Steam Navigation Company as a result of a dispute over the proportion of rates to be allocated between the railway and shipping company, and set up the rival Northern Steam Company.[278] He explained to Great North shareholders:

> ... the Great North were willing to enter into an arrangement as to the traffic with the Steam Navigation Company, but they asked a drawback of 25 percent – and the two Companies would not agree on the reduction. This was the origin of the opposition by the Northern Steam Company.[279].

The following year, the Great North gave a further subsidy to facilitate the amalgamation of the two rival steamer companies to provide a twice-weekly service

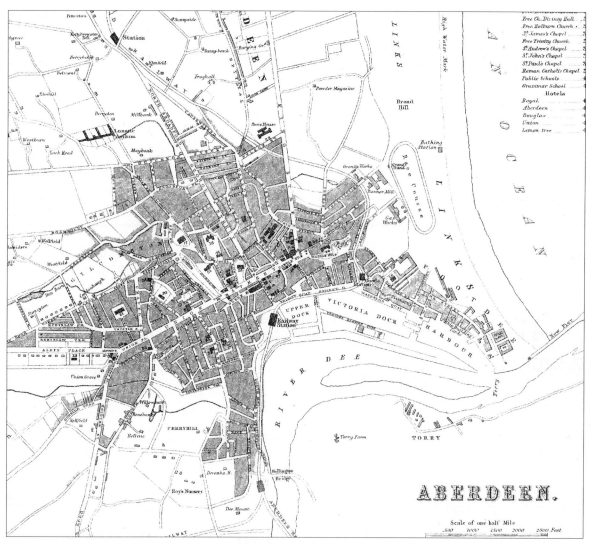

The gap between the stations in Aberdeen is illustrated on this map from Black's Guide to Scotland, 1861. The original GNSR terminus at on the north side of the town at Kittybrewster was outside the built-up area, while Waterloo, beside Victoria Dock, is erroneously marked here as a 'Goods Station'. Guild Street, terminus of the Scottish North Eastern Railway, was to the west of the Upper Dock. The tramway along the quay carried goods wagons only, drawn by horse power. (Keith Fenwick collection)

from Aberdeen to London.[280] Elphinstone announced that Stewart had refunded the subsidy given:

> Since we last met, the controversy with respect to the Steam Companies has been brought to a successful conclusion. The rival companies have now been consolidated into one, and communication with London has been established at such rates for goods as must not only prove of considerable importance to the district from which the Great North and its tributaries run, but to the trade and commerce of Aberdeen. And I am happy to say – what it is only just to say – that we owe this result, in a great measure, to the sagacity of my friend, Mr Stewart, and I have also to notice the straightforward and honourable manner in which came forward and refunded the subsidy which we had resolved to give last year.[281]

With no continuous rail link across Aberdeen and with their terminus conveniently located at the docks, the Great North continued to show favour to sea transport for goods traffic south of Aberdeen, engendering resentment within southern railway companies that had naturally expected to derive increased traffic from the opening of the line between Aberdeen and Inverness. As late as 1863, Stewart was still justifying the Great North's policy:

> The citizens of Aberdeen have been accommodated for possibly half-a-century, first by their magnificent smacks, then by their steamers. And I do not think we have any cause to complain, really, if the Great North should divert as much traffic as ought legitimately to fall into that channel. By steamboat communication, you can carry heavy goods, which cannot go South by rail. And by this means we must derive some advantage, in bringing in goods from the districts on our own line, and from which we get local rates – goods which, but for the facility of shipping them per steamer at Aberdeen, would never have been lifted from our locality at all.[282]

Two of these southern railway companies had amalgamated in 1856; the Aberdeen Railway and the Scottish Midland Junction Railway had merged to form the Scottish North Eastern Railway.[283] Attempts were still being made in 1860 to provide the link required between the Great North's line and the trunk line to the south that had been anticipated in the Great North's parliamentary act of 1846. A meeting was held in May 1860 between the Scottish North Eastern, the Great North and the Inverness and Aberdeen Junction companies '... in regard to the formation of a Locomotive Junction between the Railways at Aberdeen' and the participants agreed to raise matter with their respective boards.[284]

Ever since the Great North had obtained powers to construct the line between Aberdeen and the highland capital, Inverness interests had harboured resentment at the enforced detour that the route via Aberdeen entailed, which added time and cost to the journey. In addition to the transhipment required at Aberdeen for goods traffic as a result of the discontinuity of route, the chaotic nature of the arrangements for passengers provoked an angry letter to the press in August 1858 from James Merry of Belladrum, one of the new highland landowners who had earned his substantial wealth in the coal and iron industries of the central belt of Scotland. Merry's letter of complaint, signed also by six others, including James Grant, Provost of Elgin and chairman of the Morayshire Railway, was recorded in the Great North's minute book, which initially suggests that this stinging public criticism had made some impact within the boardroom, but the reply, written by Great North secretary Robert Milne and approved by the board, indicates that Great North was somewhat impervious to censure at this time.[285]

To the Directors of the Great North of Scotland Railway 5th August 1858

For ourselves and on the part of others who have been as we consider very ill treated, we wish to represent to you that the Mail Train from the South arrived today late as sometimes happens at this season of the year. On the arrival of that Train all were aware that a few minutes only could be calculated upon, and all made every possible speed to reach the Station of the Great North of Scotland Railway [,] the Post Office authorities taking the lead followed closely by a lot of cabs. The officials at the station seemed predetermined to cause disappointment for the moment the Mail Bags were within the portals of the establishment, and which were carried off with more than usual rapidity, the Gates were shut in the faces of the Passengers, who naturally demanded immediate admittance. This was refused and when we got entrance, the latter end of the train had not quitted the platform, and the Clock of the station shewed that the starting time had only then arrived and that had we been allowed in, when admittance was first demanded, we could have all been seated in time for the starting of the train. So great was the hurry of the officials that the lady and luggage of one gentleman was admitted when the husband was shut out. Such conduct under such circumstances we believe to be inexcusable. If the Proprietors of two main lines of Railway are to keep their Stations a few hundred yards apart from factious motives or party squabbles, with which the public having nothing to do, to the injury and inconvenience of the community and are so to work as to disappoint the public by such acts as above related it is high time that the making of a more direct and continuous line of Railway in the North should be resolved upon. It is all very fine to talk of punctuality in starting of trains [;] in cases such as the present all know what half a minute is worth, particularly to a line that ends at Keith when coaches have to do the rest of the work and when a minute or two had been practically shown to be of little consequence. We and the others had our arrangements made in the North, had our horses and conveyances appointed to meet us on the arrival of the Train and the Coaches connected herewith and the disappointments and evils inflicted upon us are greater than can well be imagined and we leave it to you to say if the practice applied to us is to be expected from you by the public in future. On application to the officials for a Special train it was peremptorily refused. We are, Gentlemen, your obedient Servants.

(signed)
James Merry, Belladrum, Inverness
Charles Carnegie, Ardgay, Forres
James Grant, Provost of Elgin
Geo. Cameron, Sheriff Substitute, Dingwall
WH Mills, Rothes, Morayshire
Sidney Hadwen, West Garty, Sutherland
Lurgan, Lurgan, Ireland.

To which Robert Milne replied :

Aberdeen 6 August 1858
To James Merry Esq
Belladrum, Inverness
Sir.

A letter of the 5th inst. signed by yourself and six other gentlemen, addressed to the Directors of the Great North of Scotland Railway Company, complaining that the doors of the Waterloo Station at Aberdeen were yesterday shut to the exclusion of certain parties wishing to travel by the 3 o'clock PM Mail train of yesterday, has been received and laid before the Board. This complaint can best be answered by a simple statement of facts.

The advertised time of the arrival at Aberdeen of the Mail Train from the South is 2.18PM, but on the occasion referred to, it did not reach the Guild Street Station of the Scottish North Eastern Railway Company (five minutes drive from this Company's Station) till nearly Three o'clock. The doors of this Company's Station were shut in terms of the Company's Time Tables, at three minutes before Three o'clock, but were again opened to admit the occupants of three or four cabs, who arrived at the Station before Three o'clock – the advertised starting time of the train – all of whom with the exception of one gentleman, who appeared to be engaged in settling with his cabman, and who failed to come into the Station – although repeatedly and urgently called upon to do so – as is collaborated by several bystanders, including the cabman – were admitted to the Station and got on by the train, although too late to get Tickets, the Booking Office being shut, and the train just starting. Some other parties did not arrive at the station until after Three o'clock,

and the train was started shortly after that hour, according to the Company's Clock, which is five minutes behind that of the Scottish North Eastern Railway, the Post Office Clock and the Town's Clocks. Had the departure of the train been delayed for the rest of the Passengers from the South Train with their luggage and dogs, the whole of the Company's Train arrangements for the day would have been seriously interfered with, thereby causing inconvenience to many more than those who are now complaining. The request for a Special Train it was impossible to comply with; it being absolutely necessary in all such cases to send due notice along the line by the previous Train, to warn the platelayers and other workmen on the line who cannot be advised by Telegraph.

In conclusion, it may be remarked that it appears somewhat unfair to attack the Directors of this Company for the consequences of delays on other lines, over which they have no control, the only offence charged against them being too great a respect for punctuality, the want of which has proved such a fertile source of accident elsewhere, and the importance of which can scarcely be over-rated, particularly on single lines. Your letter having appeared in a public newspaper, this letter will also be published.

I am, Sir, etc.
(signed)   Robert Milne, Secretary.

The Great North was under no immediate pressure to finance an expensive railway link across Aberdeen. Traffic was growing, revenue was rising, and its shareholders were being rewarded with substantial dividends. A new line was unlikely to generate additional traffic for the Great North, but would simply re-direct the existing flow from sea to rail at Aberdeen at a considerable cost to the company and its shareholders. The Great North favoured the *status quo*, but that view was not shared in Inverness, or in the boardrooms of the companies forming the southern trunk route, which saw valuable railway traffic from northern Scotland diverted to shipping at Aberdeen.

James Merry's observation that 'a more direct and continuous line' should be made reflected the wider views long held in Inverness. The Inverness railway web was still devoid of its southern strand, the central objective in its unsuccessful parliamentary plans of 1846. Invernessians had never lost sight of that goal, but the web promoters were still grappling with the capital difficulties that had arisen from the construction of the Inverness and Aberdeen Junction Railway and the new pressures emerging in financing the Inverness and Ross-shire Railway. Yet within two years of Merry's critical letter to the directors of the Great North of Scotland Railway, a new direct line from Inverness to Perth and the south was to be promoted, which contributed appreciably to the rapid collapse of the Great North's monopoly and its subsequent major financial crisis.[286]

CHAPTER 8

THE GREAT NORTH AND ITS BRANCHES

With the lapse of the powers to construct the railway to Inverness, Great North strategy turned to extending and consolidating its control in north-east Scotland by providing support to nominally independent branch line companies that were expected to feed traffic to the main line. In 1846, Parliament had approved a network of lines centred on Aberdeen to serve Deeside, Buchan, and the Alford Valley in addition to the planned branches of the Great North to Banff, Portsoy, Garmouth and Burghead, but the collapse in the supply of railway capital in the aftermath of the great railway mania had prevented the ambitious and integrated plans of the Aberdeen promoters from being realised. Although powers for the Alford Valley Railway lapsed, the Deeside Railway was re-incorporated in 1852, but now independent of the Aberdeen and Great North of Scotland Railways.[287]

In the period immediately following the mania, the railway press soon began to question the value of extensions and branch lines to their parent companies. In 1848, *Herapath's Railway Journal* concluded that where the receipts of a railway company had been reduced, 'the cause will be found chiefly in the addition of branch lines'.[288] Two years later, *Railway Times* attributed the fall in the value of railway shares to the issue of preference and guarantee stock that had been required to build branches and extensions and argued for a more equitable distribution of profits:

> ... the rapid demand for extensions and branches fully justified the creation of preference shares at the time ... But, now that so great a revulsion has taken place, and when the general dividends are in many cases reduced below that accorded to the outlay on branches and extensions, which, without the assistance they have all along derived from the trunk line, would never have been called into active use, it is only reasonable and just that some other arrangement should be resorted to, by which a more equitable distribution of profits may be extended to railway proprietors of every class and degree.[289]

The parliamentary powers granted to the Great North of Scotland Railway in 1846 to raise £1.5 million in share capital and £0.5 million from loans had been predicated upon construction of the full line from Aberdeen to Inverness and its related branches, but even the revised powers of 1851 authorised share capital of £1,107,440 and borrowing powers of £300,000.[290] In the event, the company's 1852 proposal to construct the line as far as Elgin had been restricted to the section between Aberdeen and Keith by the intervention of the two new Inverness companies in building from Inverness via Nairn and Elgin to Keith.[291] Nevertheless, the confinement of the Great North to half of its projected main line did not affect its profitability and its extensive capital-raising powers gave scope to expand and protect its territory. This new-found investment capacity was outlined by chairman Sir James Elphinstone at a meeting of the promoters of the proposed Formartine and Buchan Railway in 1857:

> ... the promotion of the line beyond Keith by an independent Company had left a large reserve of funds in the hands of the Great North, part of which they had resolved to apply to the promotion of independent branch lines ... the Great North's unexhausted available capital amounted to £500,000 which would enable them to fulfill all their engagements and have a considerable balance.[292]

Elphinstone's statement referred to the remaining balance of unissued share capital, and not to the company's ability to raise it. By July 1857, the Great North had acquired £567,689 from the sale of shares and £248,963 from debenture loans, a total of £816,652, or almost three-fifths of its combined capital raising powers of £1,407,440.[293] Credit was dear: in November 1857, the bank discount rate reached 10%, but fell back to 6% by January 1858.[294] Moreover, the capital account of the Great North was in deficit by £42,077 in 1858 with an additional £50,837 owed to banks.[295] After the Inverness and Aberdeen Junction Railway had opened to Keith in August 1858, the flow of northern traffic over the main line resulted in a marked improvement in the Great North's finances, aided also by a period of cheaper credit between 1858 and 1860 during which the bank discount rate varied between 2½% and 4½%.[296]

BRANCH POLICY AND PRACTICE

The Great North's policy for branch line development was defined in 1855 by Sir James Elphinstone when seeking the support of his shareholders for lines to Old Meldrum, Banff, Alford and into Buchan:

> ... where the proprietors and other parties in the various districts are unable of themselves to develop, by railway, their resources fully, we come forward to aid them, thinking that if we could direct their traffic into our own line, we would at once be serving them and the shareholders of our line ... as a Company, we have nothing to do with these undertakings, but in working them with our plant and holding a limited amount of their stock[297]

Elphinstone explained the benefits expected to accrue to Great North shareholders by channelling the traffic of these districts onto the Great North's main line to Aberdeen:

> He wished clearly and distinctly to state that he

had always advocated the policy of bringing out the branch lines, for the purpose of developing the traffic of the county of Aberdeen ... The Directors did not make branches themselves, but subscribed a certain sum, more or less, to help the parties locally ... and thus the traffic of the different districts flowed into the Great North of Scotland lines, to the great benefit of its Shareholders, who would be amply repaid for the original outlay.[298]

Elphinstone's expectation of ample returns to shareholders ultimately proved to be in sharp contrast to the severe financial consequences that impacted upon the Great North as a result of the company's foray into branch line development. His speech to shareholders contained the hint that the Great North proposed to work the Buchan line at 'prime cost', which implied that, by simply covering its costs, the Great North did not expect a profit from operations, relying instead on the additional traffic generated for the Great North itself.

Elphinstone had no difficulty in securing the support of his shareholders for Great North subscriptions to four proposed railway companies: £40,000 to the Banff, Macduff and Turriff, £2,000 to the Old Meldrum, £15,000 to the Formartine and Buchan, and £15,000 to the Alford Valley. Shareholders were very content to allow the directors to pursue their branch line expansion while the dividends paid on their ordinary shares continued to rise, but *Railway Times* was unimpressed with Great North branch line policy and issued early warnings:

> The next duty of the directors, it might be imagined, would have been to secure some return to the ordinary shareholders. Instead ... it would appear that the board is rather disposed to encourage extension, and to further mortgage their own line to such branches as can be induced to connect themselves with it ...[299]

> The Great North of Scotland main line is a good property, and will remain so unless weakened and endangered by hasty extensions.[300]

Elphinstone's statement of branch line policy was not reflected in company practice for, while the lines were promoted principally by local residents often with considerable encouragement from Aberdeen, the Great North provided much of the capital and worked the lines, securing in return strong or majority representation on the company boards. The Great North, however, dictated a strict commercial policy for its allied branches. John Stewart, who chaired the general meetings of the company and its allied branches when Elphinstone was absent, later described the financial principles applied:

> ... we determined to charge the branches all deficiencies upon borrowed money as a debt against them, until we had three years' experience of their working; and if, at the end of that time, they did not pay the interest upon that borrowed money, that we would carry it to a suspense account, to be charged against the

line when it was able to pay it.[301]

Interest was charged on the use of Great North plant for working the branch lines at 5% annually and interest charged on loans and advances was, if the branch company could not afford to pay, accumulated as a debt on the branch's general balance sheet.[302] Thus, any financial difficulties experienced by branch companies were isolated within their own accounts and did not impinge directly on the Great North's accounts or its profitability.

The nominal independence of the branch companies disguised the absolute control exerted by the Great North, which was strengthened further by supplying its own management and administration to the branch companies. The financial principles outlined by Stewart were sound, but the branch policy ultimately was undermined by an over-optimistic assessment of the traffic that these branch lines would contribute to the Great North. By the early 1860s, the Great North was beginning to feel the financial pressure generated by its allied branch companies; most of which were by then drifting into insolvency.

By the end of December 1856, the Great North had approved subscriptions to seven branch companies, in addition to its short-lived investment in the Inverness and Aberdeen Junction Railway (table 7).

This branch network comprised lines with two main functions. The first were intended to feed local traffic onto the Great North's main line; the second, also local feeder lines, offered a potential extension route for the Great North to compete with the established section of the main line controlled by the Inverness companies (table 8). The true cost of securing this traffic, however, was masked while the Great North's monopoly brought rising net revenue and increased dividends. The strength in the Great North's finances emanated from the through traffic to and from the north, because its own line from Aberdeen to Keith served a predominantly rural area. Nationally, *The Economist* warned that branches could 'only be nursed into profit by a long and tedious process', while *Herapath's Railway Journal* cautioned that 'it is a mistake to suppose that all the traffic brought to the main line by the branch is new', and advocated that 'Branches and extensions should never be made unless their own traffic will yield at least 5 percent on their cost'.[303]

Although Great North shareholders asked few questions about branch subscriptions, the company's contractors, who held substantial amounts of company stock, raised objections, seeing potentially unproductive investment reducing dividends and share values. In November 1856, for example, contractors John Brebner and David Mitchell objected unsuccessfully to Great North proposals to raise the subscription to the Formartine and Buchan Railway from £15,000 to £50,000 and to subscribe £5,000 towards an extension of the Macduff line beyond Turriff.[304]

The crisp financial principles that Stewart had outlined were not applied consistently or universally, but were adapted to meet the financial and trading circumstances of the particular branch companies. Capital contributions varied year by year and included

Table 7: Subscriptions agreed by the Great North of Scotland Railway to other Railways, December 1856

Company	Subscription (£)
Inverury and Old Meldrum Railway	2,000
Alford Valley Railway	15,000
Banff, Macduff and Turriff Railway	40,000
Banff, Macduff and Turriff Extension Railway	5,000
Formartine and Buchan Railway	50,000
Banff, Portsoy and Strathisla Railway	2,000
Keith and Dufftown Railway	1,000
Inverness and Aberdeen Junction Railway	40,000
	155,000

Sources: National Archives of Scotland, BR/RAC(S)/1/14 and BR/GNS/1/2.

Table 8: Railways worked by the Great North of Scotland Railway, 1855–66

Company	Act	Working arrangements
Feeder branch lines to the Great North system (with Great North directors on the board)		
Inverury and Old Meldrum	1855	Worked by the Great North at cost and leased in perpetuity at rent of £650 per annum from 1858.
Banff, Macduff and Turriff (Aberdeen and Turriff, 1859)	1855	Worked by the Great North at cost price for 10 years from 1857.
Alford Valley	1856	Worked by the Great North at cost price for 10 years from 1859.
Banff, Macduff and Turriff Extension	1857	Worked by the Great North at cost price for 10 years from 1860.
Formartine and Buchan	1858	Worked by the Great North at cost price in perpetuity from the opening of the first section in 1861.
Branch lines with through route potential (with Great North directors on the board)		
Keith and Dufftown	1857	Worked by the Great North at cost price from opening in 1861 but no formal agreement signed.
Strathspey	1861	Worked by the Great North at 40% of gross revenue from opening in 1863 but no formal agreement signed.
Independent companies with through route potential for the Great North		
Morayshire	1846	Worked by the Great North at 45% of revenue from 1863 on the opening of the Strathspey Railway.
Banff, Portsoy and Strathisla (Banffshire, 1863)	1857	Independent working until 1863 when the Great North began to work the line initially at 65% of revenue.

Source: National Archives of Scotland, BR/GNS/1/5, pp.346-47.

declared subscriptions, temporary advances, guarantees for debenture interest and hidden subsidies. Some lines were worked at cost while others were charged a share of gross revenue. Moreover, not all transaction details appeared in the accounts or general balance sheets of both the Great North of Scotland and the branch companies.

Expectation of increased traffic on the Great North as a result of branch line development was reflected in comment on the company's prospects in *Herapath's Railway Journal*:

> We are glad, but not surprised, to find that the line is obtaining a very considerable traffic. The recent opening of the Banff, Macduff and Turriff line is calculated to aid it.[305]

John Stewart was equally optimistic when he addressed Great North shareholders at their general meeting in November 1857:

> The Old Meldrum branch was remunerative to the Company; the Inverury and Turriff line was also of that character; the Banff, Macduff and Turriff would add much to their traffic; and the Alford Valley was progressing.[306]

He went on to announce that the Turriff line, opened two months earlier in September 1857, was already adding £140 per week in traffic to the Great North in return for the subscription of £40,000, and he assured shareholders that 'we need not be alarmed for the Alford branch' in which £15,000 had been invested. Stewart

gave his assessment of the Great North's progress with its allied branches:

> The great secret why we have been so successful with the branches lies, I think, in this, that we help them to help themselves. The policy of other lines has been to take the whole children upon their back, and they were paid for at too high a price.[307]

Stewart's words were intended to rally Great North shareholders, but they were already buoyed by the news of a twenty-five percent rise in passenger traffic and a fifteen percent rise in goods following the opening of the main line to Keith, and the declaration of a 4½% dividend on their ordinary shares.[308] Yet the acute financial weaknesses of the majority of branch companies were inherent from the opening of their lines, and were gradually transmitted into the finances of the parent company despite the clear intent to isolate their affairs. Within nine years, Great North shareholders found themselves contemplating the absorption of their multifarious and increasingly insolvent branch line system, as the Great North board stared into a financial abyss that threatened its very survival.

The Great North's developing railway network has been aptly likened to a tree in which the main stem was formed by the main line between Keith and Aberdeen and the branches, with facing connections towards Aberdeen, leading traffic to the south-east.[309] This structure gave potential to the Great North not only to secure local traffic from the surrounding districts, but also coastal trade from the Moray Firth, and channel it across the branches onto the Great North's line into Aberdeen.

Of the five feeder branches authorised between 1855 and 1858, company records survive for all but the Inverury and Old Meldrum Junction Railway, but the Great North maintained its interests in this short branch by subscribing £2,000 towards its £22,000 share capital, nominating one director to its board, working the line and, from 1858, agreeing a lease of the line in perpetuity for £650 per annum.[310] The Old Meldrum branch opened in July 1856 and, after the first year of traffic, John Stewart explained to Great North shareholders the immediate results of their investment in the line:

> We have got no dividend from that undertaking and we do not expect any – they have given us something like £2,500 in traffic during the last year.[311]

The perilous financial existence of the other branches, the Banff, Macduff and Turriff Junction, the Banff, Macduff and Turriff Extension, the Alford Valley and the Formartine and Buchan, described below, illustrate starkly the growing predicament faced by the Great North in maintaining its branch line policy. Only the latter branch company, with plans to connect the two important Buchan ports of Peterhead and Fraserburgh with Aberdeen, offered some realistic hope, albeit distant, of providing any return to its shareholders.

BRANCHES TO TURRIFF AND MACDUFF

Sir James Elphinstone, chairman of the Great North, met fellow landowners in October 1854 to outline proposals for the Banff. Macduff and Turriff Junction Railway; Great North secretary Robert Milne acted as clerk. This scheme revived plans originally made in 1845 as the Great North of Scotland (Western Extension)

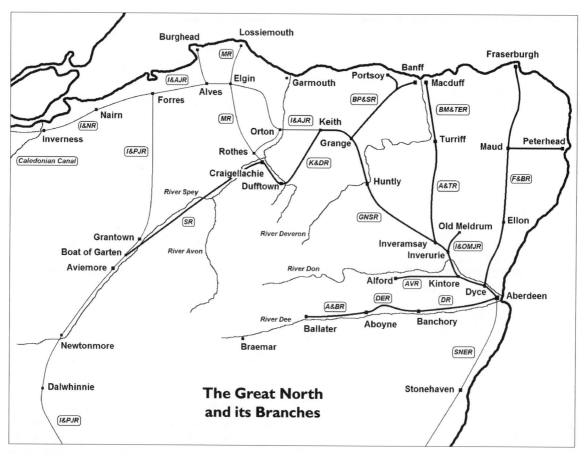

The Great North and its Branches

Key			
Great North and allied branches		**Other companies**	
GNSR	Great North of Scotland Railway	A&BR	Aboyne and Braemar Railway
A&TR	Aberdeen and Turriff Railway	BP&SR	Banff, Portsoy and Strathisla Railway
AVR	Alford Valley Railway	DR	Deeside Railway
BM&TER	Banff, Macduff and Turriff Extension Railway	DER	Deeside Extension Railway
F&BR	Formartine and Buchan Railway	I&AJR	Inverness and Aberdeen Junction Railway
I&OMJR	Inverurie and Old Meldrum Junction Railway	I&NR	Inverness and Nairn Railway
K&DR	Keith and Dufftown Railway	I&PJR	Inverness and Perth Junction Railway
SR	Strathspey Railway	MR	Morayshire Railway
		SNER	Scottish North Eastern Railway

Railway, for which a parliamentary bill was lodged but then withdrawn.

At this early stage, the terms of a working agreement were set out, allocating fifty percent of the net receipts to the Great North, which Elphinstone asserted would still produce a 4½% return to the new company.[312] The line was to run from Inveramsay on the Great North northwards to Turriff, with plans to extend to Banff and Macduff on the Moray Firth to tap potential traffic from the whole district north of the main line and the coastal traffic from the Moray Firth seaboard, although several present, representing local interests, wished to see the full scheme implemented immediately.

The Great North exercised full authority over the Banff, Macduff and Turriff Junction company from its incorporation, providing £40,000 of its £120,000 share capital and taking seven of the nine directorships.[313] Local landowners, including Elphinstone and the Earl of Fife, via his commissioner William James Tayler, offered land at a feu duty, but the lowest tender for construction of the line was £109,550, which left little margin within the authorised limit for cost increases.[314] In 1856, the estimate for the line rose to £138,000 and, with only £124,000 of assets available, a £30,000 loan was obtained from the National Bank of Scotland with security provided from company debentures and a £10,000 guarantee from the Great North of Scotland Railway.[315]

The Turriff company provides an example of the widespread use of guaranteed shares in railway finance, whereby an individual or institution guaranteed the railway company against loss on a number of un-issued ordinary shares if the company had not been able to sell those shares at least at par value within a given period of time; in the case of the Turriff company, that time period was two years.[316] Such guarantees were often used by railway companies as security for short-term credit. Lord Fife's trustees gave a 500 share guarantee in 1857, which allowed the company to obtain further credit of £5,000 from the National Bank.[317]

With the line under construction, a steady flow of capital was required. Unpaid calls amounted to £36,000 in October 1856 and so, in two board meetings in early 1857, additional funds were raised from the allocation of three-quarters of the company's £40,000 borrowing powers, issued as debenture loans paying 5% interest; £25,000 was provided by the National Bank of Scotland and £5,000 from the Northern Assurance Company.[318] With a further £6,000 debenture subsequently issued as security for an additional loan from the National Bank to complete the line, ninety percent of the company's authorised borrowing powers had been assigned by July 1857, purely as security for temporary loans from financial institutions.[319]

The final call on shares was made in July 1857 and, by the end of August, the Banff, Macduff and Turriff Junction Railway had raised £75,748 in share capital, well short of its target of £120,000. Indeed, throughout its independent existence, the company never received more than £85,290 from shares, a maximum of seventy-one percent of its authorised amount. Like their rivals in Inverness, the railway promoters of north-east Scotland had to rely on banks and other financial institutions to supply a substantial portion of the capital required to construct the lines, but these loans required servicing by the payment of interest, which had to be drawn from what was to prove to be a meagre stream of revenue.

The line opened to Turriff in September 1857, but at the meeting of Great North shareholders one year later, John Stewart's previously ebullient tone had changed. He reported that the Turriff line was being worked for 1s 9½d per mile, less than the 2s 5d per mile recorded on the Great North's main line, and so he concluded that the financial problems being experienced by the branch company were not due to the level of operating costs. The cause was to be found in revenue:

> But what have been the receipts? Why, the miserable amount of only £6,769 ... This line has already cost something line £145,000, and will require some other £5,000 to complete it ...[320]

Stewart announced that the sum raised from the district served by the line only amounted to between £14,000 and £15,000, which represented less than an eighth of the company's authorised share capital. 'Now it is high time that this state of things should come to an end', he declared in the same speech, but the Great North was already heavily committed to the branch and had already spent £18,000 on the purchase of land.

The first year of operation produced a small revenue surplus of £200, although the revenue account of the Turriff company slipped into deficit in 1859 and remained so until 1865, the year before it was absorbed into the Great North, when the princely surplus of £11 was recorded. Gross revenue, in fact, fell initially from £7,589 in 1858 to £6,945 in 1860 and then rose only slowly to reach £8,969 in 1865, but almost half of it was required each year to meet interest charges.[321] Stewart presided at the 1861 meeting of Turriff shareholders and commented on the trend in revenue:

> In the Turriff Line, the traffic strangely enough continued to go down and down from the first year of opening. Now, however, it would appear that it had reached so low that it could not get lower.[322]

Elphinstone chaired the annual Turriff shareholders' meeting the following year and adopted his customary optimistic approach at public gatherings, even though the accounts revealed a deficit of £24,783 on the capital account and a revenue loss for the year of £278 after paying the Great North's working charges, which was at least some improvement on the deficit of £899 reported the previous year:

> This line is in the position of most of the other branches, overcoming its difficulties and gradually improving every year as the country is more developed and improved. I have no doubt in my own mind that these branches will pay ultimately...[323]

Stewart supported his chairman and attempted to offer encouragement to the Turriff shareholders:

> ... there is life in the concern yet; that by and by, if it goes on at this rate, the shareholders would

be within sight of a dividend.[324]

By this date, however, the improbability of this and most of the other branch companies ever paying a dividend on its ordinary shares must have been apparent to the Great North's chairman and its directors. The capital account of the Banff, Macduff and Turriff returned a consistent deficit between 1856 and 1864. By 1859, almost two years after the line opened, capital expenditure had risen by almost one quarter above the parliamentary estimate and stood at £148,345. To try to raise additional funds, the directors sought new parliamentary powers to convert 3,722 ordinary shares, which were to be forfeited because of arrears in the payment of calls made on them, into a 5% preference stock.

The resulting parliamentary act of 1859 also included a clause to change the company's name to the Aberdeen and Turriff Railway to avoid confusion with a new railway promotion.[325] The Great North had concluded that the branch's financial position would not improve until the line was extended, as originally envisaged, to the Moray Firth coast and so a separate company, the Banff, Macduff and Turriff Extension Railway, was authorised in 1857 to build from Turriff to Macduff.[326] Capital for the new line was set at £81,000, with borrowing powers of £27,000, to which the Great North agreed to subscribe £5,000. As the Great North held tight control of the Aberdeen and Turriff line, it took only two of the six Extension directorships, perhaps anticipating the further financial difficulties that were to follow.

Once parliamentary powers were obtained to issue preference stock, the control exercised by the Great North within the Aberdeen and Turriff company was demonstrated. With six directors present in November 1859, four of whom were also directors of the Great North, the Turriff Board was informed that the Great North would increase its existing temporary advance to the company to £25,000 at 5% interest, but the loan was to be backed by £37,220 of the new preference stock taken as collateral.[327] With little possibility of raising new capital from the open sale of preference shares given the company's weak trading position and its remote location, the Great North's offer was accepted and part of the proceeds were used to redeem £15,000 of the loan already held from the National Bank of Scotland.[328]

It was only the consistent support of the Great North that allowed the insolvent Aberdeen and Turriff Company to remain operational, despite its relatively economic construction for, by 1859, the line had cost only £8,241 per mile to build.[329] The slow growth of revenue offered little scope of the company repaying its debts, let alone producing the 4½% return that Elphinstone had cheerfully forecast in 1854. But, if the results of the Banff, Macduff and Turriff Junction Railway had been disappointing to its shareholders and the Great North, the financial performance of the Banff, Macduff and Turriff Extension Railway was to prove to be even weaker.

The nominated Great North directors initially refused to join the Extension Railway board due to 'the present financial position of the Company and seeing the great deficiency in the amount of the Subscription List …'.[330] By February 1858, it was reported that 'the state of the funds was not at all satisfactory'; only £27,000 of the share capital had been subscribed, one-third of the £81,000 authorised.[331] The Great North set conditions before it would participate further, including a refusal to accept any responsibility for the construction contract, which had already been signed by other directors, unless funds were available to meet it.[332]

A detailed agreement was reached in July 1858 by which the Great North was to work the line at cost for ten years and appoint three of the six directors of the company, but with the chairman to be appointed from one of the local representatives.[333] That burden fell to William James Tayler, commissioner to the Earl of Fife and also a director of the Inverness and Aberdeen Junction Railway. The line opened in June 1860 but, within a year, the company had to defer the payment of debenture interest because there was insufficient revenue to pay it when due.[334] The trend of gross revenue was static: receipts of £3,108 in 1861 rose to £3,438 in 1863 but then fell to £3,313 in 1864 and £3,240 in 1865. The revenue account returned a consistent deficit throughout the six years of the nominal independence of the company, with half of the gross receipts absorbed by interest payments in every year.[335]

Although the capital account recorded an increasing deficit from 1860 until 1865, by when it had reached £7,625, capital expenditure was maintained within the limit of the company's authorised capital powers, principally because, for much of its length, the line crossed land owned by the Earl of Fife who accepted feu duty as recompense, and so land costs represented less than four percent of the capital expended by 1860. In August 1862, two years after the line began operating, capital expenditure amounted to £82,374, only £1,374 above the parliamentary estimate. The company's financial problems arose not from the cost of construction, but from the difficulty in raising share capital. Like its neighbour, it had to rely on authorised and temporary loans, and its static gross revenue proved to be insufficient to meet both its operating costs and the interest due on these loans.

By 1862, it was clear that both the Aberdeen and Turriff and the Banff, Macduff and Turriff Extension Railways, which connected the Great North's main line across the northern agricultural hinterlands to serve two established Moray Firth ports, could neither establish any firm financial stability nor demonstrate any sustained economic progress that would allow them to redeem their debts and begin to generate a return for their shareholders. The companies became increasingly reliant on the intervention of a major shareholder, the Great North of Scotland Railway, which was also wrestling concurrently with the finances of another branch company serving the Alford Valley to the west of Aberdeen.

ALONG THE ALFORD VALLEY

The Alford Valley Railway received parliamentary sanction in 1846, but, with the universal shortage of capital following the great railway mania, *Railway Times* reported in December 1851 that the company had been wound up:

> Alford Valley shareholders have had £2 16s returned on their payments per share and the line may now be held to be abandoned.[336]

The capital of the company had been set at £100,000 in shares of £50 and so shareholders received back just over a half of the £5 deposit paid on each share.

Plans to tap the agricultural traffic of the district were resurrected in 1855. Two competing schemes were proposed, one westwards from the Great North main line at Kintore and another by a nominally independent company extending north from the Deeside Railway, which had been re-incorporated and opened between Aberdeen and Banchory in 1853, with John Duncan, former director and chairman of the Caledonian Railway, as its chairman.[337]

Parliament approved the scheme that connected with the Great North, which was authorised to subscribe £15,000 of its £85,000 share capital.[338] The Great North held six of the seven directorships, ensuring absolute control of the branch company. It saw a strategic need to support this branch company not only for the potential traffic that it could generate for its own line, but also to protect its territory from any incursion by an off-shoot of the Deeside Railway.

The need for additional investment from the Great North was immediately apparent. In September 1856, the cost of a line as far as Whitehouse, two-and-a-half miles short of Alford, was estimated as £80,500, but the company was only able to identify capital of £72,500, which included a further £10,000 from the Great North above its authorised subscription of £15,000, £12,500 from the line's contractor, and full use of the company's borrowing powers of £28,000.[339] Only £7,000, less than a tenth of the capital required, was expected to be raised by the sale of shares in the district.

In 1858, the board of the branch company agreed to extend the line into the small village of Alford, acknowledging that they faced a shortfall of £20,000 in the amount of capital required to meet the new estimate of £100,000.[340] The Great North was to advance £15,000 to the Alford Valley company, which also accepted a £14,000 loan from the North of Scotland Bank, secured by company debentures and Great North preference shares.[341] By the use of contractors' bills, through which the company aimed to defer payment of instalments due to the contractor for one year, £15,000 of the shortfall could be bridged, but such bills required the payment of interest on the sums due.

The line opened in March 1859 and was worked by the Great North at cost price. After five months of operation, the company's first revenue account showed a surplus of £512, which induced the directors to declare a 2% dividend on its shares, but perversely on the same day the board asked the Great North to increase its advance to the company as it faced a deficit of £28,256 on its capital account.[342] The Great North agreed and, although the Alford Valley capital accounts for August 1860 recorded a temporary loan from the Great North of only £7,437, Great North secretary Robert Milne reported at the Alford Valley shareholders' meeting in November that £30,000 had been advanced on which the Alford Valley company was paying 5% interest, pointing out that 'if they had borrowed it from any other quarter than the Great North, they would be paying at the rate of 7 percent'.[343] The balance was buried in the company's general balance sheet under the heading "sundries due on account" amounting to £26,622, which included loans and contractor's bills of exchange. The Great North's financial support of the Alford Valley company was by now substantial for this £30,000 temporary advance was in addition to its subscription of £15,000 invested in ordinary shares.

The financial fortunes of the Alford Valley reflected those of the Banff, Macduff and Turriff and its extension. Gross revenue remained static throughout the independent existence of the company; receipts of £5,987 for the year to August 1860 fell to £5,009 by 1863 but then rose to £5,864 in 1865. With the exception of 1865, when a surplus of £241 was reported, the revenue account returned a deficit from 1860 until 1866 when the company was amalgamated into the Great North. The dividend of 2% paid in August 1859 after only five months of operation remained the only return paid to its shareholders.

The weakness of the capital structure of the company was sharply revealed in 1860. At the general meeting of shareholders, specific local representation on the board was sought by shareholder Dr Garden:

> ... at least one of their number, an independent shareholder, who is neither a Director nor shareholder in the Great North, should be in the Direction of this Company, to watch over their interests.[344]

This view received short shrift from the chairman of the meeting, Great North director John Stewart, who pointed out that of the £44,000 of £10 shares taken, £15,000 was held by the Great North and £12,000 by the trustee of the line's late contractor, John Brebner, with only £4,000 subscribed from the district served by the line. He suggested that, had the full £85,000 of share capital been raised, a dividend of 3% might have been possible. The Alford Valley had experienced the universal difficulty of raising railway share capital in northern Scotland, which resulted in a heavy dependence upon loans.

At the meeting of Alford Valley shareholders in the following year, John Stewart commented on the decline in revenue:

> The history of this line was a marked contrast to every railway with which he was acquainted. For the first year, they had a larger revenue than the second, and for the second they had a larger revenue than the third.[345]

Yet the Alford Valley Railway was not as unique as John Stewart alleged. In the previous year, Stewart had used virtually the same words during the general meeting of Aberdeen and Turriff shareholders:

> It was a rather singular circumstance that the second year's earnings on this line was less than the first year's, and the third year's less than the first. Of course, this was a state of things that could not go on ...[346]

Unfortunately, that 'state of things' did continue. By 1861, the trend of static revenue and rising debt had become a characteristic of these branch companies allied to the Great North. The Alford Valley board adopted the ubiquitous strategy of creating new preference shares from forfeited ordinary shares to try to raise new funds to meet capital shortages. The accounts for 1861 show that only 3,195 of the 8,500 authorised ordinary shares in the company had been paid in full, and that a further 4,517 shares had been issued on which arrears were due.[347] Parliamentary approval to convert ordinary stock was obtained in 1862 and 4,606 £10 preference shares were created, but on which the company was to pay an expensive 6% dividend.[348] The usual optimistic tone of Sir James Elphinstone was less apparent when he, rather than his deputy John Stewart, chaired the general meeting of Alford Valley shareholders later that year:

> 'All we can do is to hope that the railway will improve.[349]

By 1862, the finances of the Alford Valley company had become unstable. The deficit on the capital account, which had been rising since 1858, reached £38,508. The revenue account was in deficit by £2,017, while the proportion of gross revenue absorbed by interest charges had been growing alarmingly; 51% of gross revenue was paid in interest charges in 1860, rising to 68% in 1861 and peaking at 76% in 1863.

The Great North was forced to intervene to avoid the financial collapse of the Alford Valley company. Powers were included in the Great North's Amendment Act of 1862 to authorise an additional subscription of up to £48,000 in Alford Valley preference shares.[350] Preference shares were then taken up in 1863 to liquidate £39,420 of debt due by the Alford Valley to the Great North, which resolved the deficit on the company's capital account, although no new funds were generated as a result of this transaction.[351] The weakness of the revenue account remained as a legacy for the Great North.

The financial history of the Alford Valley Railway exemplifies the gradual inability of the Great North to sustain its branch line policy and keep its own financial affairs entirely separate from those of its allied branch companies. The line was built economically, returning a cost of just £6,310 per mile by 1859, and aided particularly by the widespread acceptance of feu duties by landowners.[352] The company, however, could produce no sustained growth in its gross revenue and, with a heavy reliance of loans, steadily accumulated copious amounts of debt. The Alford Valley became, like the Turriff lines, insolvent with no prospect of repaying its debt from revenue.

INTO BUCHAN

The region to the north of Aberdeen attracted early proposals for railways, but the parliamentary powers granted in 1846 for the Great North of Scotland (Eastern Extension) line from Dyce to Peterhead and Fraserburgh lapsed following the delays in building the Great North main line.[353] The Buchan district attracted renewed interest in 1855 from a proposed Formartine and Buchan company supported by the Great North and a rival Aberdeen, Peterhead and Fraserburgh scheme promoted by John Duncan, chairman of the Deeside Railway.[354] The Great North regarded the Buchan area as its legitimate territory, and a long contest ensued before the Formartine and Buchan bill was approved on its third application to Parliament in 1858.[355]

The Formartine and Buchan lines to Peterhead and Fraserburgh formed more of a mini-system than a branch, 54 miles in length, the cost of which was estimated at a meeting of promoters held in September 1857 to be £280,000.[356] The Great North offered to work the lines at cost and provide £50,000 in capital, but with an expectation that £50,000 would also be raised from shares and share guarantees in the district. Great

This photograph of Fraserburgh dates from its opening in 1865 and is one of the few early ones of railways in the north east of Scotland. The station was built adjacent to the harbour on the right. The original train shed was replaced when the St Combs branch was opened in 1903 and demolished in the 1980s. The engine shed survives in industrial use but so heavily rebuilt as to be hardly recognisable.
(GNSRA Collection)

North directors took five of the nine seats on the first Formartine and Buchan board, which agreed not to start construction without additional local subscriptions and to build only the twenty-nine mile section between Dyce on the Great North's main line and Mintlaw because of the shortage of capital.[357] The board also resolved not to start work until land settlements 'be effected in moderate terms', a condition that John Stewart repeated forcefully to Great North shareholders:

> ... we shall not put a spade in the ground until we have obtained liberal and satisfactory land settlements.[358]

Stewart also challenged the residents of the district to demonstrate their support for the line:

> Furnish us with £2,000 per mile and we will construct the whole line from end to end in its integrity.[359]

He suggested that £2,000 per mile for a fifty mile railway costing £400,000 was 'a comparatively small amount' for the district to raise, but the cost of the Dyce-Mintlaw section alone was now estimated at £240,000 and a shortfall in capital of £25,000 remained.[360] The Aberdeen Town and County and North of Scotland Banks advanced £50,000 each on security of Buchan and Great North shares, in effect providing temporary loans equivalent to the loan capital of £100,000 authorised in the company's parliamentary act as the company could not yet issue debentures because half of its share capital had not been paid up.[361] Difficulties with landowners arose. The company's law agents reported in December 1858 that 'some show a disposition to get the highest terms they can ...' and, by March 1859, only half of the twenty-four landowners between Dyce and Mintlaw had offered to accept a feu duty.[362]

The shortage of capital became acute with just £57,303 of the £300,000 authorised share capital raised by August 1859.[363] A plan of dubious legality was instituted to allow the release of borrowing powers by which the company's contractor was to pay the 10% deposit on 15,648 ordinary shares using funds already borrowed by the company from the North of Scotland Bank, thereby allowing a claim that half the share capital had been paid up.[364] The company then added £15,648 to the contract price to allow the contractor subsequently to repay the advance and the company to recover the shares. The Great North had objected to a similar subterfuge by the Inverness and Aberdeen Junction Railway in 1857, and so may have learned a creative financial technique from its rival to apply to its own advantage two years later.

The Formartine and Buchan board agreed to extend the line to Peterhead in 1860 after a local deputation guaranteed the £20,000 subscription required.[365] The line opened to Mintlaw in 1861 and to Peterhead in 1862, when the company offered to build a line to Fraserburgh if the district subscribed £45,000.[366] Although only £34,000 was identified, a new act was obtained in 1863, which also authorised a new 5% preference stock to reduce company debt, while the Great North obtained powers to increase its subscription to the line from £50,000 to £100,000.[367] By 1865, the Buchan lines had cost £11,544 per mile to construct, well above the costs of other Great North branches.[368]

Just over two-fifths of gross revenue on the Buchan line was absorbed by interest payments between 1862 and 1864, limiting any scope to consider paying a dividend, but the first year of operation to Mintlaw produced net revenue of £1,388 in August 1862 and a dividend of 1¼% was declared. The finances of the company scarcely justified that decision, for the capital account was in deficit by £48,967 and £84,100 was held in temporary loans from the Great North, but the dividend was probably paid to try to attract new investment in the company. The capital account reveals a rising deficit as the extensions to Peterhead and Fraserburgh were constructed, reaching £132,365 in 1865. In 1863, £100,000 of 5% preference stock was allocated to the Great North in substitution of temporary loans and advances, following the pattern adopted in other branch companies.[369]

Unlike the other branches authorised between 1855 and 1858, the accounts of the Formartine and Buchan show a rising trend of revenue as extensions were completed to the two principal Buchan ports. In 1865, after preference share dividend was paid, a revenue surplus of £1,680 allowed a dividend of 1¼% to be declared on ordinary shares. Although the company's financial structure remained weak, this branch system was showing evidence of some capacity to improve and repay its debt, albeit over the long-term.

The Great North's branch line strategy was increasingly undermined by mounting insolvency within its constituent branch companies. The uneasy financial relationship developing between the Great North and its allied branches was identified by *Railway Times*:

> However well established this undertaking is in itself, it must be confessed that it is not yet happy in its extensions. As a large contributor to as well as promoter of the Formartine and Buchan, the Great North of Scotland undoubtedly obtains the advantage of traffic from the far north-east of a hitherto unexplored territory; but the actual results of the new line are distinctly discouraging.[370]

It was not the costs of construction that caused the financial difficulties of these branches, but the shortage of share capital, which resulted in a heavy dependence upon loans and placed an unsustainable pressure on the companies to meet operating costs and interest payments from modest streams of revenue. With the exception of the Buchan lines, the branches produced little or no growth in revenue and debt was increasingly accumulated outside the main accounts with little or no prospect of its redemption. The extensive financial support given by the Great North to the branches, initially to secure traffic for its main line and subsequently to postpone their slide into insolvency, increased the financial pressure placed upon the host company that could only be sustained while it retained its share of the monopoly of the traffic from northern Scotland over its main line.

THE FRAGILITY OF MONOPOLY POWER

By 1861, the Great North had consolidated its position in the north-east of Scotland. Through use of its capital raising powers for the main line to Inverness projected in 1846, the company had been able bring into operation most of the branch lines that had been deferred in the aftermath of the great railway mania. The strict commercial policy applied to branch companies had confined the capital difficulties of those lines to the branches themselves and allowed the Great North to declare attractive dividends to shareholders. In March 1861, the 6½% dividend for the half year recommended in the Great North's report to shareholders prompted praise from *Railway Times*:

> The condition and management of this line more than continues a subject for congratulation … it proves that railway enterprise, if only once placed in an accurate groove, must run on without impediment to perennial success.[371]

The following year, *Herapath's Railway Journal* commended the Great North's half year dividend of 7½%, which was, in fact, to prove to be its apogee:

> … this high rate of dividend does not arise from any great stream of traffic. It arises from great economy in the management, particularly the capital account … If you do not keep down your capital account, it will undermine the dividend … Mr Stewart practices what he preaches.[372]

Nevertheless, there were barriers rising steadily to curtail the progress that these journals confidently expected from the Great North. There was no viable competition by land to the Great North's grip on traffic, but the company had no significant northern terminus of its own and no direct connection across Aberdeen to the trunk railway route southwards. Consequently, the Great North comprised an isolated, rural system with its profitability primarily dependent upon main line traffic from the north and the prosperity of local agriculture. Its monopoly power was therefore distinctly fragile. Sixty percent of the mileage worked by the Great North in 1861 comprised branches, within which substantial financial instability was already firmly embedded (table 9).

At the meeting of Great North shareholders held in April 1860, chairman Sir James Elphinstone recommended a dividend of 6% for the half year and claimed that the growth in traffic was 'due very much to the development of the branches'.[373] He reported, for example, that 7,687 more cattle had been transported on the Great North in the half year ending January 1860 compared with the same half year in 1859, and he specifically attributed 1,686 of these cattle to the Turriff branch and 2,321 to the Alford branch, but just 500 to the main line from Inverness. Certainly between these two half years, figures quoted by Elphinstone showed that the Great North had experienced a substantial increase in traffic, comprising 7% in passenger numbers, 16% in goods tonnage and 98% in livestock numbers.[374]

The Formatine and Buchan Railway had the problem of serving two large towns whose location in relation to the topography of the area meant that a branch was need to serve one of them. Where to site the junction was the subject of much debate. Originally proposed for Mintlaw, it was eventually situated at Maud, where a sizeable village grew up and one of the largest cattle markets in the country was established. The rising ground on the west side of the station was a favourite location for photographers. This view in the early twentieth century shows the line from Aberdeen coming in from the right and splitting into separate platforms for the Peterhead and Fraserburgh lines. The stone building on the platform survives and currently houses a small railway museum.

(GNSRA collection)

Table 9: The network of the Great North of Scotland Railway, 1861

	Route	Opened	Miles
Great North of Scotland	Aberdeen-Keith	October 1856	53¾
Allied branch companies			
Inverury & Old Meldrum Junction	Inverury-Old Meldrum	July 1856	5¼
Aberdeen and Turriff	Inveramsay-Turriff	September 1857	18
Alford Valley	Kintore-Alford	March 1859	16
Banff, Macduff & Turriff Extension	Turriff-Macduff	June 1860	11¾
Formartine and Buchan	Dyce-Mintlaw	July 1861	29
	Mileage of allied branches		80
	Mileage of the Great North system, 1861		133¾

Source: Data from HA Vallance, *The Great North of Scotland Railway*, appendices 1 and 2.

Table 10: Capital subscriptions and advances to feeder branch lines, Great North of Scotland Railway, 1861 and 1864

(£)	July 1861	July 1864
Inverury and Old Meldrum Junction	2,000	2,000
Aberdeen and Turriff	40,020	74,129
Alford Valley	15,000	59,920
Banff, Macduff and Turriff Extension	5,085	27,065
Formartine and Buchan	50,000	175,000
Total of subscriptions and advances	**112,105**	**338,114**
Total of Great North capital expenditure	1,079,546	1,669,392
Proportion of Great North capital spent on these five branches	**10.4%**	**20.3%**

Source: National Archives of Scotland, BR/RAC(S)/1/14.

Yet these halcyon years were to be short-lived. The 'perennial success', which *Railway Times* had anticipated for the Great North in 1861, was already threatened by factors to which that journal chose not to refer in the glow generated by the high dividends being paid by the company. Inverness had blocked the Great North's northerly advance towards the highland capital in 1858 and, from 1861, the branches placed an ever increasing burden on the Great North's finances. In 1861, ten percent of the Great North's capital had been spent on these five branches but, by 1864, this proportion had risen to twenty percent (table 10).

The Great North recognised the need to protect its market dominance. Its support of branches to secure territory was extended to a local ten mile line running south-westwards from Keith to Dufftown. The Keith and Dufftown Railway was incorporated in 1857; the Great North was to subscribe just £1,000 of its £50,000 share capital and appoint one of the nine directors, although both John Stewart and Alexander Jopp of the Great North are named in the company's parliamentary act.[375]

Like other branches, great difficulty was experienced in raising capital for this local line and only a third of that required for the parliamentary submission had been subscribed by December 1856.[376] By June 1857, £37,920 of the £50,000 share capital had been subscribed, of which £5,620 came from 181 local shareholders, including £1,800 from the directors and £1,000 from the Great North, £7,500 from the line's contractors, but £24,800 from the company's Edinburgh law agents.[377] The use of the law agents as nominees ensured sufficient deposits were paid to meet parliamentary Standing Orders, but the scale of this nominal involvement is indicative of the severe shortage of capital. By October 1858, construction work had been halted due to a lack of funds. The directors sought further support from the Great North, but their report to shareholders states:

> … in consequence of the numerous engagements of that Company, their Directors have hitherto declined to say if they will take up the Line.[378]

Major landowners, including the Duke of Richmond and the Earl of Fife, had given verbal support, but the Keith and Dufftown minute book records that 'the Directors have as yet been unable to get any of them to fix definitely to what extent'.[379]

Two years later, however, the Great North perceived new strategic potential in this short branch railway. The Inverness and Aberdeen Junction Railway had denied the Great North access westwards once the Inverness-Keith line via Orton opened in 1858. An alternative route to Elgin via Rothes had been considered in the 1850s by both the Great North and the Inverness and Aberdeen Junction, but it was not pursued.[380] The little independent Morayshire Railway, in dispute with Inverness in 1859 concerning running rights over part of the Aberdeen Junction line in order to connect its two isolated railways from Elgin to Lossiemouth and Rothes to Orton, announced plans to construct 'a direct line through the Glen of Rothes as was originally intended …'.[381] The Morayshire's projected line gave the Great North an opportunity to reach Elgin if it secured control of the neighbouring and ailing Keith and Dufftown company.

The Great North therefore offered to complete the Dufftown line and obtained powers to subscribe £25,000, half of its share capital, and nominate four of the eight directors.[382] With new legislation for the Keith and Dufftown Railway approved in May 1860, the Great North moved swiftly to secure its position and produced a draft agreement with the Keith and Dufftown and Morayshire companies.[383] The Great

Craigellachie was where the Strathspey line really started. This early view of the station, taken from the hill to the east, shows a train which has come down the valley in the branch platform. The through line from Keith came in from the left to the main platform in the foreground. It continued towards Elgin on the connecting line over the river which was built in 1863 to link with the Morayshire Railway's original terminus. The Strathspey line disappeared round the hill in the centre. The River Spey is just beyond the road bridge. The site is now a car park for the Strathspey Railway. (GNRSA Collection)

North's renewed interest in the Dufftown line prompted landowners to give £10,000 of share guarantees and land via feu duty.[384] Thus a proposed feeder branch to the Great North became a strategically important link in a potential new route from Aberdeen to the north.

The Great North then took total control of the Keith and Dufftown company by appointing a committee of management 'with all the powers of the Board', comprising its four Great North directors and just one local director.[385] The local directors were required to sign personal guarantees for a £25,000 subscription from the Keith and Dufftown company to a new Great North protégé, the Strathspey Railway, proposed to extend the Great North's system westwards into the Spey valley and to connect the Keith and Dufftown to the new Morayshire line through the Glen of Rothes.[386] The capital accounts of the Keith and Dufftown were used by the Great North to record elements of the financing of the early stages of the separate Strathspey Railway and so great caution is required in their interpretation. The Keith and Dufftown line opened in February 1862, although the connection to the Morayshire's new line to Elgin was not completed until July 1863.

The revenue account of the Keith and Dufftown exhibited similar weaknesses to other branches allied to the Great North. In 1863, after the first full year of operation, gross revenue was £3,187; revenue then

remained static, reaching only £3,205 in 1865.[387] Once the line to Elgin opened, the costs of operating the line rose and the revenue surplus of just £23 recorded for 1863 then sank into a deficit for the remaining three years before the company was amalgamated into the Great North in 1866.

A high proportion of receipts were absorbed by interest payments, which rose to a peak of sixty-eight percent in 1864. Moreover, not all interest was paid when due and any arrears were added to company debt, which was accumulated on the general balance sheet outside the main accounts.[388] The Great North exercised the same strict financial policy as with other branches: interest was charged at 5% on advances and the use of plant, thereby ensuring that the considerable financial difficulties of the company appeared in the Keith and Dufftown's accounts and not its own. While the financial structure of this small company was therefore very insecure, its value to the Great North was not as a feeder branch line but as a strategic section of the planned extension of the Great North's network towards the highlands.

Criticisms of the Great North's use of monopoly power, particularly in pricing and standards of service, were commonplace. Even the allied branches were not immune from high goods rates charged by the Great North. Farmers and traders using the newly-opened

Banff, Macduff and Turriff Extension Railway in 1860 sent a resolution complaining that rates were greater than stipulated in the company's legislation and made a formal complaint to the Board of Trade.[389] The Great North had refused to join the Railway Clearing House, established in 1842 particularly to encourage and co-ordinate fares and rates for inter-company traffic, until increasing competitive pressures forced it to change policy. The Inverness and Aberdeen Junction Railway had appointed deputy chairman Thomas Bruce in February 1859 to be its representative at the Clearing House, but it was not until September 1863 that Sir James Elphinstone told his shareholders that the Great North was to join the Clearing House for all its traffic from the following month.[390] In March 1864, Great North directors reported a fall in traffic receipts of £3,764 in the half-year, attributed in part to the consequences of their membership of the Railway Clearing House, although an agricultural depression and new competition from Inverness were also cited.[391] Elphinstone remarked to shareholders:

> Since I had the pleasure of addressing you last we have entered the Clearing House, and we now exchange traffic with the whole railway system of Great Britain. This, however, has deprived us of the opportunity we had previously of charging somewhat higher goods rates than some of our neighbours; and although the public have gained by that transaction, we have lost by it to the tune of £1,000 for the last half year.[392]

Increasingly, the exercise of its monopoly power alienated the Great North from its northern and southern railway neighbours and its users. The price and quality of passenger service on the Great North in this period attracted criticism:

> Its stopping trains could not even be dignified with the title "slow": they set the pace of a glacier ... But one thing the Great North did thoroughly well – it charged "express" fares for the privilege of a passage on its glaciers; and these express fares were of an exceeding magnitude.[393]

Publicly, John Stewart dismissed any risk to the continuing success of the Great North, stating in September 1861 that only about five percent of its passenger revenue was received from the fares of through passengers.[394] A year earlier, Great North directors had reported to their shareholders that nine-tenths of Great North dividends were derived from local traffic.[395] This defensive view was supported by *Herapath's Railway Journal*, which saw little danger to the Great North's profitability:

> The elaborate and able speech of Mr Stewart ... will be read with interest, especially that part of it where he mentions the small amount of through traffic, and therefore the security of the Company against any great injury from a competing line for the through traffic. A fine harvest does the Company a vast deal more good than a competition could do it harm. It now pays 7 percent and the traffic is increasing.[396]

The Great North made a new proposal in 1861 for a cross-Aberdeen railway link via the Denburn Valley, but infuriated the Scottish North Eastern Railway because it 'declined to give any guarantee as to the route by which they will send Traffic arising South and East of Keith', presumably intending to protect its connections with sea trade.[397] The Scottish North Eastern was then informed in October 1861 that the Great North had decided there was not sufficient time to prepare a Denburn Valley scheme for the forthcoming parliamentary session because the route was yet to be finalised, plans could not be completed and lodged in time and, consequently, the company had declined to proceed further.[398] The board of the Scottish North Eastern expressed its regret at the Great North's decision, resolved to stop any expenditure on the scheme, and minuted that it remained 'uncommitted' to the Great North's proposal that the measure should be put forward in the 1863 session of Parliament.

The reason soon became clear. Within two months, the Great North faced new opposition from a nominally independent line, strongly backed by the Scottish North Eastern, to construct a line from the Anglo-Scottish trunk route at Limpet Mill, south of Aberdeen, which would run northwards to connect with the Great North's line at Kintore and, as a result, by-pass Aberdeen altogether.[399] The *Railway Times* despaired of the situation:

> The Great North of Scotland have got into a jar with the Scottish North-Eastern, which will probably have the effect of throwing Aberdeen off the direct route to the north. The want of a junction between the termini of these lines at Aberdeen has long been a crying annoyance.[400]

The entrenched and highly profitable position of the Great North in the railway route to the north of Scotland was about to be subjected to significant competition, not just from the Scottish North Eastern Railway and its allies to the south, but by a new direct railway line promoted to connect Inverness with Perth and the southern network, thereby avoiding the time-consuming and costly detour via Aberdeen. In reporting the plans for a junction with the Scottish North Eastern Railway via the Denburn Valley to his shareholders in April 1861, Sir James Elphinstone appeared to acknowledge that a resolution of the discontinuity in route at Aberdeen was long overdue:

> Had this desirable arrangement been compassed sooner, he believed the projected Highland from Forres to Perth would never have been thought of.[401]

Even so, a railway link across Aberdeen was not to be opened until 1867, two decades after the Great North had been granted the original powers to construct it. Already feeling the strain of branch line development, the Great North's finances were soon to come under extreme pressure and bring the company close to bankruptcy.

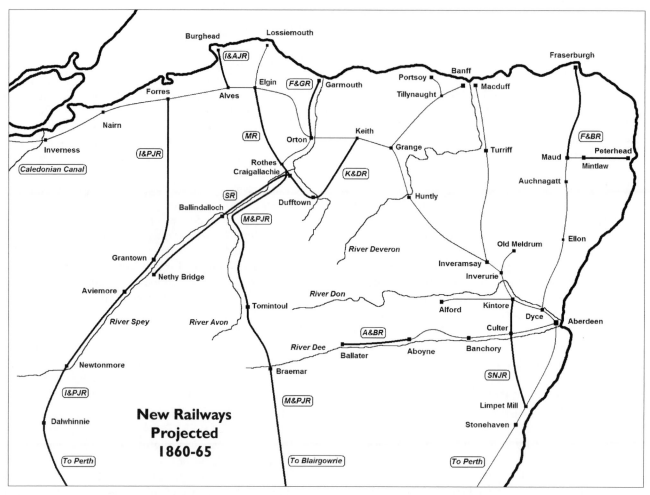

New Railways Projected 1860-65

Key	
A&BR	Aboyne and Braemar Railway
F&BR	Formartine and Buchan Railway
F&GR	Fochabers and Garmouth Railway
I&AJR	Inverness and Aberdeen Junction Railway
I&PJR	Inverness and Perth Junction Railway
K&DR	Keith and Dufftown Railway
MR	Morayhshire Railway
M&PJR	Morayshire and Perth Junction Railway
SNJR	Scottish Northern Junction Railway
SR	Strathspey Railway

CHAPTER 9

THE GALE OF COMPETITION, 1860-65

The outline of a railway system in northern Scotland had emerged by 1860, but it was focused on an elongated main line running from Perth to Inverness via Aberdeen. The two principal players north of Aberdeen, the Great North of Scotland Railway and the Inverness and Aberdeen Junction Railway, remained inter-dependent by virtue of their reliance on northern traffic crossing the joint main line, but both companies were actively planning to extend their operational compass at the expense of the other.

For the half-year ending in January 1862, the Great North paid a very attractive dividend of 7½% on its ordinary shares, compared to the 3½% declared for the equivalent period by the Inverness and Aberdeen Junction. Alexander Matheson, chairman of the Inverness and Aberdeen Junction, expressed his belief to shareholders at the general meeting held in April 1862 that, once the Inverness web of railways was completed, dividends would be comparable to those paid on the Great North.[402]

The Great North's financial standing was illustrated in *Herapath's Railway Journal* of 3rd May 1862, which reported that the company's shares were 'at upwards of £40 percent premium, indeed it is the highest stock in the whole market of ordinary trunk railways, even above the Midland considerably', and went on to attribute the Great North's success to 'faithful and economical management'.[403] Great North shares were quoted at £140-145 for stock with a face value of £100, compared to £128 for Midland Railway shares, £109 for Caledonian, and £63 for North British.

The leader writer of *Railway Times* pursued a different approach and compared developments in Inverness with the continuing conflict between the Great North and the Scottish North Eastern over the absence of a through railway route across Aberdeen, advocating closer ties between these two Aberdeen companies:

> The Inverness Companies are wise in their generation. Instead of quarrelling with each other, they combine at their inception, coalesce on their completion, and are now preparing to amalgamate the entire system … It ought undoubtedly to be the same with the eastern route …[404]

In a further article two weeks later, *Railway Times* looked beyond the current rates of dividend and predicted the ascendancy of the Inverness and Aberdeen Junction Railway:

> This company is now firmly established as one of the permanently useful and advantageous institutions in the north. It is destined, in fact, to command the whole of the north of Scotland, to control as well as accommodate the entire western coast, and to plant itself in Perth …

These various and yet uniform evidences of diligence, of sturdy self-reliance and vigorous prosecution of duties appear destined to earn a full reward; every difficulty seems to melt away in their presence; not one subscriber or shareholder, having once put forth his hand, withdraws it from the general work; thorough consension of opinion prevails, and unity or purpose presides over all.[405]

A complex pattern of lines was promoted in northern Scotland in the early 1860s as Aberdeen and Inverness strove to maintain and extend their control over northern traffic. These new developments added to the financial pressures that were already endemic in the Great North of Scotland and the Inverness and Aberdeen Junction companies as a result of the difficulties encountered in raising capital to construct earlier routes and to give support to allied railway companies.

A westward expansion of the Great North of Scotland Railway was instigated in 1859-60, using the lines of the Keith and Dufftown and Morayshire Railways to circumvent the Inverness – Aberdeen boundary established at Keith which, by 1863, created a new terminus of the Great North at Elgin. In response, Inverness brought forward plans in 1860 for the promotion of the main line between Inverness and Perth as the final and long-anticipated strand of its web of railways centred on the highland capital, by which the additional costs and inconvenience incurred by use of the circuitous route via Aberdeen were to be avoided.

As this major threat to the previously pre-eminent place of Aberdeen in the railway network was being launched from the north, a southern challenge to the Great North's monopoly was sponsored by the Scottish North Eastern Railway through its substantial financial support for a new nominally independent company, the Scottish Northern Junction Railway, by which Aberdeen and its contentious discontinuity of route was to be by-passed altogether. As both a defence and counter-attack to these simultaneous assaults from north and south, the Strathspey Railway was promoted by the Great North in 1861 as an extension of the Keith and Dufftown Railway south-westwards through the Spey valley. At Craigellachie, four miles beyond Dufftown, a junction was to be made with the Morayshire Railway's new line to Elgin via the Glen of Rothes, which itself was to be extended the short distance over the River Spey to meet the Strathspey line. But, like other allied branches, the Strathspey required extensive financial support and proved to be counter-productive to the financial interests of the Great North and divisive within its board of directors.

There were four small independent companies operating in the north in 1860, each of which held a prospective piece of the future network jigsaw. Two of these companies, the Deeside and Morayshire, were early examples of railways constructed on 'cheap' principles and both presented potential barriers to competitive expansion by other companies. The Morayshire Railway, opened in 1852, had made an agreement in 1855 with the Inverness and Aberdeen Junction for the use of part of its main line to connect the Spey valley to Lossiemouth harbour on the Moray Firth, an alliance which reinforced the check on any north-westerly expansion by the Great North from Keith towards Elgin.[406] In 1853, the Deeside Railway had opened a line running westwards along the Dee valley from Aberdeen to Banchory and extended it to Aboyne in 1859, which presented a possible obstacle to any new northerly incursions in the east of the region.

The two other independent companies operated established lines along strategically important routes. In the south, the Perth and Dunkeld Railway, opened in 1856, offered a convenient and judicious connection into the southern railway network for a direct line constructed from Inverness.[407] In the north, the Banff, Portsoy and Strathisla Railway, opened in 1859 from Grange on the Great North's main line to the Moray Firth ports of Banff and Portsoy, gave scope to develop a coastal route westwards by which the Great North might reach Elgin.[408]

WESTERN EXPANSION: THE MORAYSHIRE ROUTE TO ELGIN

An agreement was drawn up in 1856 to allow the Morayshire Railway running rights over the Inverness and Aberdeen Junction line to connect its new branch between Rothes and Orton with its established line from Elgin to Lossiemouth. Once the Aberdeen Junction's line opened in 1858, disagreements between the companies immediately arose.[409] Only weeks after opening, Inverness barred Morayshire locomotives from the main line, noting that its plant was 'not sufficient for the work' and resolving that:

> ... until the Morayshire Company are able to procure such plant, arrangement will be made for conveying their traffic between Elgin and Orton by this Company's Trains.[410]

In August 1859, the Inverness and Aberdeen Junction board minuted the 'continued attempts of the Morayshire Company to abstract and divert legitimate traffic of this Company by carriers and by sea', while the company's Order of Business Book contains the quaint note that the Morayshire Railway had 'unhinged' the agreement made between the two companies.[411]

The Morayshire responded by promoting a direct line from Rothes to Elgin to obviate the need to use the Inverness and Aberdeen Junction company's main line.[412] The Inverness and Aberdeen Junction attempted negotiation, but declined to accept the solution proposed by the Morayshire that the railway between Orton and Elgin should be doubled for which the Morayshire would agree to pay a rent of 6% of the cost of the extra line.[413] As the Morayshire's bill for its Elgin line was already in Parliament, the board of the Inverness and

Aberdeen Junction informed the Morayshire that the agreement made between the companies in 1856 would no longer be observed. The blame for the dispute was laid by *Railway Times* on the Morayshire, but it urged restraint so that

> ... there will be no foray through the Glen of Rothes, no waste of capital in forcing a useless line into the district.[414]

The new route, which represented the first significant example of duplication in the evolving network of railways in northern Scotland, offered a strategic opportunity to the Great North for expansion towards Inverness and so the Morayshire attracted competitive attention from Aberdeen. Once Parliament had granted powers to the Morayshire in July 1860 to construct its line to Elgin, the Great North produced a draft agreement in October to work both the Keith and Dufftown and Morayshire lines, thereby giving the company access to Elgin and the port of Lossiemouth and sidestepping the barrier previously established by the Inverness and Aberdeen Junction Railway at Keith.[415] The Morayshire was to extend its line over the Spey at Craigellachie to meet the Strathspey Railway, whereupon the Great North was to work the Morayshire's lines at forty-five percent of gross receipts, rising to fifty-five percent once revenue was sufficient to pay a 5% dividend. Yet, far from producing substantial dividends, this westward advance soon became a further drain on the financial resources of the Great North. Moreover, it was not until the Morayshire was absorbed into the Great North in 1880 that the route could be effectively integrated into the Great North's pattern of services

Inverness, which in July 1860 announced its intent to connect the highland capital with Perth via a new main line from Forres to Dunkeld, immediately attempted to counter the Great North's approach to the Morayshire by offering a 4½% guaranteed lease to the company provided that the proposed line between Rothes and Elgin was withdrawn.[416] Morayshire shareholders, however, accepted the Great North agreement and Inverness, already contemplating the considerable scale of the capital required to construct the Perth line, was indirectly spared a further expensive financial commitment.[417] The Perth line, incidentally, was described in its prospectus, in Inverness company minutes and in railway journals as the 'direct line', a term subsequently applied to the line constructed by the Highland Railway between Aviemore and Inverness via Carrbridge later in the century.[418]

The *Inverness Courier* denounced the Morayshire's agreement with the Great North, perceiving within it the competitive challenge posed to the monopoly of the Inverness and Aberdeen Junction's established route between Elgin to Keith:

> Miss Morayshire marrying in haste will find time to repent at leisure! The real object of the Aberdonians is to get a through line by Dufftown from Elgin to Aberdeen.[419]

Railway Times was highly critical of the Morayshire and its chairman, Provost James Grant of Elgin, and compared the proposed line between Rothes and Elgin

"HAUD AWA, BIDE AWA,
HAUD AWA FRAE ME DONALD;
WI' A' YOUR 4½ PER CENT,
YE'R NAE A MATCH FOR ME DONALD!"

ASSEMBLY BALL, ELGIN, OCT.ʳ 31ˢᵗ 1860.

Scene.__ Pause after the Parliamentary Quadrille.

Mᴿ INVERNESS.__ "May I have the pleasure of your hand for the STRATHSPEY?"

MISS MORAYSHIRE.__ "Thank you, I am engaged to Mᴿ ABERDEEN here for THAT DANCE."

Cartoon which appeared in the local press after the Morayshire AGM on 31st October 1860 showing Miss Morayshire being courted by both the Great North and the Inverness and Aberdeen Junction.
(Courtesy Jennifer Shaw, Moray Society, Elgin)

to Professor Aytoun's satirical *Glenmutchkin* scheme, published during the railway mania of 1845:

> This warlike line, with a redoubtable provost at its head, complains lustily of not having had everything its own way with the Inverness and Aberdeen ... It is in this position of their affairs that the proprietors have rejected a conciliatory offer from the Inverness and Aberdeen; and sought an alliance through the medium of glens yet untraversed and hills unpierced, with the Great North of Scotland. The latter company is to extend its line from Dufftown to Craigellachie, and so place the line of last session through the Glen of Rothes (being the veritable "Glenmutchkin" of *Blackwood*) on the Great North at Keith ...[420]

The *Glenmutchkin* analogy was more applicable to a concurrent Morayshire proposal for an ambitious main line planned to compete with the direct line from Inverness to Perth, which was to run from the Morayshire's terminus at Craigellachie to Blairgowrie where it was to connect with the Scottish North Eastern branch to that town.[421] Surveys revealed the

engineering difficulties of the line, for which the proposed share capital was £636,000, nearly seven times more than that already authorised for the existing Morayshire company by 1860.[422] Even this very substantial cost was considered to be a conservative appraisal, for the Great North was advised by its engineer Alexander Gibb that the tunnel required at the summit of the line would have to extend for at least six miles, rather than the two miles estimated by the Morayshire. *Railway Times* observed:

> To those who know the respective districts this scheme is all but impracticable, passing as it would through a desolate country ... with the gradients and other engineering works of a most costly character ... We cannot believe that the Morayshire can be serious in producing such a scheme ..."[423]

The scale of this promotion was beyond the capacity of the Morayshire, four-fifths of whose shareholders lived in the immediate locality.[424] The Morayshire scheme was ridiculed by *Railway Times*, but, surprisingly and erroneously, the journal discounted any threat to the Great North posed by the proposed line from Inverness to Perth:

> We dismiss, as altogether unworthy of notice, the bravado of the chairman of the Morayshire, whose ignorant ambition led him to calculate on a line from Craigellachie to Blairgowrie. We refuse to entertain the idea that the Inverness and Perth can inflict the remotest injury on the Great North of Scotland ...[425]

The Great North gave strong financial support to its new Morayshire ally. By July 1862, the Great North held £21,000 of Morayshire preference shares and debentures issued in return for cash advances in addition to its investment of £10,000 in ordinary shares, but Morayshire finances soon followed the pattern of other Great North branches.[426] The Morayshire had paid modest dividends consistently since it opened in 1853, but the dividend of 2½% paid in 1862 was to be its last as the capital cost of the new line from Rothes to Elgin began to impact upon its accounts and debts began to mount. By 1864, interest charges were absorbing three-fifths of the gross revenue earned by the company.[427] Annual gross revenue dipped sharply once the Inverness-Perth line opened in 1863, falling by a quarter between 1863 and 1864, and grew only slowly thereafter because the Morayshire route was nearly ten miles longer than the original main line between Keith and Elgin via Orton. *Railway Times* predicted in 1860 that the Morayshire 'will certainly come to grief' and concluded:

> ... we have only to leave the Morayshire to its fate, in the hope that its misfortune may become a warning in all time to come.[428]

Both the Morayshire and Keith and Dufftown companies that comprised this new route to Elgin were financially insecure and required significant support from Aberdeen. The Great North was warned by *Railway Times* of the financial dangers that it faced as a result, and its words proved to be prophetic:

> We venture to recommend the Great North of Scotland to look well on its right hand as well as to its left before it embarks its fortunes with the Morayshire, or to any extent takes upon itself one or more of the responsibilities of that misguided and entirely uneconomical operation ... and it would be an unhappy condition for the Great North to be fettered by a faltering Morayshire on one side, and an imperative extension through Strathspey on the other, while a not over courteous neighbour might step in at the moment of distress and convert misfortune into calamity.[429]

The neighbours, north and south, were indeed ready, willing and able to assist in converting the Great North's misfortunes into a financial calamity.

In 1866, the Great North and the Morayshire companies failed to agree terms for amalgamation because of the Morayshire's debt and operational disputes between the companies, although permissive legislation for a merger was obtained.[430] An indication of the company's indebtedness was given to the Morayshire board in November 1866 when its members were reminded that they had 'become bound as Directors and individuals on behalf of the Company to the Commercial Bank, and to the Contractors and others for sums amounting in total to £30,447 4s 3d', a sum representing over £1.5 million in current value.[431] In 1867, an approach by the Morayshire to the Highland Railway for an amalgamation was rejected once Inverness realised the scale of the Morayshire's liabilities.[432]

For a brief period in the early 1860s, the Morayshire held a strong bargaining position with the two regional railway monopolies based in Aberdeen and Inverness, but it failed to capitalise on its potential power. The company was finally absorbed by the Great North in 1880.[433] The Great North had, nevertheless, succeeded in using the Morayshire to establish a new inter-company boundary at Elgin. Disputes between Aberdeen and Inverness over the status of Elgin persisted throughout the remainder of the century, during which Inverness worked strenuously to preserve Keith as the principal point of exchange for northern traffic.

THE DIRECT LINE TO THE SOUTH: THE INVERNESS AND PERTH JUNCTION RAILWAY

The year 1860 was catalytic for railway development in northern Scotland. In January, the Great North withdrew from the board of the Inverness and Aberdeen Junction, acknowledging that Inverness intended Keith to remain the territorial boundary between the two companies. Instead, the Great North initiated its westward extension via the Keith and Dufftown and Morayshire Railways and began working this alternative route from Aberdeen to Elgin in July 1863. The strained relationships between Inverness and the Great North and Morayshire alliance, which now presented the threat of renewed competition for northern traffic, stimulated the launch of the direct line from Inverness to Perth. The railway press reported enthusiastically on this proposed new main line:

> This line will save 60 miles in the distance to the south, but it is not so much for its competitive advantage that we think well of it, as for its cheapness, and serving a new and important district of country. It is a line which ought to be made, and as it appears it can be made for about £6,000 a mile, no time should be lost in bringing about the event. We have numerous instances in Scotland and elsewhere of lines constructed at less than £10,000 per mile paying well.[434]

> This project, valuable and attractive as it is in itself, derives no small amount of importance from the hearty support it is receiving in the district it purports to accommodate. The whole of the local influences, whether accruing from residence, property, trade or social progress, are in its favour.[435]

Shareholders of the Inverness and Aberdeen Junction were informed by their directors of this new scheme at their general meeting in October 1860:

> A most important scheme for connecting Inverness and the North, by a direct line, with Perth and the general Railway System of the kingdom ... will be presented to Parliament in the ensuing session ... It will secure a free and unfettered outlet to the South for the Traffic of the Northern railways ... there is every reason to believe that it will be made at the cost of £6,000 per mile ...[436]

At this low cost, the promoters of the Inverness and Perth Junction Railway clearly envisaged the whole-hearted adoption of 'cheap railway' principles applied, not to a short branch line, but to a main trunk line of over one hundred miles from Forres on the Inverness and Aberdeen Junction Railway to Dunkeld, where a connection was to be made with the Perth and Dunkeld Railway. A standing committee, including influential Inverness directors Alexander Matheson, Thomas Bruce, Eneas Mackintosh, William Fraser-Tytler, and George Loch with Inverness banker Charles Waterston, was appointed to negotiate with landowners and to seek capital from southern railway companies.[437]

Matheson later asserted that the direct line to Perth was bought forward sooner than had been anticipated by the Inverness promoters:

> ... the Directors found themselves compelled, sooner than expected, in consequence of the obstructive policy of the Great North of Scotland, whose line interposed between them and the south, to turn their attention to the great scheme of a direct line through the Central Highlands to Perth, following nearly the original route of 1846.

> The Directors attached great importance

to this line – first, because the lines already made were far from safe so long as another Company could push into the north from the south; and, secondly, because they found that it was impossible to develop the traffic on the lines constructed along the coast, with the great detour via Aberdeen, and in the face of the obstructions which the owners of that route constantly put in the way of the northern traffic flowing to and from the south. The Inverness and Perth line was accordingly carried through with great expedition, and opened to the public in September 1863 – a little more than two years after the bill received the Royal Assent.[438]

Unsurprisingly, Matheson identified the Great North as the principal cause of the decision to proceed with the Perth line in 1860, but the Inverness and Aberdeen Junction Railway at this date was still in its infancy; the line had been open for only two years and the company was still resolving its existing capital difficulties. Moreover, the company was making further financial commitments to extend the Inverness railway web northwards into Ross-shire, where the problems of raising capital were already becoming apparent. The finance required for a major main line across the Grampian mountains to Perth at this particular juncture must have been a daunting prospect to the Inverness promoters, hence their early decision to seek support from other railway companies and local landowners. In December 1859, only a few months before the direct line to Perth was announced, Thomas Bruce, deputy chairman of the Inverness and Aberdeen Junction Railway, had suggested to the Great North of Scotland board that a subscription of £20,000 might be forthcoming from Inverness towards the cost of a Great North line across Aberdeen to connect with the Scottish North Eastern route to the south, but no subsequent progress was recorded.[439] A capital contribution from Inverness towards this long-awaited link offered the chance of substantial improvements in railway connections from Inverness with the south and at considerably less cost than a new trunk railway

from Inverness to Perth. Railway capital in northern Scotland was scarce and money was becoming dear. The bank discount rate rose from 4% in January 1860 to 6% by December and peaked at 8% in February 1861 before falling back gradually to reach 3% by the end of that year.

Matheson also indicated in this speech to shareholders that there had been some concern in Inverness that another railway company might push a line northwards towards Inverness. In 1846, the Strathtay and Breadalbane Railway had been granted powers to construct a branch from Aberfeldy to connect with the proposed Perth and Inverness Railway, but the company was left isolated when the latter scheme was rejected in Parliament. The Scottish Midland Junction Railway had seen the potential in building a branch to Dunkeld with an extension northwards to connect with the proposed Strathtay and Breadalbane line, which might also form an important section of a future through route to Inverness. At the general meeting held in August 1846, Scottish Midland Junction shareholders were advised:

> The Bill for the Perth and Inverness Railway Company's Line has been rejected, but the Bill for the Strathspey and Breadalbane Lines has been passed. A very few miles of railway are all that are necessary for uniting the Midland Branch with that Line. Already it has been suggested that the union should be made, and a Local Line extended northwards to Pitlochry, opening the Athole county, which, besides opening up the district, would be step towards the Inverness scheme ...[440]

The Scottish Midland Junction did not pursue their proposal, but a branch to Dunkeld was later constructed by the independent Perth and Dunkeld Railway and opened in 1856.[441] The line was worked by the Scottish North Eastern Railway, formed in 1856 by the amalgamation of the Scottish Midland Junction and Aberdeen Railways. The Inverness promoters of the new direct line planned to use the route of the Perth and Dunkeld to gain access to Perth and the southern

The Inverness and Perth Junction Railway had not only to contend with some barren country but it also had to pass over Druimuachdar, at 1484 feet the highest summit on a main line in Britain. The sight of the summit board was always welcomed by the crews of steam engines struggling up the hill on the northbound side. The track here was originally single, but was doubled at the beginning of the twentieth century as part of the company's investment to increase capacity and eliminate delays on its long single line.

(HRS collection)

railway network. By the time the Inverness and Perth Junction Railway was launched in 1860, the Perth and Dunkeld was well-established as a successful local line, running just over eight miles from Dunkeld to Stanley on the Scottish North Eastern main line from Perth to Aberdeen.

The strategic value, and therefore the price, of this line became apparent in 1860 when publication of the Inverness proposals for the direct line to Perth prompted the Scottish North Eastern to bid to purchase the Dunkeld company, offering a guaranteed dividend of 5% provided that the Inverness line connected at Dunkeld so that northern traffic would pass over its route to Perth.[442] The Duke of Athole, however, reported to the Perth and Dunkeld board that the Scottish North Eastern 'had started a line in opposition to the Inverness scheme from Birnam to Aberfeldy and were surveying the land between these points even against the wishes of some of the proprietors'.[443] The purpose was primarily for defence rather than opposition: the Scottish North Eastern had decided to give parliamentary notice of a bill to construct a line from Birnam to Aberfeldy and asked its engineer to prepare plans of the railway, seeking to protect its interests by securing the southern part of the Inverness-Perth route.[444] It abandoned plans for a branch to Aberfeldy and withdrew its proposed bill to lease the Perth and Dunkeld after opening negotiations directly with the Inverness promoters to provide the use of its line from Stanley into Perth.[445]

Although the Scottish North Eastern had scope to push a line northwards from Dunkeld in opposition to the Inverness and Perth Junction scheme, its records show that negotiations were conducted with Inverness over the route of the Inverness and Perth Junction line. The company recognised the potential benefits of accepting the traffic from northern Scotland onto its system without incurring new capital expenditure, which would also offset the current loss of revenue at Aberdeen caused by the Great North's use of shipping for its southern goods traffic. In September 1860, the Scottish North Eastern board instructed its engineer, John Willet, to report 'as to the practicability of having the Railway which is projected to run from Forres to Dunkeld diverted so as to join this Company's Line at Blairgowrie' whilst, at the same meeting, three directors, including their redoubtable chairman John Stirling, were deputed to meet directors of the Inverness and Aberdeen Junction 'to see if they would be parties to a scheme to make a railway from Keith to connect with the Scottish North Eastern Railway at Aberdeen', a proposal which was intended to isolate the Great North completely.[446] A request from James Grant, chairman of the Morayshire Railway, for the Scottish North Eastern to make a contribution to the parliamentary expenses for the proposed Morayshire line from Craigellachie to Blairgowrie was also firmly rejected at this board meeting, leaving that competing scheme bereft of support. The promoters of the Inverness and Perth Junction retained their proposed route to Perth via Dunkeld, but these negotiations show that the Scottish North Eastern board had the same object as the directors in Inverness, namely to remove the costs and disadvantages of the continued absence of a continuous railway route across Aberdeen and the perceived intransigence of the Great North of Scotland Railway to construct it.

The Perth and Dunkeld Railway experienced little difficulty in raising sufficient share capital and its capital account remained close to balance throughout its independent existence. Gross revenue rose steadily and, with little temporary debt, the company was able to pay modest dividends consistently. Half yearly dividends of between 2% and 3% were paid between January 1858 and January 1862, rising to 4% in the following two half years and 4½% in July 1863.[447] When, in 1861, the Inverness and Perth Junction opened discussions with the Dunkeld company to gain access over its line to Stanley, this small company was able to negotiate from a position of strength.[448] The chairman of the Perth and Dunkeld Railway, the Earl of Mansfield, informed his shareholders in September 1861 of 'the painful necessity' of recommending a dividend of only 2%, which he blamed on the Scottish North Eastern Railway and its charge of fifty percent of receipts for working the line, but he urged them:

> … not to be in too great a hurry in making an agreement with the Inverness, as he thought it would eventually be found that the Dunkeld was never more valuable than at the present moment, or that the Inverness supposed it to be.[449]

In 1863, the Perth and Dunkeld board advised Inverness of its terms; 'that an amalgamation should take place … [and] that the Perth and Dunkeld Railway Company should receive a preferential dividend of six percent …'.[450] Following a lease from June 1863, Dunkeld ordinary stock was translated into a 6% preference stock once amalgamation was finalised in February 1864.[451] The Earl of Mansfield was able to tell his shareholders that 'the effect of this arrangement had been nearly to double the value of their shares'.[452] By its strong business performance and from its important strategic position in the Tay valley at the southern extremity of the natural route between Inverness and Perth, this little company was able to exercise its market power to secure a very favourable financial settlement for its shareholders. This 6% dividend, however, represented a further cost that the directors of the Inverness and Perth Junction Railway had to meet from the revenue generated by its new main line.

The Inverness and Perth Junction Railway, also described as the Great Highland Central Railway, was promoted as 'the last section of the great central line from London' which would 'enable a passenger to travel without change of carriage from London to Inverness in 16 hours'.[453] The prospectus justified the promotion of this southern trunk route to avoid the detour via Aberdeen, but it produced a complacent response from John Stewart, who informed Great North shareholders that he had estimated a maximum loss of traffic to the company amounting to £4,302 as a result of this new line:

> Supposing the worst comes to the worst;

suppose the Highland line to be opened and in full operation, that [£4,302] is the outside that could be taken from us ... Where the inducements are to make a new line I cannot see. That, however, is not our business, and we do not need to inquire.[454]

Nevertheless, the new line presented an open challenge to the regional monopoly of northern traffic enjoyed by the Great North of Scotland Railway in its uncomfortable partnership with the Inverness and Aberdeen Junction Railway. In response, the Great North sponsored the Strathspey Railway, rejecting a request from Provost James Grant for support of the Morayshire's ambitious line to Blairgowrie and a proposal of amalgamation.[455] With both Aberdeen and Inverness embarked on schemes of competitive and costly expansion in 1860, the only truce drawn was that the promoters agreed not to oppose each other's bills in Parliament to avoid extra expense.[456] The underlying concern was aptly summarised in a letter from the Great North's law agent, Alexander Anderson, to Thomas Bruce, who had been charged by the provisional committee of the Inverness and Perth Junction Railway to try to persuade the Great North to end its alliance with the Morayshire and limit the extent of the proposed Strathspey Railway:

> ... such idle stories as you mention of our intentions to go beyond Nethy are flying about as thickly as possible ... We shall all have enough to struggle against with these Railways, if we live long, without internecine conflicts.[457]

The route of the proposed line from Inverness to Perth differed from the unsuccessful scheme of 1846 by re-locating its northerly junction from Nairn further east to Forres in order to gain traffic from the counties of Moray and Banff, to serve the important town of Grantown, and to secure the timber traffic from the Earl of Seafield's estates in Strathspey.[458] Seafield joined the first board of the Inverness and Perth Junction Railway and his commissioner, Thomas Bruce, became its chairman with Alexander Matheson as deputy chairman, a reversal of their appointments on the board of the Inverness and Aberdeen Junction Railway.[459] *Railway Times* reported in July 1860 that the line was '... supported by all the leading proprietors whose property will be traversed by it; indeed the provisional committee comprises most of their names ...', noting four months later:

> All along the route from Inverness to Dunkeld – with the single exception of Nairn, where some perhaps pardonable sulkiness has been exhibited – town and hamlet have risen up in favour of the line, while the landed proprietors, from the duke to the simple country gentleman, have come forward almost as one man in its support; and that not merely in the way of profitless praise, but with solid substantial money. This is a rare and happy circumstance ... Everyone seems to have been fully alive to the fact, that if the line is to be made at all it must be made by the people themselves ...

by the clubbing together of all the available means of the different districts – and they have acted accordingly, farmers, shopkeepers and noblemen taking stock in the concern according to their means.[460]

Parliament, satisfied that technological advances now overcame the reservations expressed in 1846 when the bill for the Perth and Inverness Railway was rejected, authorised the construction of the Inverness and Perth Junction Railway in July 1861.[461] The smooth passage of the bill through Parliament evoked comment in *Railway Times*:

> Seldom is it, indeed, that a new line, extending beyond 118 miles in length, is permitted to pass though committee with a merely formal opposition, and the whole inquiry be conducted and concluded in less than a couple of hours ... not one of the landowners along its entire route being other than an ardent supporter of the project.[462]

The first elected board of fifteen directors included four peers, three baronets and two members of parliament and all were highland landowners or commissioners of their estates; moreover, three-fifths of the board held directorships of other Inverness web companies.[463] For a quarter of its length, the new route passed over land belonging to the Duke of Atholle, who abandoned his initial reluctance for a line through his property, urged support for the promoters, and joined the first board:

> I am now convinced as to the great advantage that a line of railway to the north would be to the north country ... We all ought to put our shoulders to the wheel and help the promoters of this railway as much as we can.[464]

> I can make sacrifices for a through line, which I believe will be a great national benefit, as well as a benefit to the districts locally affected ...[465]

In view of the scale of the undertaking, the promoters agreed to ask the Edinburgh and Glasgow and Scottish Central Railways to subscribe £200,000 and work the southern half of the line from Perth to Dalwhinnie.[466] The parliamentary act authorised subscriptions from six railway companies, comprising £80,000 from the three established Inverness companies, £15,000 from the Perth and Dunkeld, and £120,000 each from the Scottish Central and Edinburgh and Glasgow. Had all of these permissive subscriptions been translated into the purchase of shares, just over half of the authorised share capital of £654,000 would have been available to the new company.

The southern companies did not provide any funds, however, with the result that shortage of capital immediately became a critical problem faced by the Inverness and Perth Junction board. By December 1860, subscriptions amounted to £148,000, representing less than one quarter of the authorised share capital, and £37,000 was borrowed from the Commercial Bank towards the parliamentary deposit, secured on the personal guarantee of seven provisional committee members, including Matheson, Bruce, Mackintosh and

Construction in progress near Kingussie. Although few mechanical aids were available, the line from Forres to Dunkeld was constructed in a remarkably short time.
(Courtesy Hamish Stevenson)

Seafield.[467] Bruce was placed in charge of arrangements for 'careful supervision of details and strict economy of expenditure …' at a salary of £500 per annum from January 1861, and confirmed in 1863 as 'Managing Director of all the Company's lines …' on the same salary.[468]

Capital problems intensified. In April 1862, Bruce informed the board that £100,000 above the company's authorised capital powers would be required to complete the line and it was agreed that loans were to be arranged from the Commercial, National and Caledonian Banks for that amount, a duty delegated to Matheson and Bruce.[469] An advertisement was placed for debenture loans at 4½% in July 1862 in anticipation of the release of borrowing powers at the shareholders' meeting due to be held in October.[470] With bank discount rates at 3%, the advertised interest on debentures was attractive and £165,690, just over three-quarters of the authorised loan capital of £218,000, was received by the beginning of December 1862, although only eight percent of these funds were from England.[471]

By mid-January 1863, £202,678 had been received from the sale of debentures and the inflow of funds not only financed the construction in progress but also moved the capital account from deficit into a small surplus of £20,271 in February 1863.[472] This improvement was to be short-lived, for only thirty-five percent of the share capital had been subscribed by February 1863 and the accounts for August that year show that £171,441 was held as temporary debt on the general balance sheet, a very substantial portion of which represented loans obtained from bankers to balance the capital account

deficit of £173,883.[473]

The Inverness and Perth Junction followed the convention of the Inverness web companies and recorded all items of temporary debt on the general balance sheet under the single heading of 'sundries' with the result that the composition of this debt was not revealed to shareholders unless specific questions were asked at general meetings. Nevertheless, the reliance placed on temporary bank advances is evident in the records of the company. In August 1863, the Commercial Bank and National Bank of Scotland in Edinburgh each agreed to lend £50,000 to the company for two years at 4½% interest.[474] Less than five months later in January 1864, the National Bank advanced a further £50,000, and the Commercial Bank gave an 'occasional overdraft' of £45,000 in March 1864.[475]

The shortage of capital prompted the company to seek the agreement of shareholders in October 1863 to convert £254,000 of unissued ordinary shares, comprising almost two-fifths of its authorised share capital, into 4½% preference stock.[476] Thus, one month after the full line had opened to traffic, just over half the total of the company's authorised capital in the form of debentures and preference shares carried fixed interest and dividend payments, the costs of which presented a prior charge on the revenue to be earned from the new line.

The railway was constructed in only twenty-three months and strict economy was exercised; stations were built in wood and contractors' huts were used initially to house railway staff.[477] In March 1865, at the last general meeting held before the Inverness and Perth Junction was amalgamated with the Inverness and Aberdeen Junction to form the Highland Railway, the directors forewarned shareholders that capital expenditure on the line was not yet complete and that 'a considerable sum' remained to be paid for the settlement of land claims.[478]

The prospectus for the Inverness and Perth Railway had advertised that the line could be constructed at a cost of £6,000 per mile including land, although the parliamentary estimate suggests a slightly lower figure of £5,813 per mile.[479] Either of these costs was exceptionally low for a main trunk route crossing the Grampian mountains, albeit using a single line of railway. Yet in October 1865 at the first general meeting of Highland Railway shareholders, when a dividend of 2% was recommended compared to the 4% declared in the previous half year by both the Aberdeen Junction and the Perth Junction companies, chairman Alexander Matheson attributed the lower dividend to the cost of the Inverness web of railways.[480] He announced that the Inverness-Perth line had cost £1,056,000, a figure three-fifths above its parliamentary estimate, and land 'estimated to cost £50,000 … has actually cost nearly three times that sum'.[481] Inaccurate estimates were identified by Matheson as the fundamental cause of the financial difficulties inherited by the new Highland company.[482]

Joseph Mitchell gave the cost of the 104 miles of railway between Forres and Dunkeld as £8,860 per mile for construction, land, law and engineering.[483] The capital expenditure reported by Matheson, however, produces a cost of £9,387 per mile if his statement related to the Dunkeld-Forres main line and the Aberfeldy branch, although if the cost of acquiring the amalgamated Perth and Dunkeld Railway is included in the calculation, the figure falls to £8,745 per mile, very close to Mitchell's assessment.[484] Matheson did not elaborate on the composition of the capital expenditure that he reported to Highland shareholders but, despite the undoubted inaccuracy in its estimates, a capital cost for this ambitious main line of circa £9,000 per mile represented a remarkable achievement in comparison to the costs of earlier trunk railways in Scotland. Great North directors, for example, had informed their shareholders sixteen years earlier in November 1849 of the costs per mile already incurred for the trunk route to Aberdeen and quoted figures for the Caledonian Railway (£30,000 per mile), the Scottish Central Railway (£27,000 per mile), the Scottish Midland Junction Railway (£20,000 per mile) and the Aberdeen Railway (£26,000 per mile).[485]

The Inverness and Perth Junction Railway paid a 3% dividend in January 1864 following the opening of the full line in September 1863 and shareholders were told that 'the Directors consider the success of the undertaking placed beyond all doubt'.[486] The line relied almost exclusively on through traffic for its revenue and the distinctly seasonal nature of the traffic, already apparent on earlier Inverness lines, featured strongly. The average of weekly gross revenue between January and March 1864 was £1,043 whereas the average for the period between July and September 1864 was £2,574,

with a peak of £3,029 received in the week ending 14 August.[487] The company secured a seven-year mail contract for northern Scotland in June 1864, not just to serve Inverness-shire and counties north but also the counties of Nairn, Moray and Banff.[488] The directors reported to shareholders that the revenue earned from this contract was equivalent to 1½% dividend paid on the ordinary shares of the company, but its more significant and instantaneous effect was to remove this guaranteed traffic from the rival Great North line via Aberdeen. The transport of mail was to remain a staple source of railway revenue for the Inverness railway web throughout the century.

The impact of the Inverness and Perth Junction on the Great North of Scotland was immediate. Chairman Sir James Elphinstone told Great North shareholders at their general meeting in September 1864:

> The opening of the Highland line took place on 9th September 1863; but its full effects were not known until nearly a month afterward. It very speedily showed that it was to act very detrimentally to the interest of this Company. In the first place, we have had the mails taken off, which is equal to £95 per week; then we have lost the through traffic amounting to something like £300 per week.[489]

Elphinstone's admission of the loss of £395 per week in revenue exceeded considerably the estimate given by John Stewart to Great North shareholders four years earlier in October 1860, and quoted above. Stewart had predicted that the maximum that the Great North could expect to lose following the opening of the Inverness and Perth Junction line was £4,302, but Elphinstone's much grimmer appraisal was confirmed in the subsequent company accounts, which showed that annual gross revenue fell from £113,165 in July 1864, to £93,214 in July 1865, a reduction of almost eighteen percent.

The opening of the line to Perth in 1863 marked the culmination of the strategy of the Inverness promoters to develop a network of railways radiating out from the highland capital over which the traffic of northern Scotland was to be channelled. Two years earlier, *Railway Times* had predicted the strength that would arise once the new company was consolidated into a single railway enterprise in Inverness:

> When the Inverness and Perth is completed, which will be in about three years from this date, the entire confederacy will no doubt be legally united, and a strong as well as prosperous and independent interest be established in the central district of the north of Scotland. The territory, though large, will be thoroughly secure – sufficient in itself to occupy the attention of a diligent and eminently practical board; the east coast will continue under the active development of the Great North of Scotland, a generous rivalry taking the place of unreflecting competition, so that energy shall not descend into extravagance, or enterprise into folly.[490]

Yet in the few years since *Railway Times* had

advocated 'a generous rivalry' between Inverness and the Great North, new and energetic competition had been launched from both north and south of Aberdeen to challenge the previously dominant place of the Great North of Scotland within the network of railways in northern Scotland. From the north, the new Inverness and Perth Junction Railway had, within two years of its opening, inflicted rapid and serious injury to the financial fortunes of the Great North. Simultaneously, the Great North was also subjected to a southerly assault on its regional monopoly, caused by its apparent reluctance to construct a railway link across Aberdeen and the consequent loss of traffic from railways to sea transport.

COMPETITION FROM THE SOUTH: THE ABERDEEN LINK

In his address to Great North shareholders in September 1861, John Stewart denied that the board had vacillated over the construction of a railway across Aberdeen to link the Great North with the Scottish North Eastern's line to Perth and the south. The parliamentary act incorporating the Inverness and Perth Junction Railway had been passed two months earlier, and its repercussions were concentrating minds in the railway boardrooms of Aberdeen. Stewart sought to lay the blame for the delay in building the cross-Aberdeen link via the Denburn Valley on the Scottish North Eastern:

> This brings us now naturally enough to the Denburn scheme ... it is not true, as has been reported, that we stood in the way of that scheme. It has been well known for many years that we were ready to subscribe £50,000 or one half of the undertaking. Our friends the directors of the Scottish North Eastern did not see their way to it. They do now.[491]

The Scottish North Eastern recognised publically that the Inverness and Perth Junction would have some effect on its traffic. Chairman John Stirling told his shareholders in March 1861 of their initial plan to lease the Perth and Dunkeld Railway:

> We thought it our duty to endeavour to make an arrangement with the Birnam and Dunkeld line, for the purpose of leasing it, because the Highland line is not a beneficial line to us, from several circumstances. We have now made an arrangement with the Inverness line ... the Inverness line will affect us to a certain extent in our passenger traffic. Our goods traffic received very little benefit from that quarter.[492]

Scottish North Eastern shareholders were well aware that the company had lost goods traffic to shipping because of the lack of a continuous railway route across Aberdeen, but the publication of the prospectus for the Inverness and Perth Junction Railway prompted the Great North to prepare a bill for a line across Aberdeen.[493] The board of the Scottish North Eastern appointed a committee to meet the Great North, but it reported back that the Great North had refused to give any guarantee as to the route by which they would send traffic southwards, thereby implying that the company intended to continue the use of steamer services. A further meeting had been held, but the Great North 'would not concede the point ...'.[494] Undaunted, the Scottish North Eastern re-appointed a committee to meet the Great North again and required it to obtain a joint report and estimate of the cost of the line and to prepare a draft agreement with the Great North.

Railway Times anticipated that the threat posed by the Inverness and Perth Junction Railway would be sufficient to induce consensus in Aberdeen, although it expressed some concern about the difficulty of acquiring the land required for the route:

> The new line through the valley of the Denburn, by which uninterrupted communication will be secured ... between the north and south, may now be considered as resolved upon. The alacrity with which the Inverness and Perth Junction has been carried out, and the formidable position that project already occupies as the highway between Edinburgh, Perth and Inverness, have undoubtedly led to the harmony and opinion of purpose which now subsists between the Scottish North Eastern and the Great North of Scotland ... Much town property will be required – property over which the municipal authorities possess absolute control. The general conduct of civic dignitaries in these affairs has not been such as to inspire either confidence or respect, and it is still doubtful whether the proceedings of the municipal body in Aberdeen will form an exception to the prevailing rule.[495]

The gap between the Scottish North Eastern and the Great North of Scotland lines had been a contentious issue ever since Aberdonian railway interests fractured in 1848 and caused the Aberdeen and Great North of Scotland Railways to abandon their plans for amalgamation. Sporadic but unsuccessful attempts had been made to achieve this important link; Great North shareholders were informed in November 1856, for example, that 'the Directors had revived the original scheme of bringing the Great North line down the valley of the Denburn, and so concentrating all the railway traffic at one place, as it there joins the south line'.[496] The directors of the Scottish North Eastern Railway set out their perception of events in their report to shareholders issued in March 1862:

> The Shareholders generally are aware that the only connection between this Company's line and the Great North of Scotland Railway at Aberdeen is by means of a tramway for horse haulage along the quays of the harbour, by which much inconvenience and detention in the transmission of through traffic is occasioned. Many of them, however, may not know that the Great North of Scotland Railway was originally intended to form a junction with the Scottish North Eastern by the Valley of the Denburn, and that powers were conferred upon that Company for that purpose ... The portion ... between their line at Kittybrewster

and this Company's railway – about one mile in length – is a distinct part of the Great North Company's undertaking. They had never obtained authority to abandon this part of their scheme, but their powers to execute the works have been allowed to expire; and having made a branch to the harbour in another direction, they decline to complete this section of their original design. Hence the break at Aberdeen, which is the only interruption in the through line of railway between London and Inverness.[497]

Dissatisfaction with the break in route at Aberdeen extended far beyond the north of Scotland. Several years later in 1866, Thomas Cook was warning tourists of the inconvenience they faced there:

> … the Great North of Scotland Line has an independent station, denominated the Waterloo, at a distance of half-a-mile or more from the Guild Street Station; and this is the only positive disconnection of rails between Penzance, in Cornwall, and Inverness, a distance little short of 900 miles.[498]

Projected costs for the connection were high due to the urban environment. Estimates received in November 1861 for the 1¾ mile line through the Denburn Valley ranged from £147,032 to £159,000, with an additional £80,378 required for approach work, but, with the deadline for prospective parliamentary legislation imminent, the Great North board decided to delay any submission until the following year.[499] The Scottish North Eastern expressed their regret at this delay, but its directors were already exploring alternative plans to isolate the Great North.[500]

Any new railway following a south-north axis to by-pass Aberdeen faced a potential conflict with the Deeside Railway, which ran westwards from Aberdeen to Aboyne. The Deeside Railway, originally authorised in 1846, was re-incorporated in 1852 with a share capital of £106,250 to build a line from Aberdeen to Banchory.[501] Two key individuals joined the Deeside from the outset. John Duncan, who had been appointed a director of the Caledonian Railway in March 1850 and its chairman from December that year during the critical period following its financial crisis of 1848-49, became Deeside chairman in 1851, while William Black Ferguson was appointed its secretary in 1853.[502] Both were later to assume similar posts in the Great North of Scotland Railway at the height of its financial crisis and were central in its subsequent recovery.

Once opened in 1853, the Deeside quickly established itself as an exemplar of a financially secure branch railway built on 'cheap railway' principles and it returned a steady increase in gross revenue without the burden of large temporary debt. Strong dividends made the company attractive to investors; 5% dividend was paid consistently between 1854 and 1858 and 6% throughout the next three years, reaching 7¼% in 1861 before settling at 7% from 1862 to 1866. In 1859, *Railway Times* commented on the Deeside's performance:

> The sole secret of this success lies in economy of construction, and a rigid regard to outlay of capital. There is no forcing of traffic; no high speed; no competition.[503]

A westward extension to Aboyne was promoted in October 1856 for which the parliamentary authorisation specifically required the shareholder lists of the two concerns to be separated until dividends were equivalent.[504] The Deeside subscribed £5,000, worked the line and managed extension affairs through its board but with the addition of two directors to represent the interests of extension shareholders.[505] Capital for the extension proved to be difficult to raise and the company had to resort to temporary loans until 1862, when, as a defensive measure, the Great North bought all unallocated stock to secure control of the route.[506] A favourable lease of the Deeside and its extension by the Great North from 1866 provided guaranteed dividends of 7½% to Deeside shareholders and 3% to Deeside Extension shareholders rising to 3½% in the second year, with both to share any gross revenue received above an annual amount of £27,000.[507] The company was finally amalgamated with the Great North from August 1875 by retrospective legislation.[508]

COMPETITIVE LEVERAGE: THE SCOTTISH NORTHERN JUNCTION RAILWAY

The Scottish North Eastern board regarded a cross-Aberdeen link primarily as a Great North responsibility, but its construction remained a principal objective despite the prospect of a significant outlay of capital to achieve it. In July 1861, the capital account of the Scottish North Eastern was in deficit by £74,039, although in the previous half year the company had paid the first dividend on the ordinary shares of the former Aberdeen Railway since amalgamation in 1856, amounting to just half of one percent.[509] In contrast, the Great North's capital account showed a surplus of £49,258 in July 1861 and the company paid a 7% dividend on its ordinary shares.[510] The Great North therefore felt little pressure to embark on an expensive railway link that was expected to transfer existing traffic between routes rather than increase its overall volume. With half year dividends of 7½% and 7% declared in 1862, *Herapath's Railway Journal* commented on the Great North's striking results:

> Now really the Great North of Scotland Shareholders have nothing to thank for this excellent result but economy and good management. The traffic of the Great North of Scotland Railway cannot be said to be by any means large. It is no great matter for 58 miles of railway to have under £50,000 of gross revenue in a half-year, but we think it is rather an unusual circumstance to find an English Railway Company paying 7 percent dividend.[511]

The traits of a complacent monopolist were evident at the general meeting of the Great North of Scotland Railway held in September 1861. John Stewart, deputising for company chairman Sir James Elphinstone, claimed that the Great North gained little benefit from through traffic with the Scottish North

Eastern, although the Great North had offered to pay half the cost of the Aberdeen connection. He stated that Railway Clearing House figures showed that only five percent of the gross passenger revenue received by the Great North was identified as through passenger traffic:

> We don't owe such a debt of gratitude to parties as to put our hands into our pockets for the advantages of the City of Aberdeen and of through passengers – for you see the value that they are to us. Nevertheless, it is important, and we are willing to play our part.[512]

Stewart did acknowledge that 'it is essential to the city of Aberdeen that there should be through communication', but he issued a veiled threat to Aberdonian commercial interests by identifying the proposed Strathspey Railway as an alternative route for through traffic:

> Our wish is to bring it by Aberdeen; but if we cannot get facilities here, we are under no obligation to do so.[513]

The dissatisfaction of the Scottish North Eastern with the stance of the Great North resulted in the promotion of a new line in December 1861 that avoided the break in route at Aberdeen. The Scottish Northern Junction Railway was to connect Limpet Mill, three miles north of Stonehaven on the main line between Perth and Aberdeen, to Kintore on the Great North's line from Aberdeen to Keith. The perceived independence of the Scottish Northern Junction was purely nominal because the Scottish North Eastern agreed to be joint promoter of the new company, to supply £90,000 of its proposed £150,000 share capital, to pay its parliamentary expenses, to work the line, and to pay an immediate 4½% guarantee on the stock once the railway opened 'provided the Gross Revenue of the Line is sufficient for that purpose'.[514]

This new line crossed the Deeside Railway and therefore the Scottish North Eastern sought an agreement to lease the Deeside lines, offering ultimate guarantees of 8% on Deeside shares and 4% on Deeside Extension shares in addition to the purchase of all unissued Deeside Extension stock, thereby outbidding a Great North offer of 6% on Deeside shares.[515] In a rapid defensive move, the Great North purchased all unappropriated Deeside stock within two weeks of the Scottish North Eastern offer, aided by John Duncan who used his casting vote as chairman of the Deeside Board to secure acceptance of the Great North's terms.[516] A bitter legal wrangle ensued over the Deeside's decision in favour of the Great North, which resulted in the issue of interdicts by both Deeside shareholders and the Scottish North Eastern that prevented the transfer of the Deeside to the Great North and delayed the lease of the Deeside by the Great North until 1866.[517]

The Scottish Northern Junction Railway may have been conceived as a competitive lever to try to force action from the Great North to provide the Aberdeen link, although it required the Scottish North Eastern to make a significant financial commitment in its promotion. The Scottish Northern Junction bill was provisionally approved by Parliament in June 1862, but the act prescribed that no construction was to be undertaken before 1st January 1863 and, if the Great North had submitted a bill for a cross-Aberdeen scheme by that date, then the Scottish Northern Junction Railway Act was to be further suspended until the Great North's bill was either passed, rejected or withdrawn.[518] Furthermore, if the Great North's bill was passed in Parliament by 1st September 1863, the powers conferred on the Scottish Northern Junction Railway were to be withdrawn.

If the Scottish Northern Junction was intended as a catalyst, then the Scottish North Eastern achieved its goal. Parliament had given another opportunity to the Great North to create the through route across Aberdeen which had been approved originally sixteen years earlier. *Railway Times* saw merit in an amalgamation of the two companies:

> The Scottish North Eastern board has undoubtedly exhibited greater courage and enterprise than the direction of the Great North of Scotland. The latter have been cautious, perhaps timorous ... It now remains, under the passive condition to which the Scottish North Eastern is reduced, for the Great North of Scotland to make a large and effective movement in the right direction.
>
> But we have been looking for something more than a mere physical junction of the undertakings. The Inverness and Perth is making rapid progress; it will sharply be in communication with the North British, the whole of the central district of Scotland, from Dingwall if not further north, being brought under one management. The map will prove all that we assert when we advise consolidation of the various interests which occupy the country from Perth to Aberdeen, and thence to the whole of the east coast of Scotland.[519]

In September 1862, the Great North and Scottish North Eastern briefly considered proposals for a joint-purse agreement and an ultimate amalgamation, but terms were not agreed.[520] Conflict between the two boards was resumed in October when the Great North announced its abandonment of the direct Denburn Valley route for the cross-Aberdeen link and selected a line around the west side of Aberdeen with a reversed junction, which attracted the title of the 'Circumbendibus' and aroused vigorous opposition, not least from the residents and authorities in Aberdeen itself.[521] Shareholders of the Scottish North Eastern were informed of the Great North's proposals:

> ... to carry the junction around the City, thereby increasing the distance nearly a mile and a half and preventing the formation of the direct through station without securing any conceivable advantage.[522]

An offer by the Scottish North Eastern of £30,000 to re-instate a direct line was rejected by the Great North, but a parliamentary application by the Scottish North Eastern to release powers to construct the Scottish

Northern Junction route was refused.[523] *Railway Times* referred to 'the war into which these two companies are evidently drifting', and despaired of the situation:

> … the directors of the two boards can neither arrange an amalgamation of their companies, nor can they live at peace … The two lines are connected merely by a tramway along the quay.
>
> The directors of the Great North, instead of encouraging the transmission of traffic by the railway south of Aberdeen, have arrangements with a steam company for the conveyance of the traffic to London by sea. The Scottish North Eastern exclaims loudly against this … And in the end the Scottish North Eastern and the Great North will be amalgamated, as they ought to be; but only after both have been spending their funds in contests …[524]

Even John Stewart, by now formally designated as deputy chairman of the Great North, recognised that amalgamation might bring benefits to both companies. Commenting on a statement made by a shareholder at the general meeting of the Scottish North Eastern held in September 1863, which anticipated 'a time when the Great North and the Scottish North Eastern will be one undertaking', he told Great North shareholders that:

> I have no instructions from the board on the subject; but I say broadly, that the public would get increased facilities by the amalgamation … because one management would do in place of two; and the management of railways is very costly.[525]

Faced by further delay and with strong local resistance to the Great North's 'circumbendibus' route, Parliament emasculated the Great North's bill submitted in 1863 for the western suburban route by inserting clauses that granted powers to the Scottish North Eastern not only to select the route but to construct the line.[526] As a result of these amendments, the legislature postponed the Great North bill for a further year to allow time for the Scottish North Eastern to bring in its own bill for a direct connection via the Denburn Valley.[527] That bill was submitted to meet the required timetable and the subsequent act transferred the financial powers granted to the Scottish North Eastern to invest in the abortive Scottish Northern Junction to the Denburn Valley scheme.[528] The Great North was to subscribe £125,000, the sum it had proposed to spend on its 'Circumbendibus' route around the city. To try to avoid future conflict, the Scottish North Eastern offered to reduce the Great North's subscription of £125,000 by £17,000 provided that they agreed the plans submitted and left that company to construct the line:

> … and that they also agree to leave the whole execution of the Works of the Line and Station to the Scottish North Eastern Company without any interference therewith on their part, it

being understood that when finished the whole Works are to be to the entire satisfaction of Mr William Johnstone, Manager of the Glasgow and South Western Railway and to be pronounced sufficient by him …[529]

The Great North consented and a further attempt was made to secure an amalgamation of the two companies.[530] Initially, the Scottish North Eastern expressed interest in a union excluding Great North branch lines, which were nominally independent of the parent company, but requested the accounts of the branch companies after it was suggested that the Great North 'should take upon themselves the liabilities attached to the Branches …' so that the Great North was considered as one unified organisation in the negotiations.[531] The financial condition of the branches must have discouraged immediate progress because the Scottish North Eastern did not seek to resume discussions until March 1865.[532] By November, however, the Scottish North Eastern had concluded an agreement for its own amalgamation with the Caledonian Railway from August 1866, following the Caledonian's absorption of the Scottish Central Railway in July 1865, which finally gave the Caledonian control of the full route from the Scottish border to Aberdeen that it had sought two decades earlier.[533]

The Great North remained isolated and disconnected from the southern railway network until the Denburn Valley link finally opened in November 1867, by when the potential economic advantage of a northern trunk route via Aberdeen had already been lost as a result of the opening of the new main line between Inverness and Perth in 1863. *Railway Times* considered that the Denburn Valley line would be a 'great public convenience', but warned:

> … the capital expended on it will, we fear, be unremunerative for many years to come. It is one of those schemes of public utility which are forced, as it were, upon railway companies, who, having the monopoly of trade of a large district of country for a series of years, must, even when under a temporary cloud, study the interest of the public before their own. That the Great North of Scotland, as one of the parties, has done so ungrudgingly, is not for a moment to be doubted.[534]

The capital expenditure to which the Great North was committed as a result of the Denburn Valley Railway Act merely added to the tribulations of the company. The Great North was already sinking into severe financial difficulties as the result of its branch line investment and the destructive effect on its traffic unleashed by the Inverness and Perth Junction Railway. It had mounted a forlorn response by promoting a line south-westwards through the Spey Valley, the consequences of which were to add further pressure to its capital account and cause a major division within its boardroom.

CHAPTER 10

DEFENCE AND COLLAPSE OF THE ABERDEEN MONOPOLY

Plans for an extension from the Keith and Dufftown line into the Spey Valley emerged in July 1860 at the same time as the proposed line between Inverness and Perth was announced to the public.[535] Great North shareholders were advised by their directors that the Strathspey Railway 'will suit our purpose as well as any branch we could recommend to you to make'.[536] That view was not shared by *Railway Times*, which professed:

> We cannot, notwithstanding the reputable parentage of the Strathspey, bring our minds to believe in its reality.[537]

Railway Times also reproduced the opinion of the *Inverness Advertiser*, which unsurprisingly roundly condemned the Great North's proposals to construct the Strathspey Railway:

> There is not traffic to warrant the formation of the projected line of railway by Speyside ... The character of the aggressive policy which suggested this remote extension of the Great North system has been more unmistakeably un-masked by the connection with the Morayshire, which establishes a rivalry for the traffic to and from Elgin eastwards, as well as for a participation in the direct through and Strathspey proper traffic, and this without legitimately subserving the public accommodation. Better far to complete the connection of the termini at Aberdeen, the want of which is so loudly complained of, than enter into a crusade professedly for the benefit of the upper districts of Strathspey, where their officiousness is not wanted, and cannot prove beneficial, as it is really out of place ... No-one can pretend that there is traffic enough in Strathspey proper for the railways ...
>
> The Strathspey ... is in no respect a sound commercial enterprise. Its sole purpose from the outset was to strangle, if possible, and to damage the through line. It is just another exhibition of the antagonism of certain parties in Aberdeen to north country interests ... The luxury is to be sought at the expense of the Great North shareholders, and they would do well to call a reckoning before the whistle is paid for out of their pockets.[538]

THE GREAT NORTH'S GLENMUTCHKIN: THE STRATHSPEY RAILWAY

Initial plans for the proposed Great North branch envisaged a terminus at Grantown, but an extension to Nethy Bridge was subsequently included to try to capture the whole of the valley traffic, arousing opposition from Inverness because of its proximity to the proposed line between Inverness and Perth.[539] Even so, Thomas Bruce, chairman of the Inverness and Perth Junction company assured his shareholders at their general meeting in September 1861 that 'we shall have so very much the best line, that any line running into it could do it no harm ...' and he referred to negotiations with the Earl of Seafield, whom he served as his commissioner of estates, 'which would have the effect of giving this company the whole traffic from his lordship's extensive forest in Strathspey which would be very important to the Company'.[540]

The Strathspey displayed all the characteristics of Professor Aytoun's satirical *Glenmutchkin* scheme. It ran through a sparsely populated area, it had no terminus of significance and quickly encountered financial difficulties. The Strathspey Railway was incorporated in 1861 with powers to raise £270,000 in share capital, of which the Great North was authorised to subscribe £100,000 and the impecunious neighbouring Keith and Dufftown Railway £25,000.[541] Of the ten Strathspey directors appointed in 1861, five were also directors of the Great North and they formed the Finance and General Purposes Committee to run the affairs of the company.[542] The Great North provided its subscription in the form of a cash account on which the Strathspey company could draw.[543]

By August 1862, only £27,205 had been raised from the sale of shares, exclusive of the Great North's subscription.[544] Borrowing powers were released in November 1862 and, although published accounts show that £89,999 of the £90,000 limit authorised to be raised from loans had been obtained by August 1863, company minutes reveal that the authorised limit had been breached and £143,941 of debentures had been issued.[545] Of this total, £50,000 of debentures were issued in January 1863 as security for bank loans from the North of Scotland and National Banks.[546] The debentures readily attracted lenders because the Great North guaranteed the 4% interest paid on them.[547]

Shortage of capital resulted in a mounting deficit on the capital account, which rose sharply from £22,339 in 1863 to £59,815 in 1864 and £68,406 in 1865. Capital expenditure rose above estimate and by August 1864, one year after the line opened to traffic, £289,988 had been spent which rose further to £298,599 by July 1865.[548] Great North accounts for July 1864 show that, in addition to its subscription of £100,000 to the Strathspey, it had also made temporary advances to the company totalling £43,576, for which retrospective parliamentary sanction was obtained.[549] The dependence of the Strathspey on the Great North was starkly illustrated in 1866, just prior to amalgamation, when Great North directors reported that their company had subscribed £192,700 to the Strathspey, whereas only £12,360 had been raised from other sources which included £11,000 from the Keith and Dufftown Railway.[550] The subsequent act of amalgamation confirmed that the Strathspey had raised £205,060 in share capital and so local support for the Strathspey had amounted to only £1,360, representing just half of one percent of its authorised share capital.

The Strathspey Railway paid no dividend and returned a consistent deficit on its revenue account during its brief existence. The financial weakness of the company was exemplified in the accounts for the year ending August 1864, which show that gross revenue of £5,930 was earned but that £7,449 was due as interest on debentures, bank loans, temporary advances and contractors' bills in addition to the Great North's charge of £1,890 for working the line. In April 1865, the directors of the Great North informed their shareholders that a loss of £1,888 17s 4d had been incurred in working the Strathspey Railway since 31st August 1864.[551]

Although planned as part of the Great North's strategy for expansion and defence, the Strathspey represented yet another branch line with severe financial weaknesses. Throughout its nominal independence between 1861 and 1866, the Strathspey company remained insolvent and added to the financial burdens already being carried by the Great North. John Stewart sought to justify both the working agreement made with the Morayshire Railway and the promotion of the Strathspey when he addressed the general meeting of Great North shareholders in March 1863:

> When the [Morayshire] line is completed, we shall have an independent entrance to Elgin on the one hand and down to Lossiemouth on the other. The Strathspey proper – I speak of it as extending from Craigellachie to Grantown and Abernethy – goes through a country that which none in Scotland is more susceptible of improvement. For self-defence, the project was all but necessary. When our friends north of the Spey promoted their through highland line, they were already within our district at Keith, and would have been in a condition almost to have dictated terms to us, had we not been in a position to have dealt with the traffic westwards and southwards.[552]

The dire state of Strathspey finances caused friction within the Great North's boardroom as the effects of the competing line between Inverness and Perth and the full impact of branch line development became apparent. At a board meeting held on 11th December 1863, a majority decision was made to seek retrospective legislation to authorise £75,000 already granted in advances to the Keith and Dufftown, the Strathspey

Stations on the Strathspey Railway were simple stone buildings which, in general, were sufficient to handle all the traffic offered throughout the time the line was open. Grantown justified a slightly larger building, but it was over half a mile from the town. The Highland station was closer and its services more useful to the townsfolk. The line had been losing money for many years when British Railways first proposed closure in 1956. In a last-stand effort to improve its finances, 4-wheeled diesel railbuses were introduced in 1958, but that did not stave off closure as part of the Beeching changes in 1965. Here, the railbus has arrived from Aviemore on its way to Elgin. Enthusiasts outnumber passengers. (Douglas Hume)

and the Morayshire Railways, but deputy chairman John Stewart and fellow director Joseph Rowell disagreed with this approach and wrote to company secretary Robert Milne to register their dissent.[553] They pointed out that they held almost £250,000 of Great North stock compared to the £1,830 of stock held by the other five directors present at that board meeting. In particular, Stewart questioned the significant Great North investment made in the Strathspey, arguing that taking Strathspey stock in return for advances was of no value to Great North shareholders because it yielded no return. In a written response to the board, Great North chairman Sir James Elphinstone placed the blame on his deputy chairman for the difficulties that the Great North was experiencing:

Mr Stewart took the leading part on urging the Board to enter upon the Strathspey undertaking, and I do not hide from myself, that his opinions, founded as they were upon the Board with reference to his large holding [of Great North shares], frequently received more weight than they ought to have done ... I was certainly ignorant (standing as it does to a great extent in other's names) that his and Mr Rowell's holding had reached this enormous amount of £250,000 and I am satisfied that I should have no difficulty in showing to the Shareholders or to a Committee of the Houses of Parliament that it is not for the general advantage that such an amount of stock should be held in this way.

I cannot help remembering with much pain, that it was owing to Mr Stewart's influence that in 1860 and 1861 we did not come to an Agreement with the Scottish North Eastern and Inverness and Aberdeen Junction Boards ... and the hostile attitude in which the Companies have since stood, would have been averted, and the large amount of money which has been expended in various ways in shielding our Company from the threatened inroad from Limpet Mill to Kintore would have been saved and it is the opinion of many, and opinion I myself have consistently maintained and expressed, that had it not been for the circumstance to which I refer we would not now have had to compete with the Highland Line.[554]

Elphinstone had been chairman of the company since 1849 and so could not escape his share of responsibility for the Great North's decline. He served as Member of Parliament for Portsmouth from 1857 to 1865 and again from 1868 to 1880 after he left the Great North board, but Great North and branch company records show that his attendance at board meetings was spasmodic.[555] Of the 104 board meetings of the Great North held between October 1860 and December 1862, for example, Elphinstone chaired only thirteen; for each of the other meetings, the directors present elected one of their number as chairman. John Stewart, however, was always called upon to chair shareholders' meetings in Elphinstone's absence, although it was not until

March 1862 that company records began to refer to him formally as vice-chairman or deputy-chairman of the Great North.

Elphinstone's acknowledgement of the deteriorating state of the Great North contrasts with his reassuring statement given to Great North shareholders at their meeting held only three months earlier in September 1863:

It is my opinion, based upon considerable inquiry into the subject, as well as knowledge of the north of Scotland, that the Highland line, if it affects our prospects at all, the effects will be only of a very temporary character ... I have always thought that the Highland line will operate to the advantage of the lines in which we are interested in ... I believe that whatever decreases in traffic may arise to us from the Highland line will be of a temporary and very trifling description.[556]

In November 1863, he had delivered an equally optimistic outlook to shareholders of the Strathspey Railway, despite the deficits returned on both the capital and revenue accounts of the company:

This line appears to me to turn out pretty well ... The amount of traffic passing over the line is remarkable.[557]

John Stewart responded by making a formal proposal to the Great North board that no funds should be paid to any branch lines without the approval of shareholders or without satisfactory security, but the motion was lost.[558] Stewart then attempted to block the progress of the draft parliamentary bill that was to legitimise the advances already made to the three branch companies, arguing that 'it would be greatly to the injury of the interest of the Great North of Scotland Railway Shareholders to subscribe for more shares in the Strathspey railway than they have already sanctioned and paid for ...', but that motion too was defeated by the five votes of Elphinstone and four other directors to the two of Stewart and Rowell.[559]

Stewart's position as deputy chairman became untenable. He wrote to Milne in March 1864 to complain that five directors had 'pretended to put me out of the chair and another gentleman into it for the carrying out of their views' with the result that a motion to call a shareholders' meeting to approve the parliamentary bill authorising branch subscriptions had been passed, despite his refusal as chairman of the meeting to accept it.[560] Stewart steadfastly refused to sign fifty-five sets of company minutes dating back to November 1863 because he 'disapproved of several'.[561] He was replaced as deputy chairman in September 1864 by John Duncan, chairman of the Deeside Railway, who had been appointed to the Great North board in March that year.[562]

The directors' report to Great North shareholders in September 1864 showed the scale of the capital cost that had been incurred to secure the Great North routes to Elgin and into the Spey valley in competition with the Inverness companies.[563] The newly authorised subscription limits of £150,000 to the Strathspey,

John Duncan, whose arrival on the Great North board introduced some realism into its relations with its branch companies.

(GNSRA collection)

£36,000 to the Keith and Dufftown, and £35,000 to the Morayshire, to which Stewart and Rowell had objected, sanctioned the temporary advances already made to these companies. The Inverness lines, however, were able to produce a rising stream of revenue in contrast to the negative revenue balances returned almost universally from the Great North's subsidiaries. By January 1865, the Strathspey owed £64,159 to the Great North, its revenue was insufficient to meet expenditure, and its survival depended on amalgamation with the Great North.[564] John Duncan, in his new role as deputy chairman of the Great North, advised shareholders of the need to absorb the Strathspey and the Keith and Dufftown into the Great North:

> … I think we must place this line, and also the Keith and Dufftown lines, in something like a more intimate relation to the Great North of Scotland than they at present stand. I mean there must be some consolidation of these three companies established in such a manner that in place of being fragments, they shall be made adhesive; and the reason is this, that of the Strathspey railway we hold the whole stock. We have £170,000 in it, so that there is scarcely any other Proprietor than the Great North. That line, then, having been constructed as it has been with the money of the Great North, it should be made an integral part of its system.[565]

A short southerly extension of the Strathspey was authorised in 1865 to provide a link into the Highland main line at Boat of Garten, but the Strathspey was never likely to carry substantial flows of through northern traffic, despite the confident report given by Duncan to its shareholders that, as a result of amalgamation, it 'would become part of the trunk line which they wished to see established, carrying goods coming by

the Highland line over to the great part of the Great North System'.[566] Amalgamation of loss-making branches simply relocated their financial instability into the parent company. Nevertheless, the Great North, already weakened by its branch line policy and the results of competition, saw latent possibilities for a westward incursion into the territory of the Inverness web companies via a coastal route using another independent branch company, the Banff, Portsoy and Strathisla Railway.

A NORTHERN COASTAL ROUTE: THE BANFFSHIRE RAILWAY

The Great North had intended to serve the Moray Firth ports of Banff and Portsoy by the lines approved in its parliamentary act of 1846, but the subsequent shortage of capital caused those plans to be abandoned. In 1856, as part of its branch line policy, the Great North offered to subscribe £2,000 to a new company which proposed to build a railway from Grange on the Great North's main line to Banff and Portsoy, and to work the line at cost.[567]

The Banff, Portsoy and Strathisla Railway was incorporated in 1857 and its board included Thomas Bruce and William Tayler, commissioners to the Earls of Seafield and Fife respectively, both of whom were already directors of the Inverness and Aberdeen Junction Railway.[568] Bruce was appointed chairman of the Strathisla; his fellow director Tayler was chairman of the neighbouring Banff, Macduff and Turriff Extension Railway, also serving Banff but controlled and operated by the Great North.[569] The Strathisla Act authorised a working agreement with the Great North and Tayler was charged to arrange one, but terms must have been unsatisfactory because the company purchased its own rolling stock in 1859.[570] The company thus remained independent, but subject to the influence of Inverness and Aberdeen through two of its directors.

The Strathisla company encountered the same difficulties in raising capital that other branches further east were experiencing. When the line opened in July 1859, £46,002 had been raised, just over half of the authorised share capital of £90,000, and concern about the arrears outstanding on share calls prompted the board to approve a circular to shareholders threatening prosecution if the sums due were not paid.[571] Borrowing powers were released in July 1859 and, within six months, almost the full limit of £30,000 had been obtained from two banks using company debentures to guarantee the loans. The North of Scotland Bank advanced £15,000 in September 1859, while the Royal Bank of Scotland provided £13,400 in January 1860 with the 4½% interest due on the loan personally guaranteed by the railway directors.[572]

The capital account remained in deficit from the opening of the line in 1859 to its amalgamation into the Great North in 1867. A temporary loan of £38,000 was agreed with the North of Scotland Bank in March 1861 with railway stock supplied as security, a significant sum given that the railway's annual gross revenue that year was only £5,331 and the accounts recorded a revenue deficit for the year of £895.[573] Gross revenue rose slowly, reaching £6,535 in 1866, but it was insufficient to meet working expenses and interest between 1861 and 1867. The company was insolvent with little prospect of repaying its debts in the foreseeable future.

With the outburst of competition between Aberdeen and Inverness in 1860, however, this little company attracted attention from both. It offered the potential for an expansionist route to the west for the Great North, but conversely it could provide a defensive block for Inverness against any advance by the Great North. In April 1862, Thomas Bruce recommended to the Inverness and Aberdeen Junction board that a working agreement with the Strathisla was advisable, but in June the Great North successfully concluded an agreement with the company to work the line in perpetuity from February 1863 and to promote a westerly extension to Buckie, Portgordon or to 'a point east of the Spey'.[574] Under legislation approved in 1863, the Strathisla was renamed the Banffshire Railway and the Great North was authorised to subscribe up to £80,000 and to guarantee Banffshire loans.[575] Thus, the branch finally assumed its delayed place within the Great North's branch line system; the companies were amalgamated in 1867.[576]

Inverness responded by promoting its only defensive branch, the Fochabers and Garmouth Railway, as a short northerly extension from its main line to the coast to try to block any further Great North advance westwards.[577] The Great North was, however, already slipping into financial chaos as a result of competition and branch line commitments and it was unable to progress the westward extension even to Buckie.[578] Inverness, too, was coming under severe financial pressure and powers for the Garmouth line were abandoned in 1869.[579] The coastal route to Elgin was ultimately constructed by the Great North, but not opened throughout until 1886.

The Banffshire Railway provides a further example of a small branch company that sank into insolvency as a result of difficulties in raising share capital, becoming reliant on authorised and temporary lending as a result and with only a modest revenue to service its debt. Its strategic value to the Great North rescued it from bankruptcy, but its transferred debts added further to the mounting financial difficulties of the Great North.

THE SIGNS OF FINANCIAL COLLAPSE

The rapid decline in the fortunes of the Great North of Scotland Railway was clearly displayed by the dividends declared on its ordinary shares. From 7% paid in 1863, the year that the Inverness and Perth Junction Railway opened, dividend fell to 5% in 1864 and to zero in 1865.[580] Thereafter, no ordinary dividend was paid until 1874, which indicates the scale of the financial crisis that faced the Great North. The railway journals, which had eulogised the progress and success of the Great North, reported the disappearance of dividend in 1865 with some alarm and explored reasons for the collapse. *Railway Times* saw little hope of any immediate improvement:

The catastrophe for which the shareholders in this company have been preparing themselves appears to have come upon them with a greater force than had been anticipated ... it had not been generally concluded that the revenue would be so deficient as it had proved. Not only is there no balance whatever to retain for next half-year, but the whole of the preference charges cannot be adequately met.

A great part of the traffic has been diverted to the central line, and there is not the slightest possibility of any portion of it being brought back ... The branches with which the Great North of Scotland has been filling up the country are natural failures for the time. Not only are some of them worked at a loss, but others have had the expenses of construction thrown upon the undertaking before they could earn anything on their own account.

These extensions, although protective batteries against invasion for all time to come, must remain a burden upon revenue for several years, and hence the necessity of looking the fact full in the face, that the return of prosperity can only be by pensive steps and slow.[581]

Railway Times also reproduced an article from the *Buchan Observer* for its national readership, which reported the sudden deterioration in the Great North's financial position with some incredulity and attributed the causes to high interest rates, the rapid extension of unproductive branches, the withdrawal of the mail traffic and the impact of the new Highland line:

Although the Great North of Scotland has perhaps a greater number of bitter enemies than any similar corporation, it is scarcely to be credited that any one will rejoice at the unfortunate position into which its financial affairs have fallen.

This is a sudden and somewhat startling revelation. A concern which only three years ago paid 7¼ percent to be now unable to pay a penny; shares which only a few weeks ago were worth £90 now sticking in the market at £40 or £45 – this is a result almost without precedent in legitimate commercial transactions.[582]

Herapath's Railway Journal produced a similar analysis in its review of the Great North's report to its shareholders, prepared for the ordinary general meeting held in April 1865:

We are amazed at the information conveyed in the present report of the Directors, that there is nothing for the ordinary dividend in the past half-year. In 1862, the dividend reached 7¼% per annum, while for the past half year it is nil.

The report explains *why* the Great North of Scotland has thus fallen from its high estate. The opening of the competing Highland line has cut into their vitals, added to which is loss from new extension lines recently opened ... The report speaks of the suspension of dividend being "temporary". We hope it is so

... we deeply regret the sudden disappearance of the Great North of Scotland dividend. The effect is to undermine confidence in the security of railway property.[583]

To Great North shareholders, accustomed to high rates of dividend, the content of this director's report must have come as a severe shock. Not only were funds insufficient to pay any dividend on ordinary shares, the fixed dividend of 4½% due on the preference B shares issued in 1862 was reduced to ½%. At the shareholders' meeting, deputy chairman John Duncan optimistically assured shareholders that 'the line will speedily recover', but he clearly identified the problems that the company was facing, pointing out in particular that the Highland line was 'running away ... with £14,000 per year' and that this traffic was now lost to the company:

The Great North of Scotland Railway Company has had a long time of prosperity; and now it is getting a rub the other way ... now we are deprived of the through traffic between Inverness and the south.

You must keep resigned to having lost the through traffic between Inverness and Perth ... but there is yet a wide field for the development of local traffic.[584]

Duncan's recognition that the recovery of the Great North depended on the development of local traffic brought the corporate and financial status of its allied branch companies under close scrutiny. He informed shareholders that the Great North's main line had cost 'about £1 million to construct and the branches £0.5 million ... so that nearly a third of the capital is on these branches', and reported that, for year to January 1865, traffic had yielded £85,000, of which £29,000 had come from the branches.[585] Although these figures suggested that the branches were contributing one third of the Great North's gross revenue, Duncan also reminded shareholders that some of the branches had been constructed not primarily as feeder lines but to 'protect yourself from invasion'. As a relatively new director and only recently appointed deputy chairman, John Duncan was able to deliver these blunt yet perceptive messages to Great North shareholders. With a certain inevitability, the shareholders' meeting appointed a committee to inquire into the affairs of the Great North comprising six members, including one each from Liverpool and Manchester to represent shareholder interests in those places.[586] These two specific appointments indicate that the influence of English railway investors remained strong in Aberdeen.

The confinement and isolation of the Great North within a distinct area of north-east Scotland were later very aptly described by Duncan as the board wrestled with the insolvency of the company and the threat of bankruptcy:

It is a very difficult thing to make a comparison between the Great North and the Southern Companies, because we are placed in a corner, on a siding as it were. We are not in possession of a line which is a thoroughfare from one part of the kingdom to another ... we are in a great degree dependent upon the traffic in the locality wherein the line is placed.[587]

The Great North was not the only railway company in Aberdeen affected by the new direct line from Inverness to Perth. Although the Scottish North Eastern had been denied much of the goods traffic carried over the Great North's main line because of the use of sea transport southwards from Aberdeen, its chairman John Stirling explained to his shareholders in October 1864 that their company had also lost revenue:

There is no concealing from ourselves that we have suffered a large loss from the opening of the Highland line ... In the month of July, our passenger receipts fell no less than £800. We have also suffered a considerable loss upon goods, though we do not know what that may amount to, as they come over the Great North line.[588]

The outburst of railway competition in northern Scotland during this brief period between 1860 and 1865 added considerably to the financial pressures that were already building within the Great North of Scotland and the Inverness companies. Local funds supplied principally from large landowners remained the prime source of railway investment in the north, but the difficulty of raising share capital had persisted. The widespread conversion of unissued ordinary shares into guaranteed preference stock and the extensive use of bank advances to raise the necessary finance required the railway companies to make regular payments of fixed dividends and interest, which placed additional strain on the flows of revenue that the new lines were able to generate. The Inverness and Perth Junction Railway, the final strand of the Inverness railway web, at least offered the prospect of a relatively secure and growing revenue stream and its temporary loans were assured by the personal guarantees of some of its wealthy directors. Nevertheless, the substantial debt accumulated by the company and transferred to the Highland Railway in 1865 had to be serviced until it was repaid, which constrained any capacity to pay dividend to ordinary shareholders.

From this intense period of competition, Inverness appeared to derive tangible advantage at the expense of Aberdeen, but the profound repercussions of the methods adopted by the companies to finance both these and earlier railway developments were not revealed fully until the amalgamations of 1865-66. Both the new Highland Railway and the re-constituted Great North of Scotland Railway were seriously weakened by the financial consequences of their expansive development. The directors of each company stared into a financial abyss in 1866, just as another major monetary crisis erupted in the national economy.

CHAPTER 11

GREAT NORTH AND HIGHLAND FINANCES, 1865-67

The regional commercial centres of Aberdeen and Inverness had each proposed plans in 1845-46 for the extension of the railway network into the north of Scotland, but the inability of the Great North of Scotland Railway to realise the substantial scheme that Parliament authorised it to construct had allowed railway promoters in Inverness progressively to challenge the Great North's monopoly during the ensuing two decades. During this time, the Great North had supported the development of a range of allied branch line companies in north-east Scotland, intended to consolidate its territorial control and to channel the traffic of the region south-eastwards through Aberdeen, while the Inverness and Aberdeen Junction Railway had assumed a central role in the management of a web of railways radiating out from the highland capital of Inverness. Almost all of these relatively remote northern railway companies had encountered persistent difficulties in raising share capital, which forced a reliance upon funds requiring guaranteed returns and, in particular, on bank loans and other forms of temporary credit to complete their lines.

The intense promotional competition that was waged in northern Scotland between 1860 and 1865 only added to the financial pressures that both of these two regional monopolies were already facing. By 1865, the scale of the debts that were to be inherited by the newly-consolidated Highland Railway and the re-constituted Great North of Scotland Railway had become all too apparent in their respective boardrooms and the consequences of those debts were about to challenge the continued independent existence of each company. The severe monetary crises faced by both the Great North and the Highland and the methods adopted to overcome them not only illustrate the considerable range of dilemmas and risks that their directors had to confront, but also the resilience and fortitude displayed in each boardroom, which enabled the companies eventually to emerge, weakened but intact, from the financial storm.

In December 1864, *Herapath's Railway Journal* reviewed the financial results of the branch companies allied to the Great North and their correspondent concluded:

> I think there are far too many of these small Scottish Companies.[589]

Herapath's Railway Journal had already advised its readers that 'amalgamation is the order of the day in Scotland', while *Railway Times* reported that:

> The purpose of amalgamation has taken a thorough hold of the intentions of shareholders; and the public itself is ripe for the consummation.[590]

Scotland experienced a widespread amalgamation of railways in 1865-66, through which directors intended to strengthen company finances whilst also seeking to consolidate their regional control. The North British Railway amalgamated with the Edinburgh and Glasgow and Monklands Railways in 1865, while the Caledonian absorbed the Scottish Central Railway in 1865 and the Scottish North Eastern Railway in 1866, thereby finally acquiring the trunk route to Aberdeen that it had first sought in 1845.[591] These amalgamations largely rationalised a plethora of constantly shifting alliances between Scottish railway companies, which produced a wry comment from *Railway News*:

> If their alliances continue to be so fluctuating and changeful as of late years, it will soon come to pass that every company will have been united at some time with each of the others ... The Edinburgh and Glasgow Railway Company has been singularly fickle in regard to its engagements. It has espoused at different times the Scottish Central and the Caledonian ... and now it has suddenly renounced the Caledonian, and while maintaining a left-handed intimacy with the Scottish Central has flung itself into the arms of the North British.[592]

Coalescence of the Inverness railway companies had always been a stated objective of the web promoters; the Inverness and Aberdeen Junction Railway had amalgamated with the Inverness and Nairn in 1861 and the Inverness and Ross-shire in 1862. Future amalgamation was specified as a condition for the subscription made by the Inverness and Aberdeen Junction to the newly-promoted Inverness and Perth Junction in 1860, and these two companies merged as the Highland Railway in 1865.[593] The act of amalgamation included clauses intended to provide some protection to the Great North, which required the Highland Railway to grant:

> ... all needful accommodation, facilities and conveniences ... by Through Booking, Through Rates and, so far as reasonably may be, Through Wagons and Carriages and Through Trains and in all respects conduct forward, carry on, and accommodate all such Traffic on equal Terms with and as well as if it were their own proper Traffic ...[594]

At a special general meeting of Inverness and Aberdeen Junction shareholders called to seek approval of its amalgamation with the Inverness and Perth Junction Railway, chairman Alexander Matheson reminded those present of the original vision of a unified railway system controlled from Inverness and outlined the expected benefits:

> It had always been the intention of the promoters of the Companies who were parties to the bill that an amalgamation should eventually take

place ... The line was projected in 1846 by one Company, and at that time it was impossible to carry through the scheme but all along since then they had never lost sight of it, and felt assured that some day or other it would be carried into effect ... the general management and working of the railway could be carried on more cheaply, it would confer great advantages on the Company in the development of the traffic and in perfecting the lines themselves.[595]

At the first shareholders' meeting of the Highland Railway held in September 1865, Matheson, now chairman of the new company, contended that amalgamation had been essential to avoid any chance of competition between the two companies, even though a working agreement existed between them:

> But the Directors felt that although an agreement of this nature existed, misunderstandings between the companies might arise which would prove disastrous to both. Indeed, no two railways existed capable of inflicting greater injury upon each other. The Junction might have sent all the through traffic via Aberdeen, while the Perth, in order to retaliate, might have pushed their line into the north, and so stopped the stream of traffic flowing to and from the south. It was under these circumstances that the directors of both companies were unanimous in promoting the amalgamation bill of last session.[596]

The commonality of directorships across the two companies suggests that such competition was most unlikely to arise locally, but the Caledonian Railway had expressed interest in 1865 in subscribing £50,000 to the Inverness and Perth Junction under the powers previously given to the Scottish Central, and a further £50,000 to the proposed west-coast Dingwall and Skye line.[597] There had also been indeterminate proposals to link the Highland's Aberfeldy branch to the Caledonian's Callander and Oban satellite company near Killin.[598]

Unlike the Highland Railway, which was to operate a main line from a connection with the Anglo-Scottish trunk route at Perth to Inverness, with a northerly extension to the border of Sutherland at Bonar Bridge and an easterly extension from Inverness to Keith, the Great North's system comprised a main line of just over fifty miles between Aberdeen and Keith, supplemented by a series of branch lines. John Duncan, elected deputy chairman of the Great North in September 1864, acknowledged that many of these branches failed to yield much return:

> If you look into the report you will find that the amount of money expended in construction of the main line was about a million, while the company has on all these branches half a million, so that nearly a third of this capital is on these branches. There are many of these branches unproductive, but there are many of them yielding a considerable amount of traffic to the main line.[599]

Duncan estimated that branch traffic accounted for just over one third of the revenue derived from the Great North's main line.[600] Despite the serious financial condition of many of these branch companies, the Great North could not abandon them to bankruptcy because it would lose some of the traffic that they generated, incur a large capital write-off on its branch line investment, and face the possible severing of its independent route to Elgin if a rival company bought out one or more of the branches. The Great North therefore amalgamated with its allied branches in 1866, formalising the control that had been exercised in all but name, although amalgamation with the Banffshire Railway was delayed on a financial technicality until 1867 and an agreement with the Morayshire was not finally concluded until 1880.[601] Of shareholders present or giving proxies at the Great North meeting that approved the amalgamation bill in June 1866, 120 were Scots but 41 gave English addresses, 12 of whom were from Liverpool, which confirmed the continued English influence within that company.[602]

The Scottish amalgamations of 1865-66 produced five comparatively large railway companies, a structure which remained until the grouping of 1923. From a Scottish railway system comprising 1,043 route miles in 1854, the Caledonian, North British, Glasgow and South Western, Great North of Scotland and Highland Railways controlled 2,193 of the 2,244 route miles in operation by the close of 1866.[603] Of these, 242 miles were worked by the Highland from its formation in 1865 and 276¼ miles by the Great North after its amalgamations of 1866, which rose by 11 miles in October 1866 once the Great North began to work the Aboyne and Braemar Railway, which extended the Deeside line westwards from Aboyne to Ballater.[604] The sizes of the two companies' systems were similar, but the nature of the constituent lines within them was very different.

INSOLVENCY IN THE GREAT NORTH

For several years, the half-yearly results of the Great North had attracted compliments from the contemporary railway press, but the rapid disappearance of dividends aroused concern. Deputy chairman John Duncan remarked in response:

> Well, it may be distressing, but ... those men who invest in railway stock must have laid their calculations that they would get their fingers burnt on some day or other ...[605]

The Great North began to lose its northern traffic immediately the Inverness and Perth Junction line opened in 1863, but in April 1865 its directors also reported 'the great disappointment in the Traffic of the Strathspey, Keith and Dufftown and Morayshire Railways'.[606] The debt burden of the branches remained confined to the accounts of those companies until amalgamation, but the Great North's capital account, which had recorded a surplus in ten of the previous eleven half years, slipped into deficit in July 1865 prior to the reconstitution of the company.

Although the gross revenue of the Great North rose

steadily from 1861 until 1864, the extra costs of working the new Morayshire route to Elgin from July 1863 caused a rise in expenditure, reducing the revenue surplus available for dividend in 1864 (table 11). Thereafter the sharp fall in revenue surplus was reflected in the cessation of dividend paid on ordinary shares.

The elimination of ordinary dividend and the default on payment of some preference dividend for the half year ending in January 1865 resulted in shareholder unrest and, at the general meeting held in April, a committee was appointed to investigate the company's financial position and prospects.[607] *Railway Times* endorsed the shareholders' decision:

> The investigation committee, if it acts firmly and honestly, must effect much good. It will, in the first place, convince the local shareholders that the present distress is to a great extent due to their over-confidence in the resources of their district, as well as their refusal to look on the Inverness line as certain to injure them before the branches could come into profitable operation.[608]

The committee reported promptly later that month and identified that the Great North had expended the substantial sum of £684,524 on branch lines, which represented over a third of the company's total capital expenditure of £1,847,610 shown in the accounts of July 1865. Of this sum, £86,982 had been spent in the purchase of shares in the Deeside Railway and a further £7,450 on shares of the Montrose and Bervie Railway that had been acquired without parliamentary sanction during the competition with the Scottish North Eastern Railway and, additionally, £19,249 had been spent above authorised limits on the Strathspey, Keith and Dufftown and Morayshire Railways.[609] The Committee were blunt in their assessment of past policy, but noted that shareholders had given their consent to the Great North's support for branch companies:

> Your Committee cannot see any justification for a large portion of this expenditure, which has led to such disastrous results, and regret that the Shareholders should have given the Directors authority for its expenditure, as it appears to your Committee, that the character of the country through which several of these Lines pass, did not in their opinion warrant the outlays.
>
> With regard to the purchase in the Deeside Railway, your Committee while thoroughly condemning the outlay of money without Parliamentary sanction, can yet find some

justification of the purchase as a measure of protective policy, but for the amount expended, and yet to be paid for the Montrose and Bervie Railway, your Committee cannot find the slightest excuse, and must characterise it as a wasteful expenditure of your funds.

> Your Committee are fully satisfied that your Financial difficulties and the loss of Dividends are to be entirely attributed to this very large outlay upon lines, particularly those constructed north of Keith, from which the actual returns are so very unprofitable.[610]

The committee recommended that the Great North's commitment of £78,500 made towards the cost of an extension of the Banffshire Railway westwards should be postponed, but supported the investment of £25,000 to link the Strathspey Railway to the Highland main line at Boat of Garten in the expectation of an improvement in traffic over the Strathspey line as a result. Despite the trenchant criticism, however, the committee could make no recommendations other than 'to leave the Directors to administer the affairs of the Company, so as may be best calculated to develop and render productive the branch lines as early as possible … and to promote friendly relations with neighbouring companies'.[611] This anodyne conclusion prompted comment in *Railway Times*

> The sudden shock of "no dividend" had so paralysed the proprietary generally that they seemed to be prepared for rank exposures, enormous losses, and indefinite insolvency.
>
> The treatment of the report of the committee of investigation by Mr Duncan was equally clever and candid. The learned gentleman, while admitting certain results to have been faulty, made not a single excuse for the origination of any measure from which disappointment or disaster have flowed instead of the success anticipated.[612]

At the shareholders' meeting called to consider the report, Professor Fuller of Aberdeen University reminded those present that no-one had taken the trouble to examine the company's accounts when dividends were high, but his motion to replace the board was not carried:

> I think it may also be well to have a new board of directors, because our line has been completely mismanaged by the present board. It may be said that these gentlemen have done their best, but their best has proved utterly ruinous.[613]

The financial storm clouds were gathering over the

Table 11: Revenue account of the Great North of Scotland Railway, 1861–66

(£)	July 1861	July 1862	July 1863	July 1864	July 1865	July 1866
Total annual revenue	89,895	100,608	109,611	113,165	93,214	103,785
Total annual expenditure	37,557	41,136	37,986	59,169	52,286	71,919
Revenue surplus	52,338	59,472	71,625	53,996	40,928	31,866
Change in revenue surplus	-	13.6%	20.4%	- 24.6%	- 24.2%	- 22.1%
Dividend to 31 January	6½%	7½%	7%	5%	0	0
Dividend to 31 July	7%	7%	7%	5%	0	0

Source: National Archives of Scotland, BR/RAC(S)/1/14.

Great North. By the end of January 1866, the Great North owed £245,150 to banks and the company was refused further credit. The North of Scotland Bank declined a request for an additional £32,000, stating that 'The Sum owing to us by the Railway Company is … already very large and, if the Directors feel that they could increase the sum at all, it could only be upon additional and much more available security', while the National Bank replied that they 'are not disposed to give any further advances'.[614] These two banks relented to the extent of £10,000 each and the Great North also arranged a loan of £30,000 from bankers Fenwick and Woods of Newcastle, but this £50,000 of new borrowing required the deposit of £104,350 of preference and ordinary shares and debentures as security, which indicates the poor credit status of the company and the low value of its stock.[615]

The Great North's bill for amalgamation with its branches requested permissive powers and, by the time the Great North sought the approval of its shareholders in June 1866, terms had been agreed with five branch companies, the Aberdeen and Turriff, the Banff, Turriff and Macduff Extension, the Alford Valley, the Keith and Dufftown and the Strathspey Railways. The Great North had subscribed to £363,231 of stock in these branches, compared to only £133,480 provided by the public.[616] Terms had not yet been agreed with the Formartine and Buchan or the Inverury and Old Meldrum Junction Railways, but the Great North had also invested £175,000 in the former and £2,000 in the latter. These two companies, however, were amalgamated into the Great North along with the other five branches from 1st August 1866. The Great North of Scotland Railway (Amalgamation) Act of 1866 converted the stock of the branch companies into new Great North stock. In recognition of the now cancelled ordinary shares previously held by the Great North in these branches, Great North shareholders were allotted £142 of new ordinary stock for every £100 of Great North stock previously held, providing them with some nominal return as a result of the amalgamations.[617]

The Great North was not only unable to pay an ordinary dividend in 1865 but also had insufficient funds to meet all of its preference dividends. Although the 5% preference and the 4½% preference A shares had received their dividends in full, holders of the 4½% preference B shares received only ½% in April and 1½% in October. The 5% preference and the preference A shares dated from 1859 and so held a priority for payment over the preference B shares, which had been issued in 1862.

Preference B shareholders were paid only ½% again in April 1866, but default on preference dividends increased further in October when £3 13s was paid on the 5% shares and £3 6s on the A shares, just under three quarters of the expected dividend, and nothing was paid on the B shares. Arrears on the original 5% preference shares were paid to shareholders as deferred warrants, which simply added to the accumulating debt of the company.[618] Not surprisingly, holders of the 4½% preference shares felt aggrieved that they were not similarly able to receive deferred warrants, but John

Duncan explained that the 1866 act of amalgamation required the 4½% preference A and B stock to be paid annually out of revenue and therefore 'in the event of deficiency in revenue in any one year, they have no claim on subsequent years'.[619]

Prior to the shareholders meeting in October 1866, the Great North's board agreed to ask its shareholders to elect a new board to represent the all the interests within the new amalgamated company. At the meeting, deputy chairman John Duncan explained their decision:

> I do not mean by any means to say that the gentlemen who are presently on the Board retire from it in disgust, or from dissatisfaction with themselves, but that they do it in implement of the duty which they consider they have to perform.
>
> The directors are at the disposal of the shareholders as their seats are at their disposal; and it will be for you to select such men as you think best qualified to carry out such objects as you may think will most conduce to produce to the shareholders the most flattering returns.[620]

A decision on the composition of a new board was postponed, first to December 1866 and then to the following February to give shareholders time to consider their preferred membership.[621]

By January 1867, the Great North had become financially unstable. Of the £3,085,817 raised in capital, £1,381,530 was represented by preference shares and £755,042 by debenture loans, all of which required fixed interest payments. Almost seventy percent of the company's capital therefore placed a prior call on the revenue earned by the company. In addition, the Great North owed £345,972 to its bankers, held outside the main company accounts on the general balance sheet but which also required the regular payment of interest.[622] Although gross revenue was increasing slowly, expenditure was also rising and, once interest on debenture loans was charged to revenue, the company remained unable to pay any ordinary dividend or to meet the full amount of dividend due on its preference shares (table 12).

A confidential report was commissioned by the board from the company's auditor, accountant Robert Fletcher of Aberdeen, to assist the finance committee in renegotiating bank lending and allow the company time to try to build its recovery and repay debts.[623] In it, Fletcher highlighted bank loans as the most pressing liability on the company, but he indicated that, while revenue was sufficient to pay interest on these loans, the £437,390 of stock held by the banks as security was mainly 'of an unmarketable description'.[624] The company was advised to seek shareholder approval to issue a pre-preference stock which would rank before all other preferences, using receipts from its sale to repay debt, thereby reducing the amount of interest that had to be paid and consequently enhancing the value of existing company stock. But, with £267,379 of debenture loans due for renewal in 1867, Fletcher issued a sharp warning to the board to expect an increase in interest costs in order to renew these loans as a result of

Table 12: Finances of the Great North of Scotland Railway, 1867–68

(£)	January 1867	July 1867	January 1868	July 1868
Capital account balance	- 269,905	- 278,030	-363,741	- 182,695
Temporary loans from banks	345,972	303,171	350,348	181,549
Gross revenue for the half year	79,112	86,466	90,112	90,656
Gross expenditure for the half year	46,956	54,204	56,838	58,426
Surplus before debenture interest	32,156	32,262	33,274	32,230
Debenture interest for the half year	9,034	16,501	17,482	18,317
Surplus after debenture interest	23,122	15,761	15,792	13,913
Dividend on ordinary shares	0%	0%	0%	0%

Source: National Archives of Scotland, BR/RAC(S)/1/14.

the financial weakness of the company:

> It is not an overestimate to assume that if the Company's credit is not completely re-established, it will ultimately pay on the whole Debenture debt 1 percent higher than Companies enjoying, as this Company formerly did, first-class credit. One percent on the authorised debenture debt of £801,586 is yearly £8,000.[625]

Robert Fletcher reminded the directors that the average interest paid on what he termed 'irregular debt' over the last two years had been almost 7%. His report concluded that the availability of any 'temporary accommodation' from its bankers would depend upon 'what was done meanwhile in strengthening Direction and in placing the irregular debt on a permanent footing at a moderate rate of interest', but Fletcher also pointed out the dilemma faced by the banks in protecting their funds already lent to the company and obtaining the interest due to them:

> The Banks have a most material interest in this question; if the depreciated credit of the Company compels it to give high rates for a large amount of Debentures, a very serious inroad will be made in the Balance of the Company's Revenue available for payment of interest on the debt to the Banks.[626]

Nevertheless, the Great North was facing bankruptcy if the banks decided to recall their advances. On 16th November 1866, only two days after Fletcher's report was received at a special meeting of the Great North's board, the National Bank of Scotland demanded £10,670 in interest and arrears of interest due on its loan of £50,000.[627] On 21st November, the Aberdeen Town and County Bank refused further advances, 'temporary or otherwise', and required settlement by 29th November of two accounts totalling £62,605, also demanding immediate payment of £5,000 on two debenture bonds due the previous day.[628] On 7th December 1866, the National Bank gave the Great North one week to pay the interest due before legal proceedings were instituted, and, on the following day, the Commercial Bank demanded repayment of a loan of £4,500.[629] Robert Fletcher negotiated a temporary loan of £20,000 from the Northern Assurance Company, but further demands for payments were received on 18th December, including a threat of legal action from the Railway Clearing House unless £3,800 due from the Great North was paid within fourteen days.[630] The

Great North lacked the funds to make the repayments demanded and so the banks began to sell company stock held in security to redeem some of the funds owed.[631] The Aberdeen Town and County Bank announced that it was to 'take steps for realising the securities held by the Bank' while the National Bank informed the Great North board that it had sold 4,000 Great North shares and 35 Deeside shares. One week later, clearly encouraged by the price obtained for Deeside shares, the National Bank gave notice that they proposed to continue to sell Deeside stock 'which is giving on the whole a very fair price …' in order to reduce the company's loan from £100,000 to £80,000 and re-iterated the reason:

> You are aware that our Directors are desirous of making some noticeable impression upon the amount of debt due to the Bank.[632]

In January 1867, the Caledonian Railway joined the list of creditors because the Great North owed payments for its share of the cross-Aberdeen railway under construction:

> You are aware that your Company is already largely indebted, and is being every month more so, to the Caledonian on account of the Denburn Valley Railway works. It is very desirable that some arrangement should immediately be made for a repayment to this Company of their advances in this Account.[633]

Thus, at the end of 1866 and only three years after paying 7% dividend on its ordinary shares, the Great North was close to financial collapse as the banks demonstrated their loss of confidence by selling company shares held as guarantees. The accumulated debts of the Great North's branch line system had impacted simultaneously with the loss of through traffic from its main line to the rival Inverness and Perth Junction Railway. The company was committed to substantial capital investment in the construction of the Aberdeen link line but it had defaulted on some payments, bank interest was overdue, and it was unable to pay the full guaranteed dividends on its preference stock, all of which were adding steadily to its accumulating debt. Any additional earnings from revenue were increasingly absorbed by the interest payments required for temporary and authorised loans.

In the face of this financial catastrophe, two options were available to the Great North's board if the company was to survive. The directors could try to negotiate an amalgamation or lease with another company, or they could attempt to refinance the Great North in co-operation with their bankers and apply severe economies to company operations in order to build the flow of revenue necessary to begin the repayment of debt. In its dire financial condition, the Great North attempted unsuccessfully to achieve the former and was thus forced to seek its own salvation.

THE HIGHLAND'S INHERITANCE

Towards the end of 1864, one year after the opening of the Inverness and Perth Junction Railway, the proposed amalgamation of that company with the Inverness and Aberdeen Junction Railway attracted the support of *Railway Times*:

> One of the chief measures for consolidation and aggregation of strength in the north is presented in a proposal to unite these undertakings which have not only much in common, but from the topographical condition of the country would not well be brought into antagonism with each other. As there are several independent branches already springing out of these trunk lines, and as it is more than probable that the whole of the north-west of Scotland must be made tributary to the great Highland line, it appears alike requisite and judicious that the existing interests should become united ere any misgiving or ill-regulated ambition should take its rise in any quarter with a view to disturb the harmony which so fortunately prevails.[634]

Fusion of the Aberdeen Junction and Perth Junction companies to form the Highland Railway was recommended to shareholders to achieve economies in the management and working of the lines and to assist the development of traffic.[635] The apparent prosperity of these two Inverness companies was highlighted by *Railway Times*:

> These lines have fallen not merely on pleasant places but in happy times. Heartily supported by the localities through which they sought their way, with scarcely other obstacle than what rugged Nature presented and which skill could surmount, they not merely arrived at completion, without inordinate delay or excessive expenditure, but they as it were found a traffic prepared to their hand.[636]

Although successful in operation, both companies were accumulating considerable temporary debt. In March 1865, with amalgamation imminent and the capital account in deficit by £144,306, shareholders of the Inverness and Perth Junction Railway were advised that further expense was expected:

> Your Directors are glad to be able to say that with one exception, the Contractors' claims have all been settled, and although the Land claims along the Line have been ascertained, a considerable sum under that head is still unpaid, and therefore some additions to the Capital Account may yet be looked for.[637]

The capital account of the Inverness and Aberdeen Junction Railway was also under pressure. Expenditure was still rising, due primarily to the costs outstanding from the construction of the Ross-shire lines. The deficit on the capital account had been reduced from £190,585 in July 1864 to £105,588 in January 1865, despite extra expenditure in the half-year of £89.748, but this result was achieved only by the issue of £174,804 of additional Ross-shire and Ross-shire Extension stock, a practice which was used extensively by the company to provide security for bank loans. Consequently, in March 1865, the board attempted to cap further expenditure:

> The Board, having regard to the enormous increase in the capital account and the large Expenditure on Works, and seeing the necessity of observing the utmost economy, resolved that no new works of any kind shall be commenced without being previously submitted, with a careful estimate of the expense, and approved of by the Committee hereinafter named, and being also approved by the Board on the report of the Committee ...[638]

Gross revenue was rising steadily on both lines, which augured well for the eventual resolution of the financial difficulties being experienced by the two companies, although chairman Alexander Matheson admitted to Inverness and Aberdeen Junction shareholders in May 1865 that, in working the Perth Junction line, 'we made the agreement rather too hastily, and at too low a rate of remuneration so that we have lost by that'.[639] The consistent difficulties encountered in raising capital for these northern railways had fostered a conviction in Inverness that the rapid expansion of the railway web should be checked. In 1862, Matheson had advocated that '... once they got in connection with the southern lines at Perth and had reached Bonar-bridge in the north, they ought to pause'.[640] With new railways being proposed in the north of Scotland, Matheson confirmed that objective the following year:

> We are on the best footing with the lines south of Perth ... we are quite determined to enter on no working agreement or proposal of amalgamation that would compromise our independence in the north. We shall remain as we are, with our head quarters at Inverness.
>
> The Caithness people are most anxious to have a line to Wick; the people of Fort-William want one to Kingussie; and the people to Skye are urging one from Dingwall to the West coast. I have received various communications from those parties, who are very anxious about those lines, and my answer to them has been, that if they subscribe the capital and make the lines, they will find us anxious to afford them all reasonable assistance and encouragement in order to complete them, and to work them afterwards when they are completed. But for my own part, I consider that before we enter on new undertakings we should consolidate what we have on hand, and see that it gives us a fair return for our capital.[641]

The combined capital deficit of both Inverness companies in July 1864 was £334,607, which suggested the wisdom of a pause in expansive ambition. In September of that year, Matheson declared to shareholders of the Inverness and Aberdeen Junction that the anticipated amalgamation of their company with the Inverness and Perth Junction would complete the highland system:

> The traffic on the Inverness and Perth line has exceeded our most sanguine expectations. Arrangements are in progress for the amalgamation of the Junction and Perth lines … When this amalgamation is carried out, our system will be complete from Keith and Perth to our northern terminus at Bonar Bridge; and I may here observe that it is not the intention of your Directors to recommend to you any further extension of our railway system for the present.[642]

Nevertheless, at the same meeting, Matheson announced the promotion of two new independent lines, one from Dingwall westwards to Kyleakin on the west coast and one extending the highland system northwards from Bonar Bridge to Golspie, although he pointed out that for this latter line, 'the public will be indebted to the enterprise and patriotism of his Grace the Duke of Sutherland'.[643] These proposed extensions were designed to open up large highland estates and Matheson indicated the policy of Inverness towards them:

> As both are likely to throw a considerable amount of traffic on our line, we shall deem it a duty to take a limited interest in each, and to arrange for working the new lines on fair terms.[644]

The Duke of Sutherland and Alexander Matheson, both directors of the Inverness and Aberdeen Junction and, subsequently, the Highland Railway, were principal landowners in the districts to be served by these proposed independent railways, but the 'limited interest' announced by Matheson implied further capital commitments for an enterprise already experiencing serious financial constraints and some shareholder concern was expressed. Mr Grant of Kincorth, a shareholder of the Inverness and Aberdeen Junction Railway, reminded Matheson at the general meeting held in September 1864 that the company had already decided not to grant funds to the promoters of the Fort William line because 'the line should be entirely constructed by parties interested in it, or by independent persons who chose to contribute towards the necessary funds'.[645] Mr Grant also drew attention to the route of the Skye line, identifying characteristics which might have been drawn directly from Professor Aytoun's' *Glenmutchkin* parody, and, perhaps seeing parallels with the misfortunes of the Great North of Scotland Railway, he warned of the future financial prospects:

> … he looked upon any connection with these lines with some degree of apprehension. He had known many instances of through lines that were highly productive of themselves being almost ruined in consequence of making rash connections with new lines which were not equally remunerative.
>
> Look at the country through which the Skye railway would pass. It was by no means populous, and at the same time it was very remote and unimproved. There was no concentrated population at the proposed terminus – there was no manufacturing town. What prospect therefore was there for traffic as such could possibly lead them to hope that the line would pay for many years to come.[646]

Matheson assured Mr Grant and other Inverness and Aberdeen Junction shareholders that:

... these branch lines would not form part of the Junction Company's system. They would be independent lines altogether; but a proposal had been made that they should work them at the cost price – that was to say, that the trunk line could not possibly lose by such an arrangement.[647]

This statement of intent to work the lines at cost price gave an indication that the promotion and working of highland lines was not always to be undertaken to secure maximum profit for the operator, but that the traffic of the independent lines was expected to bring increased revenue to the parent company, a policy already followed by the Great North but with disappointing results.

The amalgamation of the Inverness and Aberdeen Junction and Inverness and Perth Junction Railways was authorised by Parliament in June 1865.[648] The first accounts of the Highland Railway compiled to August 1865 showed the new company to have a capital deficit of £201,460, which the directors reported 'was divided about equally between the two constituent companies'.[649] Highland shareholders attending the first general meeting held in October 1865, aware that they were to receive a dividend of 2% on their ordinary shares compared to the 4% paid by the two constituent companies in the previous half year, were told by chairman Alexander Matheson of the indebtedness of their new company:

I may add that our liabilities to the bank are still considerable and must continue so until we are able to dispose of our stocks. But there is more than ample stock on hand to cover every liability. Your directors are still personally liable for about £280,000 of that amount.

During the last twelve months, however, accounts have been rendered for extra works, additional plant, and land claims, to the amount of nearly £300,000, the interest of which large addition to our capital now has to be provided for. I may add that all our outstanding liabilities, exclusive of loans from the banks, are now ascertained, and they do not exceed £140,000.

The amount due to the banks is about £550,000 in all.[650]

Although temporary debt was not detailed in the main accounts until 1866, the scale of these loans and guarantees revealed in Matheson's speech was highly significant. Liabilities and temporary loans amounted to £690,000 and, in addition, the company held £565,241 in authorised debenture loans. This £1.255 million of temporary and authorised debt represented a very substantial sum in comparison to the £1.838 million held by the new company in share capital in August 1865 (table 13). In current value, the temporary loans from banks equate to at least £27.5 million, while the personal guarantees of directors correspond to at least £14 million. It was fortunate that the Highland Railway board was dominated by wealthy and influential landowners, many of whom held wide commercial contacts. George Loch, a Highland director and commissioner of estates to the Duke of Sutherland, reminded shareholders that the board had a strong personal interest in ensuring the company flourished because of their appreciable investment in it:

... the large amount of stock which was held by the Directors of the Company was an ample guarantee to the Shareholders that they would use their best endeavour to promote the prosperity of the Company. They held an amount of ordinary unguaranteed stock to the value of no less than £210,590.[651]

In April 1866, Matheson, who was also a director of the Bank of England, was able to illustrate the efficacy of the directors in securing lower interest rates for longer periods:

You are aware that we have a large amount of floating debt for which we have hitherto been paying the current rates, and these have averaged 7 percent for the six months. This, on £565,000, the amount of our debt, comes to be a serious burden. But I am happy to say that we shall be independent of the bank rates in future, as the directors, by interposing their personal security, have been able to make arrangements,

Table 13: Capital structure of the Highland Railway, August 1865

Capital (31 August 1865)	Authorised (£)	Raised (£)	(£)
Dunkeld 6% Preference Shares	76,000	76,000	
Nairn 5% Preference Shares	45,000	44,960	
Nairn 6% Preference Shares	59,080	59,080	
Class A 4½% Preference Shares	513,650	460,245	
Class B 5 % Preference Shares	400,000	110,402	
Total of stock raised carrying preferential dividend			**750,687**
Ross-shire ordinary shares	215,000	209,856	
Ross-shire Extension ordinary shares	160,000	147,733	
Highland ordinary shares	740,350	729,374	
Total of share capital	2,209,080	1,837,651	
Total of debenture loans	700,880	565,241	
Total share and loan capital	2,909,960	2,402,892	
Temporary bank loans		550,000	
Total of debentures and temporary loans			**1,115,241**
Total of funds requiring guaranteed payments			**1,865,928**

Sources: National Archives of Scotland, BR/HR/1/1, pp.42-43; *Railway Times*, 4 November 1865, pp.1406-07.

whereby the money has been obtained for a period of three years at 5 percent.[652]

The Highland had managed to negotiate these loans at 5% at a time when bank discount rates had risen from 7% in October 1865 to 10% in May 1866.[653] The capital structure of the new company showed that two-fifths of the issued share capital required guaranteed payments and that preference shares and fixed-interest debenture loans formed over half of the total capital raised (table 13).[654] In addition to this guaranteed capital, the temporary loans from banks also required interest payments, and so the Highland began its existence with £1.115 million of authorised and temporary loans and £1.866 million of funds requiring guaranteed payments, placing an immediate strain on its revenue account.

The burden of fixed-interest debt on the company was considerable. Over one quarter of gross revenue was absorbed by interest payments before any preferential dividends were paid, but Thomas Bruce, deputy chairman, admitted at the shareholders' meeting in April 1866 that one-third of interest due had been paid not from revenue but from capital.[655] In the half year to August 1865, it transpired that £12,000 interest had been charged to capital and a further £10,000 in the following half year to February 1866. A shareholder claimed that this practice meant that the Highland was adding to its debt by 'paying interest on interest', to which Bruce replied that some interest had been charged to capital ever since the time of the Inverness and Nairn Railway. Nevertheless, Bruce announced that it was 'expected to halve this in the next half year and then meet most thereafter from revenue'.[656] That goal was expedited and the directors were able to report in October 1866 that the whole of the interest due in the half year to August, rather than half as anticipated, had been charged to the revenue account.[657]

The new Highland board had, in fact, clearly told their shareholders in October 1865 that they intended to charge the cost of temporary loan capital to the capital account rather than to revenue to 'represent in the fairest manner the real position of the company'.[658] The prime object, however, had been to retain revenue to pay some dividend on the ordinary shares because,

in these two particular half-years ending in August 1865 and February 1866, the revenue used for the ordinary dividend and the small revenue balance carried forward would have been insufficient to meet the interest which had charged to capital (table 14). Had the full interest burden fallen fully on the revenue account, the Highland, like the Great North, would have had to cease paying any ordinary dividend and to default on some of its preferential dividend payments.

Revenue rose slowly and reflected the marked seasonal nature of traffic that had already been experienced by constituent companies (table 14); traffic receipts for the week ending 6th August 1865, for example, amounted to £6,647, but fell to £2,431 for the week ending 4th February 1866.[659] These peaks and troughs in revenue presented a particular test to the company's officials in providing sufficient rolling stock for services without incurring unnecessary expenditure.

Both the Highland and the Great North of Scotland Railways faced serious financial predicaments, but, unlike the ailing Great North, the Highland could realistically anticipate an increasing flow of revenue from its lines and it could rely on substantial monetary backing from its directors to ease, at least temporarily, its budgetary pressures. Moreover, Matheson disclosed to his shareholders that the Inverness promoters had not expected instant returns:

It is only right to state that, after the Directors fairly embarked in the system of railway communication in the Highlands, the different extensions were to a certain extent promoted more as strategic lines than lines which would bring an immediate and large traffic, although the latter was certain to follow in time ... The result is that we have now a line perfectly secure from attack.[660]

Nevertheless, the Highland began its operations exhibiting many of the financial weaknesses of other northern lines. Matheson identified the cost of the lines as the fundamental cause of the Highland's financial problems and, in a very detailed speech to the first meeting of Highland shareholders in October 1865, he provided the latest assessment of the costs of the

Table 14: Revenue account of the Highland Railway, 1865–67

(£)	August 1865	February 1866	August 1866	February 1867	August 1867
Gross revenue	100,733	82,668	99,744	96,362	103,766
Expenditure	50,195	42,022	45,561	44,569	45,271
Interest	26,090	19,280	29,148	27,128	28,142
Net Revenue	24,448	21,366	25,035	24,665	30,353
Interest as a proportion of gross revenue	25.9%	23.3%	29.2%	28.2%	27.1%
Dunkeld 6% preference dividend	2,660	2,280	2,280	2,280	2,280
Nairn 5% preference dividend	1,311	1,124	1,124	1,124	1,124
Nairn 6% preference dividend	2,067	1,772	1,772	1,772	1,772
Class A 4½% preference dividend	9,468	8,218	8,218	8,558	8,893
Class B 5% preference dividend	166	4,153	6,980	7,202	7,267
Ordinary share dividend	8,516	3,649	3,649	3,649	7,299
Expenditure on dividends	24,191	21,197	24,025	24,586	28,636
Balance to carry forward	257	169	1,010	79	1,717
Ordinary dividend	2%	1%	1%	1%	2%

Source: National Archives of Scotland, BR/HR/1/1.

Note Shillings and pence have been rounded down and so totals may not match precisely the sum of component items.

Inverness railway web (table 15):

Matheson gave his explanation for these significant increases in costs and courted the support of Highland shareholders by referring to the long-standing conflict with the Great North of Scotland Railway:

> Now, I admit that these are large sums and there is no doubt that this excess of costs has been the means of bringing this company into its present position, for it must be observed that in no case has the traffic failed ... The chief reason of the great excess of expenditure I believe to have been the undue lowness of the original estimates. Our engineers failed to make a sufficient allowance for accommodation and extra works, as well as for the land, which, on the Inverness and Perth, was estimated to cost £50,000, while it has actually cost nearly three times that sum.
>
> I am not aware that any of the great lines in this country have been made at the original estimates, and the mistake in all cases is the same – viz. the lowness of the original estimates.
>
> At one critical moment your line would have fallen into the hands of the Great North of Scotland, if your directors had not interposed their personal responsibility for a large amount. I leave you to imagine the disastrous consequences to these northern countries which would have resulted had the Great North succeeded in their attempt to get possession of our system. I may add that our liabilities to the bank are still considerable and must continue so until we are able to dispose of our stocks. [661]

According to Matheson's figures, the constituent companies of the Inverness railway web had cost one-and-a-half times their parliamentary estimates. Despite the financial support of a relatively small number of large landowners and many small local shareholders, share capital had proved difficult to raise outside the region and the companies had been forced increasingly to finance their rising capital costs from preference stock and temporary loans. Matheson summarised the Highland's dilemma:

> ... we had not only the excess of cost to contend with, but we were placed in a still greater difficulty from the original capital not having been taken up by the public. We were compelled to raise a large amount in preference stock, and, in addition, to borrow considerable sums from banks, on our personal guarantee, and at the prevailing high rates of interest. Our revenue has thus been absorbed, leaving but a trifling sum to meet dividends on ordinary stock. [662]

He finished his address to the shareholders' meeting on a decidedly confident note:

> We have secured possession of the whole traffic of the north of Scotland ... Our dividends may be low for a short period; but, rest assured, the time is not far distant when we shall be paying 5 percent. And when we get the Sutherland, Caithness and West Coast traffic thrown on our system, I do not hesitate to predict that we shall have one of the safest and best-paying railways in Scotland. [663]

It took another six years for Matheson's aspiration for a 5% dividend on ordinary shares to come to fruition. More immediately, *Railway Times* questioned how the Highland could justify the 2% dividend that it had declared, but it recognised the strength of the Highland's railway network:

> The whole history of this noble enterprise is now before the country. There is but one grievance, and that, unfortunately, is too common amongst us to be seriously regarded. On each of the sections save one the estimates have been exceeded, and the cost of construction is now ascertained to be such as scarcely to justify the earlier dividend that had been declared. Hence the immediate fall in the half-yearly distribution, as well as the misgivings which found vent at the meeting on 27th ult. It is admitted on all hands, however, that the system is now impregnable, while the new lines (the Sutherland and the Dingwall and Skye) must add materially alike to its position and revenue. [664]

Railway Times continued by predicting the amalgamation of the Scottish North Eastern with the Caledonian and suggested 'that the Highland must be taken in hand by the North British', but it was to be the Caledonian, already ensconced at Perth, which was to offer potential lifelines to both the Highland and the Great North of Scotland Railways.

In the immediate aftermath of the opening of the direct line between Inverness and Perth, a superficial assessment might conclude that the Highland, now secure, able to pay a small dividend, and experiencing a growth in traffic, had relegated the Great North to the status of a rural railway, the very existence of which was threatened by its overwhelming debts. While the Great North was undoubtedly close to financial collapse,

Table 15: Capital costs of the Inverness railway companies, October 1865

Company	Route	Estimate (£)	Cost (£)	Excess (£)	Excess (%)
Inverness & Nairn	Inverness to Nairn	80,000	118,000	38,000	47.5%
Inverness & Aberdeen Junction	Nairn to Keith	325,000	578,000	253,000	77.8%
Inverness & Ross-shire	Inverness to Invergordon	215,000	285,000	70,000	32.6%
Ross-shire extension	Invergordon to Bonar Bridge	160,000	160,000	0	0.0%
Inverness & Perth Junction	Inverness to Perth	654,000	1,056,000	402,000	61.5%
	Total	1,434,000	2,197,000	763,000	53.2%

Sources: *Railway Times*, 4 November 1865, p.1406-1407; *Herapath's Railway Journal*, 4 November 1865, pp.1217-19.

the Highland also faced severe vulnerability from its floating debt, those sums requiring repayment but held outside the main capital and revenue accounts of the company. Even so, *Railway News* concentrated on the positive economic and social results of the Inverness railways:

> The Highlands and Islands of Scotland are now within 24 hours distance of London ... it will not be surprising to hear that Highland property is increasing in value. The shootings have greatly advanced in rental, and the sheep farms are on the rise ... it is to be hoped that we have seen the end of that periodical distress which had become chronic, and could never have been relieved by the old system of the cottages and the croft.[665]

The Inverness strategy to secure the control of railways serving the northern counties of Scotland had been accomplished two decades after Parliament had rejected the bill for the Perth and Inverness Railway in 1846, but the Highland Railway, like its rival the Great North of Scotland, had to resolve the financial frailty that had resulted from enterprising expansion and expensive competition. The budgetary difficulties faced by both companies reached their zenith as a major national crisis erupted following the failure of the respected London finance house of Overend, Gurney in May 1866, caused by its over-extended dealings in railway securities. Shortages of railway capital throughout Britain had increased the practice by which railway companies paid contractors with company stock and bills of exchange, for which financial intermediaries had established a market to convert such securities into cash.[666] The *Railway Times* summarised the consequences in the capital market:

> The failure of Overend, Gurney, and Company to meet its engagements – its inability to repay money it had borrowed on immediate call, in consequence of having lent it at enormous interest to parties who were at all times on the verge of bankruptcy – is represented as a calamity of unparalleled description ... The disastrous effects of this inveterately encouraged panic are making themselves felt on every description of security.[667]

The resulting financial crisis was described by *Railway News* as 'the most important and serious stoppage ever announced in the City of London'; bank discount rates rose to 10% and *Railway Times* estimated that over £10 million was wiped from the value of railway stock.[668] The collapse of Overend, Gurney severely damaged investor confidence in railway shares with the result that these two relatively small and remote railway companies in the north of Scotland had little prospect of raising new share capital. With no immediate solutions to their financial plight, the Highland and Great North of Scotland each turned to Caledonian Railway to explore the possibility of lease or amalgamation.

As well as its other problems, the Perth line presented the Highland Railway with the difficulty of operating some of the steepest gradients in the country. The locomotives purchased in the first half of the 1860s were hardly up to the task, but nothing new could then be afforded until 1874. This is No.21, one of the Small Goods class built in 1863-64. During the winter, this locomotive was fitted with a large snow plough and kept ready to clear any blockages. (F Moore/HRS collection)

CHAPTER 12

CALEDONIAN LIFELINES

The Caledonian's previous attempt to take control of the northern route to Aberdeen was overtaken by its financial failure in 1849, but, by amalgamation with the Scottish Central in 1865 and the Scottish North Eastern in 1866, the Caledonian finally achieved that objective.[669] The price was considerable; Scottish Central shareholders were to receive a guaranteed 7% on their ordinary stock, Aberdeen Railway shareholders were to receive 3¼% rising by ¼% each half year until the rate reached 4%, and former Scottish Midland Junction shareholders were to retain their proportional premium above that paid on Aberdeen stock.[670]

As a result of amalgamation, the Caledonian inherited the Scottish Central's commitment made in 1864 to subscribe £200,000 to the proposed Callander and Oban Railway, promoted to connect the west highland coast with the main railway network, and to work the line at fifty percent of gross receipts.[671] The Scottish Central also held an unexercised power to subscribe an amount not exceeding £120,000 to the Inverness and Perth Junction Railway under that railway's act of incorporation.[672] Both lines offered scope to the Caledonian to extend considerably its influence in the north and west of Scotland.

Shortage of capital for the Inverness and Perth Junction Railway prompted the Inverness promoters to approach the Caledonian Railway. Andrew Dougall, general manager and secretary to the Inverness companies, reported to the Inverness and Aberdeen Junction board on 7th July 1865 that the Caledonian had offered to subscribe £50,000 to the Inverness and Perth Junction Railway and a further £50,000 to the proposed Dingwall and Skye Railway, and intended to justify this investment to its shareholders by declaring that 'they have an interest in the Line from their terminal station in Perth on to Skye'.[673] Parliamentary authorisation of the independent Dingwall and Skye, however, gave permissive powers to the Caledonian to subscribe £100,000, just over one-fifth of the authorised share capital of the company, which implies some predatory intent.[674] The deeper significance of this 'interest in the Line' was the opportunity given to the Caledonian to develop its influence in the north of Scotland and, in particular, in the key strategic railhead of Inverness.

With royal assent to the amalgamation of the two Inverness companies given just eight days previously, the Inverness and Aberdeen Junction board agreed to the Caledonian offer and authorised Dougall to issue £50,000 of ordinary stock to the Caledonian once payment for the Perth Junction subscription was made. Dougall wrote to the Caledonian on the following day, and a subsequent Caledonian minute records that 'under certain conditions this Company should subscribe £50,000 towards the capital of each of the two companies'.[675] The negotiations that resulted in the Caledonian offer to purchase £50,000 of Highland stock were concluded in principle in July 1865, but in the following month, the Caledonian's general committee noted:

> The Chairman [Lt Col Salkeld] read a copy of this letter of 19th inst to Mr Dougall in reply to the overtures made by the Highland Railway Company for a more intimate alliance with the Caledonian.[676]

What this more intimate alliance might have been is not explained, but it implies that more was involved than a limited investment.[677] By recording this minute, the Caledonian received the Highland's approach formally, which suggests that this advance or proposal was made on the basis of a Highland board decision. Highland records are silent about negotiations with the Caledonian, but, given the consistent advocacy of northern independence that had prevailed in the Inverness boardroom, it is not surprising that any discussions on such a contentious issue were kept out of the formal company records. Some knowledge of negotiations must have percolated through Highland staff, because, in March 1866, the board received a 'Memorial from Head Officials':

> Read letter dated the 27th ultimo from the Heads of Departments requesting that in the event of any amalgamation taking place between the Highland Company and any of the great Companies in the South their interest be protected when the terms of amalgamation are being adjusted. Resolved to state in reply that no arrangement of the kind alluded to in the letter is in contemplation, but in the event of such a contingency occurring hereafter this Board will do their best to protect the interest of the Memorialists.[678]

The Caledonian also received a proposition from one of their own shareholders in November 1865 for the 'acquisition' of the Highland, but company records do not indicate the response of the board.[679] Some consideration of lease or amalgamation appears to have arisen at the time the Highland was incorporated, at which time its directors would already be aware of the scale of the debt to be inherited by the new company. Any negotiations between the Highland and the Caledonian were prolonged because, in April 1867, *Railway Times* was expecting a lease ultimately to be concluded at 4%, an attractive rate compared to the 1% dividend that had been paid by the Highland in each of the previous three half years:

> ... the [Highland] dividend is apparently to remain at one percent, until several capital liabilities are cleared off, and the line thereby made acceptable to the Caledonian on a lease of

four percent.[680]

Caledonian finances were also coming under increasing pressure with the absorption of the Scottish Central and Scottish North Eastern Railways and the company wrote to the Highland in August 1866 to explain that:

> ... in the present position of their finances, they were unable to take £50,000 of the Highland Company's Ordinary Stock as suggested by them last year.[681]

Negotiations continued; the draft of an agreement between the Caledonian and Highland was submitted to the Caledonian board in June 1867 and remitted to a committee of directors Buchanan, Ferguson, Johnstone and Hill to consider.[682] In July, Buchanan and Thomas Bruce, deputy chairman and managing director of the Highland, urged the board of the Caledonian to make a 'final adjustment' of the agreement and the committee was charged to 'settle the Agreement as soon as possible'.[683]

The apparent haste to finalise an agreement may reflect the financial condition of the Highland Railway. Temporary bank loans held at this point amounted to £535,000, backed by the security of company stock to that value, which had enabled the capital account to be balanced. In August 1867, the Caledonian board minuted that an agreement had been finalised 'as in draft revised in blue ink', but, in September, Andrew Dougall, general manager of the Highland, raised objections to charges proposed by the Caledonian with which the Caledonian disagreed, noting that 'Mr Dougall's alterations appear to be inconsistent with the spirit and intention of the Agreement ...'.[684] A revised agreement was prepared and, in October 1867, Caledonian directors Buchanan, Ferguson and Ainslie were deputed to meet Bruce 'with full powers to settle'.[685] In December, the Caledonian board received the agreement signed by the Highland company and minuted the terse instruction 'Execute Agreement'.[686]

The urgency displayed by Buchanan and Bruce may also indicate the increasing disquiet being expressed by Caledonian shareholders about their company, which, in October 1867, resulted in the agreement of the board 'to invite several of the more extensive, influential and commercially qualified shareholders' to examine the company's affairs.[687] The report of the committee of inquiry, published in January 1868, highlighted the financial consequences of the competitive expansion pursued the Caledonian company:

> ... [As] no separate accounts of the earnings have been kept, we are unable to place before you the results of the Scottish Central and Scottish North-Eastern Railways, but we very much doubt if either can have been beneficial to the Caledonian Proper. The Scottish North-Eastern has, we have no doubt, entailed a heavy loss, and is another fruit of reckless competition.
>
> Throughout, your attention has been drawn to the disastrous effects of competition and rivalry ... We have recommended the abandonment of every work which can be stopped without

evident injury to your undertaking.[688]

The committee of inquiry identified new and urgent priorities for the Caledonian to resolve its financial difficulties, amongst which was a recommendation that an agreement between the Caledonian and North British Railways was 'absolutely essential'. No further progress on an agreement with the Highland was recorded, but *Railway Times* had already concluded in October 1867 that a Caledonian lease of the Highland had been postponed:

> The [Highland] directors announce ... that it is not their intention to promote any bill in the ensuing session. We take for granted, therefore, the lease by the Caledonian at 4 percent is adjourned *sine die*.[689]

Nevertheless, in a highly critical article on the Caledonian in the aftermath of the shareholders' inquiry, *Railway Times* remained convinced that a firm lease had been under negotiation between the two companies:

> ... the solemn mockery of the Caledonian having actually had the temerity, or the effrontery, to offer to lock the Highland in its embrace at 4 percent ... that company now exhibits the spectacle of a madman, idly seated, and recklessly smoking, on a barrel of gunpowder. The financial policy of the Caledonian is rotten to the core.[690]

The prospect of a lease of the Highland continued to attract comment. In 1869, *Railway Times* advised Highland directors and shareholders to retain their independence:

> This undertaking is gradually emerging from its difficulties. The traffic is slowly returning to its former proportions, while the working expenses are being diminished.
>
> The proprietors will do well to keep in their present course of action; to keep the line open to all sources of communication from the south; and to abandon reliance on the Caledonian, as well as on any past and prospective offer to lease at 4 percent.[691]

A lease by the Caledonian in 1867 would have resolved many of the serious financial predicaments faced by the directors of the Highland Railway, both personally and as a board. The failure to conclude an agreement left the company to tackle a growing mountain of bank debt, which rose from £535,000 in August 1867 to £565,000 in August 1868 and £625,000 in February 1869, where it remained for three successive half years until falling back to £605,000 in August 1870.[692] At its peak, the Highland's temporary bank debt represents over £31 million in current value.

The Great North was also deeply indebted to banks. In July 1866, at the point it was to amalgamate with its branch companies, the company owed £274,527 to its bankers, which rose to £345,972 in January 1867 and peaked at £350,348 in January 1868.[693] This maximum bank debt was equivalent to eleven percent of the £3,171,552 raised by the Great North in share and debenture capital at this date. In contrast, the Highland's bank borrowing in February 1868 was £535,000 and still rising, which corresponded to nineteen percent of its £2,818,848 capital raised from shares and debenture loans, and ultimately reached twenty-two percent in 1869.[694] The dependence on bank loans was therefore proportionally greater in the Highland, but the scale of its financial difficulties attracted less attention than those of the Great North because of the improving trading position of the company, the maintenance of a small dividend on ordinary shares, and the personal guarantees given by its directors to bankers to underpin these substantial loans.

In August 1866, *Railway Times* reported a rumour that negotiations were in progress for a 'speedy amalgamation' between the Caledonian and Great North of Scotland Railways, although the journal later revised its announcement from an amalgamation to a working agreement.[695] In November 1866, the Great North proposed that the Caledonian should work its lines for a fixed percentage of receipts and suggested a figure of 38%.[696] The Caledonian requested a copy of the Great North's accounts, which revealed the working expenses of the company to be 44%, but the Great North's general manager, Robert Milne, responded that their expenses could be reduced to 40½%, assuming a curtailment in train mileage and 'the saving in the cost of fuel by land as compared with sea carriage in the event of your working the line'.[697] Milne then asked the Caledonian at what figure below 40¾% they would work the line 'with your numerous advantages and experience', but professed that 'we have gone to the very lowest point at once'.[698]

Following amalgamation with the Scottish North Eastern Railway in 1866, the Caledonian had assumed responsibility for the construction of the Denburn Valley Railway across Aberdeen to join the southern trunk route with the Great North's railway system. In January 1867, noting that the Great North already owed £25,918 plus interest for work on the Denburn Valley line, the Caledonian declined to work the Great North, but proposed that the managers of the two companies should meet 'with a view to some Traffic Arrangement':

> The Directors … regret to be unable to see their way to entering into such an arrangement. They are, however, most anxious that the two Companies should work harmoniously together ... You are aware that your Company is already largely indebted, and is being every month more so, to the Caledonian on account of the Denburn Valley Railway works. It is very desirable that some arrangement should immediately be made for a repayment to this Company of their advances in this Account.[699]

Caledonian records show that repeated attempts were made to extricate payment from the Great North for work in the Denburn Valley, which culminated in the Great North obtaining parliamentary approval in 1867 to exercise its borrowing powers of £41,600 granted in the Denburn Valley Railway Act of 1864, even though

the requisite half of share capital had not yet been paid up.[700] Whilst in conference with the Caledonian, the Great North's board had postponed decisions on the demands received from banks for repayment of their loans, but in February 1867, John Duncan had to tell his shareholders that the Caledonian was not to be the saviour of the Great North: 'For the present, therefore, I regret to say that our negotiations have terminated'.[701] As *Railway News* pointed out, the bargaining position of the Great North was weak:

> The Great North of Scotland, having a nearly exclusive occupation of the counties of Aberdeen and Banff, was only a year or two ago regarded as a very prosperous line, paying a dividend of seven percent. The construction of the Highland Railway proved a blow to its through traffic while, through rivalry with the Highland Company at the north and the Scottish North Eastern at the south, obligations were incurred for the formation of branches, which have now fallen as a dead weight on the undertaking.
>
> … the hopes of the proprietary of the Great North are rested upon a prospective amalgamation with the Caledonian, but until the company's affairs are established on a better basis, it would be in vain to expect good terms in such a transaction.[702]

The Caledonian faced no competitive pressure to obtain control of the insolvent Great North. The scale of the latter's debts and the nature of its isolated rural system precluded the need for amalgamation while the rival North British Railway and its east-coast partners still relied on two major estuary crossings for an Anglo-Scottish route to the north of Scotland. Moreover, if Great North creditors were to force the company into liquidation, its assets and routes would become available for sale at an attractive price. Given the concurrent negotiations with the Highland Railway, an agreement to secure the traffic from northern Scotland via the main line from Inverness to Perth offered greater prospective returns to the Caledonian than those from the regional traffic transported over the Great North's branch line system and transferred at Aberdeen.

Yet Caledonian plans were brought to an abrupt halt as the result of its own shareholder inquiry. The previous inquiry of 1849 had criticised the unjustified costs of the lease offered to the Scottish Central as part of Caledonian plans to secure control of the trunk route to Aberdeen and had condemned the actions of the board as indicating 'a want of judgement and discretion':

> ... with a capital barely sufficient for the original undertaking, their over-zeal induced them to embark on schemes and speculation in an extent seriously compromising the safety of the Company.[703]

The inquiry of 1867-68 revealed some parallels with its predecessor. The vigorous policy adopted by the Caledonian in acquiring control of smaller independent railways throughout Scotland had resumed once it recovered from this earlier financial crisis, and it earned for the company the title of 'The Gaberlunzie' in *Railway*

Times, a Scottish term applied to someone seen as half thief and half beggar.[704] The amalgamations with the Scottish Central and Scottish North Eastern Railways had finally brought Perth and Aberdeen within the Caledonian's empire, but, in criticising the costs of acquisition, the members of the 1867-68 committee of inquiry recognised the importance of the territorial control that their company had acquired:

> While we have directed attention to the diminished revenue which at present, and for some time may be expected to arise from amalgamations which have been entered into, it is to be kept in view that the securing, although at much too great a cost, a united line from Carlisle to Aberdeen, forming in the words of the preamble of the Scottish Central Act, "a continuous portion of the great line of communication between London and the North of Scotland, via Carlisle", has formed your line into a great national undertaking, which may at some future period enhance its value upon this account alone.[705]

Both the Highland and the Great North of Scotland Railways formed northerly off-shoots from the Caledonian's expanded railway system, giving the Caledonian a strong stake in the passage of traffic to and from the north of Scotland by either route. For a brief period, there had been a prospect of the Caledonian obtaining complete command of the northern railway system, although Parliament's rejection of the end-on amalgamation of the Glasgow and South Western and Midland Railways in 1867 suggests that a similar Caledonian, Highland and Great North arrangement might have fared no better.[706] The Caledonian's own financial affairs, however, precluded any possible monopoly of the northern network and the Great North and the Highland were left independently to tackle a rising burden of debt, which threatened their financial viability.

The Great North and the Highland were not the only companies in Great Britain to face serious financial problems at this time. One new method of managing capital was being widely considered within many British railway companies by which fixed term debenture loans were to be converted into undated debenture stock. Both companies had made full use of their borrowing powers and, by July and August 1867 respectively, the Great North had raised £756,579 from debenture loans while the Highland had raised £697,872. Debenture loans were contracted for fixed terms and at interest rates which reflected the market conditions at the time of issue. *Railway Times* described debentures as '… dangerous, they are erratic, they are uncontrollable', and argued that the original intention of Parliament had been that such loans were to be paid off and not converted into long-term debt:

> Debentures were established on the origin of the railway system in the idea that they might – nay, would – be paid off, and that the capital of a company, after constructing its works and opening its line for traffic, would consist of

nothing beyond its ordinary shares.[707]

Shortages of share capital and rising costs of construction and maintenance throughout Britain, however, had translated debenture loans into a fundamental and renewable source of railway capital. Whenever economic events pushed interest rates upwards, railway companies seeking renewal of a portion of their debenture loans could become locked into the payment of higher interest costs and many explored converting these loans into debenture stocks, which had no specific date of redemption but were offered with a fixed rate of interest to forestall the impact of future interest rate variations. Such conversions required careful timing to coincide with periods of favourable interest rates, but the issue of debenture stock made a prior call on the revenue of the company in order to pay the guaranteed dividend, which consequently left less revenue to provide a dividend to ordinary shareholders. When the South Eastern Railway in England proposed the issue of a debenture stock at 5%, the *Railway News* was critical:

> The preference shareholders are provided for, the debenture holders have power to protect themselves, but the holders of ordinary stock are entirely at the mercy of the directors …[708]

The issue of debenture stock offered some scope to the Great North and Highland railway companies to ease the costs of servicing their loan capital, but both companies were close to the limit of their borrowing powers and so had little latitude to raise new capital by this method. This article from *Railway News* was circulated by Great North secretary William Ferguson to his board and the North of Scotland Bank for their information when a similar debenture conversion was under consideration in Aberdeen in June 1868.[709] Both the Great North and the Highland began cautiously to convert debenture loans into debenture stock during 1869, but it was not until 1872, once the immediate financial crisis in each company had passed, that debenture conversion gathered pace.

A resolution of the acute financial difficulties pressing upon the Great North and the Highland Railways were some years away. In the summer of 1867, each company was teetering on the brink of a budgetary chasm. The Great North's capital account was in deficit by £278,038, it owed £303,171 to its bankers who had already started to sell shares held in security to recover some of their funds, and it had failed to obtain terms either for an amalgamation or a working agreement with the Caledonian Railway. A Caledonian lease had eluded the Highland and, though its capital account showed a small surplus of £9,069, it owed £535,000 to its bankers and that sum was rising steadily. Moreover, the prospect of any railway company in Britain raising new share capital, let alone two small, remote and impecunious Scottish companies, had been severely dented by the loss of confidence in railway shares following the collapse of the London discount house of Overend, Gurney. It was against this unpromising background that the Great North and the Highland Railways began their financial recovery.

CHAPTER 13

REFINANCING THE GREAT NORTH OF SCOTLAND RAILWAY

In October 1866, deputy chairman John Duncan had suggested the reconstruction of the Great North's board of directors following the company's amalgamation with its branches and he proposed an adjournment of the shareholders' general meeting to allow time to consider the composition of a new board.[710] Shareholders did not reconvene until December when chairman Sir James Elphinstone explained that they had the option to elect an entirely new board, to add new members to the existing board or to adjourn the meeting again. Robert Lumsden, manager of the North of Scotland Bank, commented to applause:

> I think it right frankly to say that the Board, as presently constituted, does not appear to enjoy in a high degree the confidence of the shareholders (applause) – not certainly in such a degree as is either comfortable for them or likely to promote the interest of the Railway.[711]

Lumsden proposed that the current directors should withhold their resignations for two months and, accordingly, the meeting was adjourned. Robert Lumsden was a pivotal figure in the fate of the Great North of Scotland Railway because the North of Scotland Bank, founded by Aberdeen entrepreneurs in 1836, was one of its principal creditors. Lumsden had been appointed manager of the bank in December 1864 and served until 1888 during a particularly critical period for the Great North.[712] He succeeded James Westland, who had held the post since the resignation of Henry Paterson in 1848 following the use of bank funds by directors and officials for dealings in railway shares. The Great North was also indebted to three other banks, the National Bank of Scotland, the Commercial Bank of Scotland, and the Aberdeen Town and County Bank.

The delay in reconstituting the board was agreed because the Great North was not only in negotiations with the Caledonian Railway concerning an amalgamation or working agreement but also with its bankers in the light of the report commissioned from its auditor, Robert Fletcher, on the financial circumstances of the company. Fletcher's report had recommended that the company should obtain powers to issue a pre-preference stock to raise new funds in order to reduce its debt. This new stock was to rank before any other preferences because dividends had not been paid in full on all the existing preference stock. He warned that Parliament would require the consent of existing holders of preference stock and that these shareholders would not readily agree to weakening their current priority claim on any profits generated by the company.[713]

Fletcher's warning was immediately vindicated. In December 1866, the Aberdeen Town and County Bank raised concerns about the effect of a new pre-preference share issue on the value of stock that was already held in security by the bank against the loans it had advanced to the Great North. Great North secretary William Ferguson attempted to diffuse the bank's unease by confirming that 'there was no intention to force the new bill on lenders without their consent', although he had also to tell the Bank that 'it would not be convenient for the Company to pay up your advances at present'.[714]

The Great North's difficulties in maintaining a sufficient flow of funds intensified. Lumsden's North of Scotland Bank offered a further temporary advance to the Great North in December 1866 to meet a proportion of the debenture loans coming due with the proviso that the funds were to be repaid as soon as new debentures were placed, but other banks continued to demand repayment of their loans.[715] Without the continued financial assistance of the banks, the Great North could not continue to trade. Accordingly, Duncan consulted Lumsden on the constitution of a new board and Lumsden then submitted a list of directors that would command the support of his bank.[716]

At the reconvened shareholders' meeting held in February 1867, John Duncan invited Robert Lumsden to propose the motion to restructure the board. Lumsden moved acceptance of the resignations of five directors, including the current chairman Sir James Elphinstone, the reappointment of six existing directors, and the appointment of six new directors.[717] Elphinstone had asked that the meeting be adjourned again because he was indisposed and wished to justify his chairmanship over the previous twenty years, but Lumsden, while not attributing specific blame to the out-going chairman, urged shareholders to proceed and elect a new board:

> At the last meeting I took the liberty of saying that the Directors did not appear to enjoy so fully as would be agreeable to them and beneficial to the Company the confidence of the shareholders at a distance. Any distrust or any want of confidence felt by those shareholders does not arise in the slightest degree from doubts as to the ability of the personal character of the gentlemen composing the Board ... When, in order to determine the characters of the members composing the Board, they look at it with that view, they find it composed merely of two classes of gentlemen. One – the larger class – are those who originated, and for a series of years persistently carried on a course of policy which has landed the Company in financial difficulties and for a time nearly abolished dividends. The other class – the minority – are those who, like yourself, Mr Chairman, have recently joined the Board and strenuously

endeavoured to retrieve the errors of their colleagues.

But I do not think there is any charge whatever brought against Sir James Elphinstone in connection with the administration of the affairs of the Company. He is identified with the policy pursued by the Directors. Nay, he is more than identified with that policy – he was for a long period the representative and the exponent both to the public and to the shareholders of that policy. His high social standing and his very many excellent qualities made that policy on many occasions more palatable to the shareholders and to the public that it otherwise would have been ... But I think that any delay to enable Sir James Elphinstone to make a statement from the chair is quite uncalled for. No explanation would ever persuade the shareholders of this Railway that they were better to have no dividend at all than with a dividend of seven percent – (applause) – and unless that was done I do not believe that any statement on Sir James Elphinstone's part would alter the views entertained of the past policy of the Company.[718]

Of the original directors of the Great North, only one survived the board reconstruction of 1867; Newell Burnett, an Aberdeen lawyer, served on the Great North's board from 1846 until his death in 1879.[719] Lumsden also reminded shareholders of John Duncan's previous experience as chairman of the Caledonian Railway in the crucial period following that company's financial failure almost twenty years before, and he suggested that Duncan would be a good choice as the new chairman of the Great North:

The duties of the directors of this Company, Sir, I suspect, will not be light for some time to come, and I rather think that the duties of the Chairman will be peculiarly onerous and arduous ... I suppose some gentlemen in this room recollect very well that sixteen years ago a Company in the South was in difficulties even greater than those in which the Great North of Scotland are now. That railway is now one of the most prosperous, and one of the greatest in Scotland. I recollect, Sir, well, when you took the chair of that Company. I recollect well what great and important services you rendered it in extricating it from those difficulties. I think, Sir, with the example of the Caledonian Railway Company before them ... perhaps the Directors, your colleagues, will see it their duty to invite you to accept of the chair (applause). And should they do so, I think I speak the sentiments of a very large portion of the Shareholders of this Company, when I say that it will give a very great confidence to them, and be very satisfactory to the public (applause).[720]

In reply, Duncan explained that Lumsden had persuaded him to remain as a director of the Great North, but warned the new board of the difficulties that lay ahead:

So far as regards myself, however, I must say that the duties of the office for the last three years have been very arduous. Not to make much discrimination between myself and the other Directors – for I must say no body of Directors could have worked harder or more earnestly than they did – I must say that a greater responsibility certainly did lie upon me, and rendered work imperative. I had made upon my mind to cease the connection just for the reason that I could not spare the time from my own business that I have given to the interest of the Company for the last few years. I would have carried out that determination, had it not been for the request of Mr Lumsden and others, to remain. I must say that, if I am to remain, I shall devote the best of my energies to bring the company out of its difficulties. And I can tell those gentlemen, who are coming into the Board, that they will not find it idle play, for its requires all the skill of tried financial business men to conduct the affairs of a Company such as this ... But, whatever may be the case, I hope we will be able to make a reasonable turn-out of it within a reasonable period.[721]

This shareholders' meeting and the subsequent board meeting that elected John Duncan as chairman of the Great North of Scotland Railway represented a significant watershed for the company.[722] Shareholders were also informed of changes made to the structure of responsibilities within the Great North, which brought William B Ferguson, general manager of the highly successful Deeside Railway, to work alongside his Deeside chairman, John Duncan, who explained:

... one of the arrangements contemplated in consequence of the amalgamation of the Deeside Railway with the Great North, was the introduction of Mr Ferguson, the Deeside Manager, into the Great North office. Mr Milne and he now divided the labour – Mr Ferguson taking the post of Secretary, and Mr Milne that of Manager of the traffic, being well acquainted with it. However, Mr Milne was absolutely over-worked. He need not say that they were very fortunate in having two such men connected with the Company for no body of Directors could get on without entire confidence in the officials below them.[723]

The North of Scotland Bank, as a principal creditor, continued to play an important role in shaping the planning and policy of the Great North of Scotland Railway. To try to achieve operational savings, Robert Lumsden explored with Thomas Bruce of the Highland Railway a possible closure of the Morayshire's line between Rothes and Elgin, used by the Great North, and the establishment of a joint-purse arrangement between the Highland and the Great North. Bruce replied to Lumsden's suggestion:

Admitting as a basis the sketch which you sent to me – that the Rothes direct Line should be closed, the Traffic from the competitive points be sent by the shortest routes ... it would give a considerable immediate saving to the Great North, whereas the Highland Company ... would have a considerable increase of Traffic to carry and consequently an increase of working expenses ... This would require to be adjusted in fixing the allowance for carrying extra traffic.[724]

The Great North's general manager Robert Milne consulted Thomas Harrison of the North Eastern Railway who had frequently been used by the company as an arbiter. Harrison considered that neither the Board of Trade nor Parliament would consent to closure of the Glen of Rothes line, and he warned that the Great North would be at a disadvantage if the Highland were to withdraw from such an agreement in the future:

> ... to enter on any such agreement except in perpetuity and under parliamentary sanction would be putting the Great North entirely in the power of the Highland Company, who, unless bound hand and foot, would after the traffic had been fairly diverted to their lines and the Rothes direct line probably in disrepair, find an opportunity of breaking off when it would be found impossible for the Great North Company to get it [the traffic] back again.[725]

The Great North's proposal to seek powers to issue a pre-preference stock continued to generate dissatisfaction primarily because dividend on this new stock was to be paid after the interest due on debentures but before the dividend on all existing preference stock, which affected the status and potential returns of all ·Great North shareholders. Duncan warned of difficulty in Parliament, where Lord Redesdale, chairman of the House of Lords' Private Bills Committee, was reported to be resistant to the creation of such stocks.[726] Some shareholders sought legal advice to protect their position and their advocates asked the Great North for permission to use Robert Fletcher's report on the company's finances, which had been prepared confidentially for the board.[727] The North of Scotland, Aberdeen Town and County and National Banks and the Scottish Provident Assurance Company petitioned against the Great North's pre-preference proposal, although the Great North's parliamentary agents advised the board that 'if you can give the Bankers new Stock for the securities they presently hold you will have little trouble from them'.[728]

The Great North's parliamentary bill initially included powers to create £378,000 of 4½% pre-preference stock 'to provide for the liquidation of the Floating Debt',

although the board reduced this sum to £330,000.[729] This floating debt comprised the advances accepted from banks, which in January 1867 amounted to £345,972, £64,000 for rolling stock and £86,882 for work on the railway link across Aberdeen through the Denburn Valley. In March, a circular to shareholders from chairman Duncan and secretary Ferguson announced that opposition to the proposals had been withdrawn following shareholder meetings held in Aberdeen, Glasgow, Liverpool and London.[730]

The first full accounts of the newly consolidated Great North of Scotland Railway were presented to the ordinary general meeting held in April 1867. Duncan bluntly told his shareholders that, in the half year between July 1866 and January 1867, £15,000 had been paid to meet debenture interest and that interest on the floating debt had required a further £11,700, a sum which the accounts show represented over four-fifths of the available net revenue after working expenses had been paid:

> Gentlemen, it is a deep well that has no bottom, and we are very near the bottom of the well now. I believe that we are now at that point when it is scarcely possible to figure that the condition of this Company can be worse than it is.[731]

Duncan's assessment was forthright and accurate. By the end of that half-year in July 1867 and just one year after the formation of the consolidated company, the Great North returned a net revenue surplus for the year of £39,243, but its capital account showed a deficit of £270,038 and it owed £303,171 to its bankers (table 16).[732]

Faced with the alternative of forcing the Great North into liquidation, which posed the risk of a substantial loss of bank capital, the North of Scotland, Aberdeen Town and County and National Banks agreed a refinancing arrangement with the Great North in March 1867. The Great North was to use receipts from the sale of pre-preference stock to redeem loans, while the banks were to restrict the interest charged on their loans to 4% for three years 'but no longer', provided that the Great North paid off its debts 'at the rate of not less than one fifth of the amount in each year for five years'.[733] The agreement was made dependent upon parliamentary approval of the powers to issue pre-preference capital and the final acceptance by shareholders of the proposals, but it offered the Great North the prospect of a period of some stability within which to begin to restore its financial affairs.

The Great North board recorded formally that a petition from preference shareholders against the bill

Table 16: Revenue account of the Great North of Scotland Railway, 1867–72

Annual data to 31 July (£)	1867	1868	1869	1870	1871	1872
Total revenue	165,578	180,770	180,909	184,608	196,918	209,168
Total expenditure	100,800	115,264	96,443	94,663	98,926	99,218
Surplus – before the payment of fixed interest	64,778	65,506	84,466	89,945	97,992	109,950
Surplus – after the payment of fixed interest	39,243	29,707	43,004	48,996	58,075	71,604
Data at 31 July (£)						
Temporary debt owed to banks	303,171	181,549	91,963	32,674	10,300	0

Source: National Archives of Scotland, BR/RAC(S)/1/14.

Robert Lumsden, Manager of the North of Scotland Bank, who engineered the election of the new GNSR Board in 1867. (From A Keith, 'North of Scotland Bank')

had been withdrawn, but, at the ensuing shareholders' meeting in April, the directors continued to urge shareholders to return their papers giving approval to the pre-preference issue and reinforced their appeal with a letter to 'non-assenters'.[734] The letter referred to the £400,000 of floating debt due to banks, wagon manufacturers and contractors, and reminded shareholders that the company had paid £11,700 in interest on these debts in the last half year alone.

By May 1867, shareholders representing £156,230 of stock had still to consent and the Great North's parliamentary agents reported 'the obstinacy of Lord Redesdale upon the Preference Question'.[735] The Great North's bill not only sought powers for the pre-preference stock but also parliamentary approval to raise loan capital for the Denburn Valley line and authorisation of the amalgamation of the Great North with the Banffshire Railway. Parliament agreed the latter proposals, but struck out the pre-preference capital from the Great North's bill.[736] With this rejection, the Great North's agreement of March 1867 with its bankers was rendered void as the company no longer had the means to raise new funds to redeem its debts.

Even if the powers for a pre-preference stock had been granted, the sale of all of these new shares was by no means assured. The widespread malaise in railway shares experienced across Britain at this time was reflected in two letters published in *Railway Times*:

> The condition of railway property at the present moment in England … is so fearfully depressed in value that the faith of the investing public seems staggered in the belief that railways are a property at all.

> We know that the depression in railway property has been brought on by the folly of directors and shareholders in making or buying so many extensions or branches, and still more the Legislature who have allowed it.[737]

In July 1867, the Great North held £367,940 of floating debt on its general balance sheet, comprising £303,171 owed to bankers, £31,013 for work on the Denburn Valley line and £33,756 on bills of exchange to other creditors. Moreover, the company had sold £30,000 of its Deeside Railway stock, which had been bought without parliamentary sanction, to assist in the reduction of the company's debt.[738] The Great North re-opened negotiations with its bankers, seeking to use 5% preference stock authorised for the Formartine and Buchan Railway in place of the rejected 4½% pre-preference stock in order to raise capital.[739] The banks still faced the intractable dilemma that the Great North could not afford to repay its loans, but these bank funds would be at considerable risk if the Great North was precipitated into bankruptcy. The Aberdeen Town and County Bank continued to press for payment and declined to accept a draft agreement with the Great North submitted in November 1867.[740] The North of Scotland and National Banks appeared to be more accommodating and indicated that they were 'disposed to enter into the Agreement' provided some adjustment was made to the amount of stock to be provided in return for an absolute discharge of the Great North's debts.[741]

Meanwhile, the Great North faced legal action from shareholders over the distribution of preferential dividends. In the half year ending in July 1867, £2 8s was paid on the 5% preference stock, and £2 3s on the 4½% preference A shares, in both cases just under half of the advertised dividend of these 1859 stocks, while holders of the 4½% preference B stock, issued later in 1862, received nothing.[742]

A new agreement was finalised between the Great North of Scotland Railway and the North of Scotland and National Banks in April 1868, which allowed the Great North's recovery to begin in earnest.[743] The banks agreed to purchase £110,320 of former Formartine and Buchan and Aberdeen and Turriff preference shares at par value and returned £97,340 of Great North stock that had been held in security.[744] The two banks therefore became full shareholders in the company and the Great North was required to use the proceeds from these transactions to redeem bank loans. The agreement was risky for the banks, but it offered some chance to recover their advances made to the Great North and ultimately to sell their shareholdings without loss once the company re-established a more secure financial footing.

This substantial inflow of funds allowed the Great North to reduce its floating debt significantly. As a result, the amount of interest charged on the company's debt fell, which in turn released more revenue to begin repaying other debt. Bank debt fell sharply from £350,348 in January 1868, prior to the agreement, to £181,549 in July 1868.[745] The North of Scotland Bank then purchased a further £37,500 of Buchan preference stock at par in April 1868 to clear the outstanding arrears on the Formartine and Buchan Railway bank account.[746] In October 1868, Great North shareholders were told of the progress in reducing the company's floating debt:

> An important change has been made on the debt

of the Company; £147,820 of the Formartine and Buchan and Aberdeen and Turriff 5% Preference Stocks have been realized at par, and the Proceeds applied in discharge of the floating debt. Of the (B) 4½% Preference Stock held in security, £136,010 has been returned to the Company and cancelled.[747]

The rapid impact of the refinancing package was reflected in the company's accounts and, by January 1869, temporary bank debt had fallen to £94,331, almost a quarter of its level just two years earlier. During these refinancing negotiations, the Great North had also embarked on a policy of maximum economy in the operation of its lines. In September 1868, for example, when general manager Robert Milne asked for £18,200 for replacement rolling stock spread over 6 years, the board agreed to put aside just £1,000 per half-year as an additional sum for renewals.[748] Over the following decade, the persistent drive for thrift yielded its return; between 1867 and 1879, revenue on the Great North rose by 57.6%, but expenditure fell by 15.5%, leaving an increasing margin by which the finances of the company could be stabilised and strengthened.[749] More immediately, company secretary William Ferguson warned his directors:

> It is to a reduction of the rate of interest on the debenture debt and the improvement of the Traffic that we must look for a return of prosperity and to that end all our efforts must be directed. There is nothing to hope for from reduction in working expenses and renewals as our first duty must be to keep up the value of the property judiciously and well.[750]

Ferguson suggested that debenture loans should be replaced by debenture stock to stabilise interest payments, a proposal supported by the North of Scotland Bank which advocated a 5% stock payable by instalments whilst such a rate remained attractive to investors. Secretary of the North of Scotland Bank, Edward Fiddes, who was to later succeed Robert Lumsden as its manager, wrote to the Great North board:

> The weather in money matters is too severe and it will again in the course of a few years get stormy but now is the time to put your finances in a permanently stable position ... The next two or three months promise to be remarkable for very low rates, and such a stock, as you can offer, would I think attract purchasers by advertisement in London and elsewhere.[751]

Bank discount rates in July 1868 were just 2%, but the board concluded 'that it is not advisable under existing circumstances of this Company to issue Debenture Stock at such a high rate', and it was not until October 1868 that the creation of debenture stock was agreed in principle up to a limit of £100,000, provided the offer was made available to all shareholders.[752] Any decision to proceed was made subject to the approval of Lumsden and the North of Scotland Bank, although the National Bank was also consulted and considered that a 5% interest rate was too high. A small sum of £11,915 had

been converted into debenture stock by January 1869, but it was not until the shareholders' meeting held in October 1871, by when the final £10,300 of temporary bank debt had been repaid, that approval was obtained to begin converting all debenture loans into debenture stock provided that the rate did not exceed 4¼%.[753]

In April 1869, Duncan was able to give a more optimistic report to Great North shareholders, observing that the floating debt had been reduced to £124,000, but expressing his regret that the company remained in default in paying dividends on preference shares:

> ... during the last four years, the present Board have been labouring under the most uncomfortable feeling in conducting the Company, the financial circumstances of which have been so embarrassing.
>
> We have nearly got rid of a most overwhelming load of debt ... and, although the dividends now payable to preference shareholders may be small in amount, the affairs of the Company are placed in such a position as to give increased confidence and the hope of a future more prosperous than what we had had hitherto.[754]

Railway Times confirmed the Great North's progress, but it was unable to foresee when dividends might be restored to holders of its ordinary shares:

> This undertaking is silently and gradually emerging from its difficulties ... there is little prospect, as yet, of any part of the revenue proceeds permeating towards the holders of ordinary stock.[755]

Dividends paid on preference shares were still well below half of the rate that holders of these shares expected. In the half year ending in January 1869, the 5% preference shares were paid £1.7s.9d, while holders of the 4½% preference A shares received £1 5s. Each of these payments represented just over a quarter of the expected dividend. The 4½% preference B shareholders continued to receive nothing. Nevertheless, the Great North's capital account returned the first surplus since January 1865, amounting to £47,972 compared to a deficit of £182,695 in the previous half year to July 1868. Furthermore, the surplus of net revenue earned from the Great North system began to show a steady rise (table 16).

The refinancing agreement with two banks had, therefore, provided the means for the Great North to recover slowly from its deep financial difficulties. In January 1871, the Great North's share price was quoted as £17-19 per £100, but by November, it had increased to £37-39, although still only two-fifths of its par value.[756] Progress, although slow, continued and, by April 1874, the price had climbed to £50-52, rising further to £65-67 in December that year.[757] Both *Railway Times* and *Railway News* paid due tribute to the improvement in the Great North's financial position:

> The rigorous economy and well-planned finance which have been in operation during the past four years contrast wondrously with that practised in the North British ... Not only has the credit of the undertaking been brought

back to its original standard, but the condition of the line, including the way, works and plant, have been renovated to a marvellous extent.[758]

We can scarcely point in the whole railway system to a line which has made progress more marked in its character or more gratifying alike to the direction and the shareholders ... We regard the accounts of this company as another example of the truth, that in this country honest and prudent management will ultimately bring a railway through any difficulties or disasters.[759]

Addressing his shareholders in October 1870, John Duncan contrasted the current situation of the Great North with that of the company in 1866:

It is a different thing from what it was four years ago. The difficulty then was to find who would go on to this sinking ship, and imperil his life and means to keep up a rickety concern that was going as fast as possible to the bottom ... We required some courage to go in and try to support a concern of that kind; but now when it is fair weather ... everybody is now anxious to be a director.[760]

The Great North had narrowly avoided a complete financial collapse, but holders of its ordinary shares had received no dividend since 1864 and the arrears in preferential dividends continued to mount. By January 1871, £44,555 was owed as deferred payments on the

5% preference shares, although the company's floating debt was eliminated by January 1872.[761] The company's recovery provided sufficient revenue by January 1872 to allow the full payment of preference dividends on both the 5% preference and 4½% preference A stock in March 1872, but holders of the 4½% preference B stock still received nothing.[762]

John Duncan, who had led the Great North successfully through its financial crisis, stepped down as chairman of the company in October 1871, but he remained a director until his death in 1874. He was succeeded by William Leslie, who indicated the board's intent to capitalise the arrears of preference dividend to ease the pressure that would otherwise be placed on the revenue account.[763] At the ordinary general meeting held in October 1872, the directors reminded shareholders that the company was bound to pay the arrears due on the 5% preference stock before any dividend could be restored to the preference B or ordinary shareholders and they recommended that parliamentary authority should be sought for a new 4% preference stock to capitalise these arrears, which would rank after the preference A shares.[764] Chairman Leslie explained that, without capitalisation of these arrears, it would take between three and five years to clear them by using revenue, during which time the preference B and ordinary shareholders would receive no return. Also at this meeting, he made reference to a specific financial sacrifice that had been made by one of the Great North's loyal staff during the preceding

MACDUFF FROM THE WEST.

Despite financial stringency in the years after 1866, the Great North managed to build a short extension at Macduff. The previous terminus was behind the hill on which the photographer was standing and involved a walk of three quarters of a mile to the town. Even the new terminus was still above the town, but people had to climb as far to get to their church. It had been hoped to build a goods tramway down to the harbour, but that was never realised.

(From a postcard, Bob Drummond collection)

years:

> ... some six years ago, when they were at the very water's edge, and when they set about reducing the salaries and lessening all the expenses, their efficient secretary, Mr Ferguson, had voluntarily proposed that his salary should be reduced from £600 to £350 ... the directors therefore felt bound now to propose that the salary of Mr Ferguson, whose zeal, energy, and indefatigable business habits, had done so much for the benefit of the proprietors, should be raised from £350 to £500.[765]

The continued absence of dividend for the holders of the 4½% preference B shares was a cause of concern to the Great North's board, but Leslie revealed in February 1873 that over one-half of the Great North's ordinary stock was held in Liverpool and he and his fellow directors were anxious to restore some dividend to ordinary shareholders and thereby encourage a rise in the much-depressed value of the shares.[766] The directors announced that agreement had been reached with the holders of the 4½% preference B shares whereby preference B dividends were to be restricted to 3% for five years to allow scope to pay some ordinary dividend. Powers for such a restriction were included in the parliamentary act of 1873, which authorised capitalisation of the arrears of preference dividend into a 4% redeemable preference stock.[767] The accounts for January 1874 show that 5% preference and 4½% preference A dividends were paid in full, and preference B holders received the new temporary dividend of 3%, which allowed the payment of ½% dividend to ordinary shareholders, the first such ordinary dividend declared since 1864.[768] The holders of these B preference holders are unknown, but their benevolent action for the longer-term benefit of the company suggests that many must have been closely associated with the Great North board; John Duncan had admitted to shareholders in 1867 that he was a holder of preference B stock, describing them as 'these people that are so far behind, and among whom I have the honour of classing myself'.[769]

The restoration of a dividend on the ordinary shares of the Great North of Scotland Railway attracted optimistic comment in *Railway News*:

> For a long period the line has been under a cloud ... But, as we have often shown, the line contained elements of considerable promise,

and it only required the capitalisation of the arrears, which was happily accomplished last session, to improve materially the position of every shareholder.[770]

The annual surplus on the Great North's revenue account after fixed interest was paid continued to strengthen, rising from £71,604 in July 1872 to £83,851 in July 1874. The improving finances of the company allowed the board in 1872 to agree to progress the extension of the Banffshire Railway from Portsoy to Buckie, which had been postponed in 1865 and then abandoned when the Banffshire was absorbed into the Great North in 1867.[771] The decade following the Great North's financial crisis, however, was one of consolidation for the company and new powers for the Buckie extension were not obtained until 1882, although a short extension of the Macduff line to provide a more convenient terminus was opened in 1872.[772]

The Great North successfully steered a way through the financial storm that broke upon it in 1866 by its own determination and resilience, due in no small measure to the leadership of its chairman John Duncan, supported by his former Deeside colleague, secretary William Ferguson, and general manager Robert Milne who had served the Great North since 1851. Following John Duncan's death in December 1874, the Great North's board recorded 'their high esteem and regard for their late colleague and of the value of his services to the Company', but a long road to rebuild the company's traffic and its previous reputation for attractive and reliable dividends lay ahead.[773] The Great North was still weak financially, although its system was now connected to the national railway network at Aberdeen via the Denburn Valley line. The company had justified the confidence shown in it by its two principal banking creditors, which had recognised the potential financial damage that would be caused to their own businesses by allowing this small and insolvent railway company to become bankrupt. The Great North had been saved from that fate by the recycling of its debt through the refinancing package provided from the North of Scotland and National Banks. In contrast, their northern neighbour, the Highland Railway, encountered much less difficulty in obtaining the support of its bankers, but the debt of this company was proportionately more substantial than that of the Great North and it adopted very different tactics to resolve its particular financial dilemmas.

CHAPTER 14

TACKLING THE DEBT OF THE HIGHLAND RAILWAY

The formation of the Highland Railway in 1865 brought into sharp focus the financial difficulties inherited from its constituent companies. The Inverness and Aberdeen Junction and Inverness and Perth Junction Railways had each paid a final dividend of 4% to their shareholders, but the Highland board recommended a dividend of just 2% at the first meeting of shareholders held in October 1865. Chairman Alexander Matheson assured those present of better times to come:

> For the following half-year … I fully anticipate that we shall be able to pay a considerably larger dividend, perhaps 4 percent.[774]

The Highland's finances did not improve and, in the following half year, dividend fell to 1%, which attracted comment from *Railway News*:

> … all great railways have had their period of trial and financial depression, and after a short period of apparent prosperity, that of the Highland Company had at length come.[775]

Shareholder Mr Gentle of Dell, a regular contributor to general meetings in Inverness, described the 1% dividend as 'a discouraging account of the state of our revenue' but supported the work of the board, remarking 'I believe the directors have made the best they could of the matter'.[776] Matheson predicted that the Highland would receive an increase in traffic once the lines to Skye and the far north were constructed and opened:

> The state of the money market, and other adverse circumstances, have hitherto caused the construction of these lines to be delayed. But the delay is only temporary … The opening of the Highland has given the northern counties a fresh start.[777]

He was able to announce that the Highland had succeeded in negotiating bank loans for a three year period at an interest rate of 5% compared to the average of 7% which had been paid in the previous six months.[778] By contrast, John Duncan later revealed that the Great North was paying 6% in 1867 for its bank advances:

> … why was it 6%? Simply because the credit of the Company was such that no lender would give money unless at a risky interest.[779]

The Highland Railway was perceived to pose less risk to financial institutions than the ailing Great North. The revenue of the company was rising and some of its directors were prepared to give personal guarantees for the advances given by banks. The temporary loan debt of the Highland was closely matched by the par value of company stock issued in security, whereas the Great North had to supply significantly more stock than the value of its loans, reflecting its lower credit status (table 17).

The Great North's bank debt began to fall rapidly in 1868 as a result of the refinancing package agreed with its bankers in April of that year, but the Highland's bank debt continued to rise. The scale of temporary bank loans and the personal liabilities of its directors had made an exploration of amalgamation or lease with the Caledonian Railway an attractive proposition to the Highland's board, but a successful resolution of the clandestine negotiations was denied by the Caledonian's own financial problems. Had firm proposals for a lease been published in 1867, strong opposition could have been expected from Inverness and the highland region, given the important economic contribution made by the railway to the town and the long-held desire for local and independent control of railways in the highlands, which was still evident forty years later in 1906 when the Highland board withdrew from an agreement to amalgamate with the Great North of Scotland Railway.[780]

Despite the financial difficulties facing the new Highland board, the directors were prepared to consider spending additional capital to protect their company. The Inverness and Perth Junction Railway had made an agreement with the Scottish North Eastern Railway in 1861 for use of the line into Perth.[781] The annual cost in 1866 was £9,874, but a request to convert the tolls

Table 17: Temporary bank debt and stock held in security, 1867–72

Great North of Scotland (£)	January 1867	July 1867	January 1868	July 1868	January 1869	July 1869
Balances due to bankers	345,972	303,171	350,348	181,549	94,331	91,963
Stock held in security	457,240	448,266	456,973	162,040	132,361	131,512
Highland (£)	**February 1867**	**August 1867**	**February 1868**	**August 1868**	**February 1869**	**August 1869**
Balances due to bankers	505,000	535,000	535,000	565,000	625,000	625,000
Stock held in security	505,000	535,000	535,000	565,000	524,000	524,000

Great North of Scotland (£)	January 1870	July 1870	January 1871	July 1871	January 1872	July 1872
Balances due to bankers	39,099	32,674	32,695	10,300	0	0
Stock held in security	47,061	37,636	37,538	18,400	6,000	6,000
Highland (£)	**February 1870**	**August 1870**	**February 1871**	**August 1871**	**February 1872**	**August 1872**
Balances due to bankers	625,000	605,000	520,000	450,000	0	0
Stock held in security	524,000	504,000	384,000	274,000	0	0

Sources: National Archives of Scotland, BR/RAC(S)/1/14; BR/HR/1/1-2.

Eneas W Mackintosh of Raigmore, a director of the Highland Railway from 1865 and its chairman from 1891 to 1896, served on the boards of all the Highland's constituent companies and was named as a first director in the parliamentary act incorporating the Inverness and Nairn Railway in 1854. (From 'The Iron Track through the Highlands' by JE Campbell)

into a fixed annual payment of £5,000 was refused by the Scottish North Eastern.[782] Despite mounting debt, the Highland proposed construction of its own line into Perth, although the promotion was doubtless intended as a competitive lever to seek better terms.[783] At the final general meeting of the Inverness and Perth Junction Railway, Matheson accepted that a Highland line into Perth would involve an expensive contest with the Scottish North Eastern in Parliament:

> We ought certainly to get the toll reduced to £5000 a year. That is as much as we ought to pay. If they cared to offer that, it might be better to accept it than to make a line of our own.[784]

The cost of this new line of eleven miles was estimated at £124,000, but, following an arbiter's report suggesting a compromise with the Scottish North Eastern, the directors acknowledged the strained finances of the company.[785] An agreement for use of the Perth line was finalised in June 1866 at an annual charge of £5,000 and clauses were included in the Caledonian and Scottish North Eastern amalgamation act to set this toll and to protect Highland traffic.[786]

Highland Railway records reveal a constant struggle to obtain sufficient capital. In September 1865, Charles Waterston, manager of the Caledonian Bank in Inverness, a director of the Inverness and Nairn Railway between 1858 and 1861, and a long-standing supporter of highland railway development, was elected to the board.[787] The Caledonian Bank had been a regular source of funds for the Inverness railway companies, but not all banks were so accommodating to the new Highland Railway. In November 1865, following the announcement of a reduced dividend, the Commercial Bank wrote to the Highland:

> In consequence of the recent fall in the price of the Company's shares, the Bank will require additional Stock from the Company in security of the advances made by them.[788]

To ease the shortage of funds, deputy chairman Thomas Bruce attempted to negotiate a loan of £150,000 from the Standard Insurance Company for two or three years at 4½% interest, backed by preference stock of that value and the personal security of the directors, but he was unsuccessful and reported to the board that 'there is little prospect of getting the sum required from other parties in Edinburgh'.[789] Attention turned to London and, in December 1865, £140,000 was obtained for three years at 5%, backed by preference stock and the guarantees of directors.[790] The 5% interest rate obtained may reflect the influence and financial contacts of the directors, given that bank discount rates were at 7% in December 1865, rose to 10% in the wake of the collapse of the London discount house of Overend, Gurney in May 1866, and did not fall back to 5% until September 1866.[791] Highland Railway chairman Alexander Matheson, for example, was a director of the Bank of England from 1847 to 1884. A local loan of £100,000 at 5% for 3 years was secured via Waterston at the Caledonian Bank in January 1866 and the £110,000 overdraft standing with the National Bank was extended to December 1868.[792] Thus, in this brief period, £350,000 was obtained from banks for a three year period, equivalent to over £17½ million in current value, backed by company stock and the personal security of directors.

Despite their individual wealth, the faith of the directors making this scale of financial commitment should not be underestimated. Some strain in the Highland boardroom became apparent in January 1866 when the Duke of Sutherland requested payment of an agreed subscription of £30,000 to the new Sutherland Railway, an obligation inherited from the Inverness and Aberdeen Junction and Inverness and Perth Junction Railways.[793] The Highland board reminded the Duke that he and his commissioner, George Loch, had declined to give personal guarantees in 1857 when the Inverness and Aberdeen junction had been seeking capital.[794] Sutherland and Loch were directors of the Highland Railway, but had failed to persuade the board to call a meeting of shareholders to approve the raising of funds for the subscription to the Sutherland Railway. The Highland board was wrestling with its own major financial difficulties and it felt bound to honour the Sutherland subscription only if the preference stock it was authorised to issue was found to be 'a marketable or saleable security'.[795] In the difficult financial climate of early 1866, Highland Railway stock like that of many railway companies was not attractive to investors.

In a sharp response to George Loch's letter requesting payment of the subscription, the Highland board declined to take further personal responsibility for company funds and resolved:

> That the Directors, cheerfully acknowledging the liberal Spirit in which His Grace the Duke of Sutherland has contributed to the promotion of some of the Railway undertakings of the

Amalgamated Company, must in justice to themselves remind Mr Loch that while His Grace and Mr Loch declined to undertake any personal obligations, the other Directors severally contributed largely according to their ability, to important schemes which did not reach or pass through their respective estates – that moreover from the outset of Railway projects in the North they came under heavy personal responsibility for which as Directors or otherwise there was no legal call upon them and that for these, extending over many years and still continuing in many cases, apart from the large sums held by them in ordinary stock, to larger amounts than His Grace's contributions – Railway enterprise in this part of the country would long since have been utterly crushed, and would never have reached the borders of the County of Sutherland.

That the Directors continue to hold it in the highest degree inexpedient in the present circumstances of the Company to convene a Meeting of Shareholders to consider the question of raising funds for subscriptions to the Sutherland Company, and do not feel warranted ... to incur further personal liability for the undertaking – and despair at this juncture of procuring the requisite amount on any security in their power to offer as Directors of this company.[796]

Nevertheless, the Sutherland Railway board, with just the Duke and George Loch present, recorded formally that the failure of the Highland to contribute its subscription had denied the Sutherland access to its borrowing powers, 'thus causing a deficiency of £90,000 altogether of available capital'.[797] Further pressure from Loch for the subscription revealed that all unissued stock of the company was held by directors as their security for personal guarantees given for loans and so no capital could be raised for the Sutherland Railway unless shares already held by directors were purloined:

The whole of the unissued Capital of the Company is held by the Directors who have

subscribed these Bills as a security for the advances guaranteed by their signatures. Under these circumstances no advances could be made by the Highland Company to the Sutherland line except by issuing further capital on the Security of the Directors or by appropriating part of the shares which now form their Security.[798]

Unsurprisingly, the directors declined to reduce their security held in shares or to raise the capital limit of the company and proposed to postpone raising the issue of the Sutherland subscription with shareholders until the company's financial position improved, although they expressed their regret at 'the delay and inconvenience' that had been caused to the Sutherland company.[799] The impasse was not resolved until October 1866 when the Highland board agreed to sell £30,000 of preference stock at par value to the Duke of Sutherland, using the funds received to pay the subscription.[800]

Despite the dire capital position, the performance of the new Highland Railway justified the commitment of its directors. Gross revenue, whilst reflecting the distinctly seasonal nature of the traffic carried in each of the half years, rose consistently, and ordinary dividend increased modestly but steadily (table 18). The Highland was commended for its improvement by *Railway Times*, which also reminded its readers that Highland landowners had invested in these northern lines primarily to obtain an improvement in their land values:

For a line the stock of which is so largely held by the resident gentry – by parties who look not to interest on their outlay so much as to improvement in the value of their estates – to be paying four percent is a result which must be considered throughout the locality as more than successful.[801]

The Highland was able to recycle its temporary debt when loans became due. A loan of £160,000 at 4½% was obtained from the British Linen Bank in 1867 for one year to repay the £110,000 owing to the National Bank and a personal advance of £50,000 given by director James Merry.[802] With £405,000 of temporary loans due for repayment in December 1868, chairman Matheson

Table 18: Revenue account of the Highland Railway, 1867–74

Half year data (£)	February 1867	August 1867	February 1868	August 1868	February 1869	August 1869	February 1870	August 1870
Gross Revenue	96,362	103,766	100,169	107,164	102,563	110,964	101,251	113,645
Net revenue	51,792	58,494	53,721	64,420	61,743	67,000	60,138	68,616
Interest & dividends	51,715	56,778	53,603	62,271	61,619	65,791	60,032	65,101
Balance remaining	77	1,715	118	2,148	123	1,208	106	3514
Ordinary dividend	1%	2%	1%	3%	2¼ %	3½ %	2%	4%

(£)	February 1871	August 1871	February 1872	August 1872	February 1873	August 1873	February 1874	August 1874
Gross Revenue	107,967	118,799	123,117	131,140	124,792	133,872	134,288	146,322
Net revenue	65,598	70,004	73,518	77,945	66,201	73,627	65,581	75,239
Interest & dividends	65,480	69,140	73,078	75,459	65,917	70,593	65,466	73,208
Balance remaining	117	863	440	2,485	284	3,033	115	2,031
Ordinary dividend	4%	5%	6%	6%	4¼ %	5%	4%	5%

Source: National Archives of Scotland, BR/HR/1/1-2.
Note: Shillings and pence have been rounded down and so totals may not match precisely the sum of component items.

Although little was spent on station buildings on the Perth line, the Ross-shire line stations had substantial buildings in the Italianate style which was also found on the Keith line. This is Fearn which, like many stations north of Inverness, was sited in open countryside but it did survive the closures of the 1960s and is still open today.
(C J B Sanderson)

and general manager Dougall sought renewals at lower interest.[803] A loan of £60,000 for two years was accepted from the Union Bank in March 1868 at an initial rate of 4½%, although the term was extended in August to three years.[804] Loans held with the Commercial (£95,000), British Linen (£160,000) and Caledonian (£120,000) Banks, which previously attracted interest at 5%, were renegotiated in September and October 1868 for two years at 4¼%, reflecting the general fall in interest rates since 1866.[805]

With the Highland's sound revenue account and the personal contacts and guarantees of its directors, credit was available to the company and its approval presented little risk to the banks. Bank lending reached a peak of £625,000 in February 1869, only falling back to £605,000 in August 1870, although the banks required only £524,000 of stock as security for the loans (table 17). This substantial level of temporary debt had accumulated throughout the decade as the result of difficulties in raising share capital for the Inverness railway web and the costs of construction, but the consolidated company was trading successfully. The policy of the Highland board to redeem this considerable debt, therefore, was to guarantee temporary loan capital whilst building the company's traffic, revenue and dividend, thereby making Highland shares more attractive to investors. Once the price of stock rose to par value or above, the board then intended to release stock held in security and use the proceeds from its sale progressively to repay the company's debt. The success of this policy, however, was only sustainable because of the considerable personal financial commitments made by the company's directors to secure and maintain temporary borrowing.

Like the Great North and many other railway companies, the Highland saw merit in converting its renewable debenture loans into undated debenture stock. In April 1869, Highland shareholders approved the conversion of debenture loans into debenture stock at an interest rate of 4¼%, which yielded a potential saving in interest payments and offered greater stability in managing future debt charges.[806] Debenture loan rates had been set by the board in April 1866 at 5% for a three year loan, 4¾% for a five year loan and

4½% for a seven year loan, although Dougall had been instructed not to insert the interest rate in the debenture advertisement and to arrange the loans by negotiation in order to obtain the lowest interest rates possible.[807] Debenture conversion remained modest until the heavy temporary debt of the company had been cleared, but from February 1872 the Highland's accounts show a steady growth in the amount of debenture stock issued.

Unlike the Great North, the Highland continued to pay its preference dividends in full throughout its period of financial difficulty. Dividend paid on its ordinary shares rose steadily from 2% in August 1867 to 3% in August 1868, 3½% in August 1869 and 4% in August 1870, which stimulated market interest in the Highland's stock. In January 1871, Andrew Dougall informed the Highland board that the remaining £15,400 of unissued 5% preference B stock had been taken since the last ordinary general meeting of the company.[808] Matheson and Dougall were authorised to fix the time to sell the available £8,350 of 4½% preference A stock, leaving just £71,300 of ordinary stock and £30 of 5% Nairn preference stock unissued. Moreover, the board at this meeting was able to repay £45,000 to the Union Bank and £25,000 to the Caledonian Bank to reduce further the company's temporary debt. By June 1871, £33,540 of preference stock released from security had been sold and, by September, preference share sales had yielded a further £55,505.[809]

A multiplier effect then acted very swiftly to reduce the level of bank debt. Rising market demand for Highland shares was satisfied by stock reclaimed from banks as loans were repaid and also by the release of stock previously held by directors as security for their personal guarantees. From £625,000 of temporary bank loans held in February 1869, August 1869 and February 1870, the amount fell to £605,000 in August 1870, £520,000 in February 1871, £450,000 in August 1871, and was eliminated completely by February 1872 (table 17). As receipts from the sale of released shares swiftly reduced the company's debt, the charge to the revenue account to meet all interest costs due for debenture and temporary loans, which had been £31,394 in August 1869, fell steadily to £28,862 in August 1870, £26,219 in

August 1871 and £15,511 in August 1872, a reduction of fifty percent in just three years.[810]

The main source of funds to trigger this rapid elimination of temporary debt came from the sale of ordinary shares previously unissued or held in security for loans. The Highland's capital account for August 1871 shows that £110,000 of ordinary shares had been released to the company, but £274,000 still remained in security. The board considered how to manage the sale of this large amount of ordinary stock and meanwhile authorised Matheson and Dougall to sell at a premium of £105 'if that price can be got'.[811]

At the general meeting of shareholders held in October 1871, the directors announced their intention to sell ordinary shares with a face value of £385,390 on 1st December 1871 at par to shareholders and at a small premium on the open market.[812] Highland shareholders were offered a rights issue of £20 of new stock for every £100 of stock held, provided that it was fully paid up on the specified date of issue. After Dougall reported to the board on 5th December that £127,000 of ordinary shares had already been taken, it was minuted that 'none to be sold after this week under £105' and Bruce was asked to arrange for the shares to be quoted on the London Stock Exchange share lists.[813] The immediate proceeds of the share sale were used to repay £80,000 to the British Linen Bank and £47,500 to the Commercial Bank.

In the following month, a further £78,260 of ordinary shares was sold, with £20,000 of these yielding a premium of 3% and £20,680 a premium of 5%.[814] The board also agreed to sell £50,000 of ordinary shares to director James Merry at a price of £105 per £100, but resolved not to sell any more on the market at less than £108. By 6th February 1872, all of the ordinary stock had been sold and the company had received £14,817 as gross premium over the £100 par value of the shares, giving an average premium of 3.8% per share, although at the peak of sales some shares had been sold at £110.[815] When *Railway Times* published its first quotation for £100 of Highland ordinary stock in February 1872, the price was shown as £120-125, although by contrast on the same day £100 of Great North ordinary stock was quoted at £41-43, reflecting the market opinion of the relative financial strength of the two companies.[816]

While the depth of the financial crisis for the Highland had, in absolute terms, been greater than that for the Great North, the financial backing of its directors, their ability to secure credit at relatively favourable rates, and the strengthening trading position of the company resulted in a dramatic recovery between 1869 and 1872. On 6th February, the Highland board reviewed a list of the major temporary loans taken and since repaid, which indicated the scale of the financial difficulties through which the company had passed (table 19).

The somewhat laconic entry in the Highland minute book following this list can only leave the reader to imagine the profound sense of relief that must have been felt in the boardroom at Inverness on that day:

> The Secretary stated that the Bonds, Bills and Agreements referred to in the foregoing statement were now on the table, whereupon it was resolved to commit them to the fire, which was accordingly done in the presence of the meeting.[817]

At the shareholders' general meeting held in April 1872, the directors were able to announce that the company was free of debt:

> Since the last meeting, the balance of ordinary stock amounting to £385,390 had been disposed of, and with the proceeds, the last instalment of the Temporary Loans, which then stood at £450,000, has been paid, thus enabling the Directors to make the satisfactory announcement that the undertaking is now entirely free of debt.[818]

Highland shareholders recorded their appreciation of the work of the directors and voted a sum of £1,250 as remuneration to be divided as the board decided:

> That the cordial thanks of the Shareholders be tendered to the Directors for their attention to the affairs of the Company, and especially for having interposed their personal security for the large sums of money required during many years to carry the undertaking through

Table 19: Major temporary loans taken and repaid by the Highland Railway

Source	Loan (£)	Taken out (or renewed)	Repaid
Commercial Bank (For the Inverness and Aberdeen Junction Railway)	60,500	6 August 1861	2 December 1862
National Bank	110,000	1 January 1866	11 September 1867
Royal Bank of Scotland	20,000	13 November 1866	9 November 1870
Scottish Provident Institution	50,000	15 May 1869	13 May 1871
Lord R Leveson-Gower (son of the 3rd Duke of Sutherland)	50,000	21 December 1866	15 May 1871
Lord A Leveson-Gower (son of the 3rd Duke of Sutherland)	50,000	21 December 1866	15 May 1871
Union Bank of Scotland	60,000	8 September 1868	8 September 1871
James M Graham	10,000	13 November 1866	8 November 1871
Commercial Bank	95,000	21 October 1870	3 February 1872
British Linen Bank	160,000	31 December 1870	19 January 1872
Life Association of Scotland	20,000	10 August 1866	3 December 1871
Standard Life Assurance Company	30,000	20 October 1869	26 December 1871
Caledonian Bank	20,000	3 September 1864	14 September 1867
Caledonian Bank	100,000	31 December 1864	3 February 1872
Total	£835,500		

Source: National Archives of Scotland, BR/HR/1/2, p.140.

its difficulties, whereby the interests of the Company were protected and promoted, and a Dividend even at the most depressed period, paid to the Shareholders.[819]

The diligence of the board and its staff in the financial recovery of the Highland was commended to its national readership by *Railway Times*:

> It has not been our privilege, for some considerable time past, to furnish a more satisfactory report than that of the Highland ... Meanwhile the thanks of the railway community are emphatically due to the chairman, directors, and secretary of the Highland. Probity, endurance, and cordial faith are seldom without reward.[820]

Matheson's successful work in uniting the constituents of the Highland company and protecting its territory was widely acknowledged. *Railway News* referred to 'Mr Matheson of Ardross MP, who has done so much for railway extension in the north', while *Railway Times* commented:

> Mr Matheson has served them well for many years, and to his intimate knowledge of the district and its capabilities, and to his able and successful exertions in uniting together the several undertakings of which it is composed, and afterwards in protecting it from aggression, they are mainly indebted for the successful position their property now holds.[821]

At the shareholders' meeting held in October 1875, Inverness banker Charles Waterston, who had stood down from the Highland board in December 1874 but was to return in 1876 and serve for a further twenty years, proposed that £500 should be voted to commission a portrait of Matheson, which was to be hung in the boardroom:

> The noblemen and gentlemen who form the board of the Highland are deserving of all honour for their patriotism and public spirit in taking the lead they did in this great undertaking, and in nothing did they show more wisdom than in the selection from their own number of Mr Matheson as their chairman. No chairman could have done more than he has done. He has devoted his valuable experience and much of his valuable time to our service, and along with other members of the board has largely used his personal credit in placing the finances of the railway upon a most satisfactory and economical basis.[822]

Waterston's motion was seconded by James Falshaw, now Lord Provost of Edinburgh, but who, as contractor with Thomas Brassey, had constructed the Inverness and Nairn Railway twenty years before:

> ... under his [Matheson's] management and tact these small beginnings had swollen into undertakings of great magnitude. Mr Matheson always did the right thing at the right time ... Once the line had been started then Mr Matheson's difficulties began. They all recollected how they had been bearded by the Great North, and here it was that Mr Matheson had shown his firmness. "Never", said he, stamping his foot on the floor, "while I sit in this chair shall the Great North extend beyond Keith".[823]

Matheson replied that he hardly knew how to express his feelings: 'It was quite true he had done all in his power to promote the railway system in the north ... that he had succeeded was sufficient compensation ...'.[824] In recognition of his wider contributions to commerce and the highlands, Matheson was created a baronet in 1882, taking the title of Sir Alexander Matheson of Lochalsh.

The astute management of the Highland Railway retained the premiums received from the sale of its shares in a reserve fund and, in April 1873, used £10,596 to cushion the effect of a short-term reduction in revenue as the result of a serious harvest failure in the north. The declared ordinary dividend of 4¼% for February 1873 was supplemented by a further 1¾% in order to match the 6% dividend previously paid in February and August 1872.[825] In October 1873, *Railway News* observed:

> ... the Highland occupies an unusually favourable position, and should, in its limited way, be one of the safest and best investments of its time.[826]

With wealthy directors prepared to guarantee the temporary loans provided by the banks and with a rising trend in the gross revenue earned by the company, the Highland board did not have to pursue a policy of refinancing similar to that adopted by the Great North to recover from its financial difficulties. The Highland Railway was inherently sound due to its location and the traffic tapped by its web of railway routes. The finances of the new company, however, had been placed under immediate pressure by the substantial capital debt inherited from its constituent companies and the escalating amount of temporary credit required to balance its budget. Backed by the personal resources, commitment, and expertise of its directors, the Highland bought the time necessary to allow its trading position to improve sufficiently to make the large stock of its unsold shares more attractive to investors, then using the receipts from their sale to cancel the company's debt.

The Highland directors were able to take a longer-term view of their company's potential prosperity, although the scale of its immediate financial plight was acutely apparent to them, both collectively and individually. In the absence of similar personal backing, the board of the Great North of Scotland had to adopt an urgent and short-term approach to resolving its financial emergency. After the failure of both companies to secure an amalgamation or lease with the Caledonian Railway, they were left to resolve their serious difficulties in their own singular ways, but with the threat of company bankruptcy and personal liability ever present. The story of their eventual success has left two remarkable examples of the sagacity and resolve of railway entrepreneurs in northern Scotland during the nineteenth century.

CHAPTER 15

THE GREAT NORTH AND THE HIGHLAND RAILWAYS, 1874

The decade between 1845 and 1855 had seen the plans of highland promoters for a railway between Inverness and Perth rejected by Parliament and approval given to the Great North of Scotland Railway to extend the Anglo-Scottish trunk route from Aberdeen north-westwards to Inverness. The inability of the Great North to complete that route, however, had allowed Inverness to begin to construct its web of railways centred on the highland capital. The following decade between 1855 and 1865 was dominated by the competitive pressure brought to bear on the Great North of Scotland Railway's regional monopoly, which was marked by the opening of a new main line connecting Inverness with Perth and the southern railway network and the resultant isolation of the Great North. In the following years, both the Great North of Scotland and the Highland Railways had to wrestle with the major financial consequences of their earlier regional expansion, but, by 1874, some stability had been restored within the railway system of northern Scotland.

1874 was a significant year for the two principal railway companies in the north of Scotland. The Great North of Scotland Railway was able to declare the first dividend on its ordinary shares since 1864, albeit a very modest amount. Its network of rural lines in north-east Scotland was by now connected across Aberdeen to the Caledonian main line to Perth and the south. It had repaid the large amount of temporary debt owed to its bankers, its capital account was in balance, and its gross revenue was beginning to rise steadily.

In the highlands, the railway reached the far north ports of Wick and Thurso in 1874 over the lines of the Sutherland, the Duke of Sutherland's, and Sutherland and Caithness Railways. These lines, together with the Dingwall and Skye Railway which opened to Strome Ferry on Loch Carron in 1870, were worked by the Highland Railway from the outset and completed the main arteries of the railway system in northern Scotland. Almost mirroring the previous relationship of the Great North with its branches prior to their amalgamation in 1866, the Highland acted as host to these nominally independent companies until the Dingwall and Skye was absorbed into the Highland in 1880, followed by the far north lines in 1884.

The Highland Railway had restored the dividend on its ordinary shares back to the levels which its two main constituent companies had paid prior to the formation of the new company in 1865. It had repaid a mountain of temporary bank debt, which, at its peak, was almost twice the amount owed by the Great North at the height of its financial crisis. Gross revenue earned by the Highland was rising slowly but consistently. While the capital account still showed a deficit in 1874, this sum represented only four percent of the total amount of share and loan capital raised by the company.

There were similarities in the reasons for the major financial crises that had confronted these two northern railway companies in 1865-66, not least of which had been the persistent difficulty in raising sufficient share capital to construct their lines, but the capacity of each to resolve its problems was very different. The Highland Railway held a good prospect of repaying its considerable debt because it had captured the bulk of the traffic to and from northern Scotland, it had established a rising trend of revenue, and it was able to obtain bank credit through the contacts and personal guarantees of many of its directors. Using these financial advantages, the Highland directors gained time to strengthen the company's revenue and thereby its dividend, whereupon Highland shares became more attractive to investors and the large amounts of stock held in security for bank loans were progressively released and sold to redeem the debt. Notwithstanding their personal wealth, the extraordinary feature of this successful strategy for the financial recovery of the Highland Railway was the degree of risk that some of its directors were able and prepared to accept to protect their company and their interests.

The Great North of Scotland Railway also held a significant burden of debt but, without the security of northern traffic passing over its route to Aberdeen, its future earning potential was uncertain. It benefitted from a more compact system than the Highland, serving an agricultural area and with less seasonal variation in its traffic. Nevertheless, it was unable to service its debt and faced financial collapse in December 1866 as banks began to sell Great North stock held in security to recover some of their funds. Aberdonian banks and the Great North had been closely associated since the 1840s and the Great North's salvation was to be achieved through a re-financing agreement with its bankers. The decisive role undertaken by two banks ensured the survival of the Great North as an independent concern and the North of Scotland Bank in particular helped to shape the future direction of the railway company.

The Great North and the Highland both emerged successfully from their own distinctive financial crises and remained as autonomous enterprises despite their exploration of amalgamation or leasing arrangements with the Caledonian Railway. By 1874, the Great North, confined to a network of relatively short rural lines in north-east Scotland, faced a slow and painstaking task to rebuild its traffic, customer loyalty and revenue. The Highland, operating a logical network of lengthy main line routes serving sparsely populated areas and with marked seasonal fluctuations in traffic, had to respond to new railway promotions in the far north and west of the highlands. It soon became clear that these remote highland lines were to pose the same financial dilemmas to their host company, the Highland, which the north-east branches had presented to the Great North in the previous decade.

Indirectly, both companies had been driven to observe the dictum that *Herapath's Railway Journal* had published in April 1855 and with which this book opened: 'Take care of the capital account and the revenue will take care of itself'.[827] Yet *Herapath's* advice was not entirely applicable in northern Scotland because the generation of revenue remained a critical and unremitting labour for the Great North of Scotland and the Highland Railways even after their capital problems had been largely resolved.

It was not long before the attractive dividends that the Highland Railway began to pay consistently from 1871 reawakened the interest of railway entrepreneurs in promoting highland schemes. The first signs emerged in 1874 when *Railway News* reported proposals made by engineer Sean McBean of Westminster to construct a railway between Glasgow and Inverness via Fort William and the Great Glen with a branch to serve Skye at a projected cost of £2 million. The journal commented on the 'boldness of the projector and the ingenuity with which his proposal is supported', but suggested that the capital required would 'be largely obtained locally'.[828] Scarce local capital was already heavily committed in the Highland Railway and its northern satellites and it was not until 1882 that the Glasgow and North Western Railway was promoted, albeit unsuccessfully, to run via the Great Glen to Inverness. The Highland Railway was entering a new era of competition that was to bring further financial tribulations to its board in Inverness.

Yet 1874 was a year when the directors of the Highland and Great North of Scotland Railways were able to feel some relief from the financial misery that had engulfed them for almost a decade. Much of their story in this book has been charted though the pages of the national railway journals of the time and so it is fitting that the final word on the progress of these two remarkable railway companies comes from their leader articles:

> True, the dividend just announced is only 5s for the past half-year; but the resumption of payments, however small at first, bodes well for the future of the company ... Again, however, the Great North of Scotland may be classed amongst the dividend-paying lines, and we hope ere long it will occupy the position it formerly held. (*Railway Times*, commenting on the Great North of Scotland Railway, 7th March 1874)

> We must congratulate the gentlemen by whose public spirit and energy the benefits of railway communication have been extended to the remote Highlands that their efforts have been crowned with such signal success, and that they are now reaping, in a handsome dividend, the reward of their courage in standing by the line through all its difficulties. The burning of the bonds in the board-room at Inverness, by which was signified recently the extinction of the heavy pecuniary responsibility which lay so long upon the directors, should be chronicled as among the happiest incidents of the railway's history. (*Railway News*, commenting on the Highland Railway, 20th April 1872)

After a century and a half, the Great North of Scotland and Highland Railways continue to attract the interest of historians and the public alike. The survival of the principal railway routes of these companies into the twenty-first century is due in part to the resolve of their directors, who fought so tenaciously in the mid-nineteenth century to overcome the multitude of financial and managerial dilemmas that beset them. Comparable financial dilemmas continue to face the railways in northern Scotland today, but the main lines of the mid-nineteenth century remain to serve and captivate new generations.

BIBLIOGRAPHY

Acworth, WM	*The Railways of Scotland* (London, 1890).
Alborn, TL	*Conceiving Companies: joint stock politics in Victorian England* (London, 1998).
Alderman, G	*The Railway Interest* (Leicester, 1973).
Anderson, G and P	*Handbook to the Inverness and Nairn Railway and scenes adjoining it* (Inverness, 1856).
Anderson, G and P	*Handbook from Perth to Forres, Inverness to Bonar Bridge by the Inverness and Perth and Aberdeen Junction Railways* (Edinburgh, 1864).
Aytoun, WE	'How we got up the Glenmutchkin Railway, and how we got out of it', *Blackwood's Edinburgh Magazine,* vol.58 (October 1845), 453-66.
Aytoun, WE	'The Railways', *Blackwood's Edinburgh Magazine,* vol. 58 (November 1845), 633-48.
Barclay-Harvey, M	*A History of the Great North of Scotland Railway* (London, 1949, 2nd edition, reprinted Shepperton, 1998).
Butt, J and Ward, JT	'The promotion of the Caledonian Railway Company', *Transport History,* vol. 3, No. 2, part 1 (July 1970), 164-92 and vol. 3, No. 3, part 2 (November, 1970), 225-57.
Campbell, JE	*The Iron Track through the Highlands : Glimpses of it in the Past* (Highland News, Inverness, 1922)
Campbell, RH	'The Law and the Joint Stock Company in Scotland', in PL Payne (ed.), *Studies in Scottish Business History* (London, 1967), 136-151.
Channon, G	*Railways in Britain and the United States, 1830-1940* (Aldershot, 2001).
Checkland, SG	*Scottish Banking, a History 1695-1973* (Glasgow, 1975).
Cottrell, PL	'Railway Finances and the Crisis of 1866: contractors' bills of exchange and finance companies', *Journal of Transport History,* new series, vol.III, No.1 (February 1975), 20-40.
Cummings AJG and Devine, TM	*Industry, Business and Society in Scotland since 1700* (Edinburgh, 1994).
Devine, TM and Orr, WJ	*The Great Highland Famine* (Edinburgh, 1988).
Devine, TM	*Clanship to Crofters' War: the social transformation of the Scottish Highlands* (Manchester, 1994).
Devine, TM	*The Scottish Nation 1700-2007* (London, 1999, reprinted Harmondsworth, 2000, new edition, London, 2006).
Fenwick, K	'Genesis of the Great North', *Great North Review,* vol.33, No.128 (February 1996), 242-45; vol.33, No.129 (May 1996), 283-92; vol.33, No.140 (August 1996), 306-11.
Fenwick, K	*The Inverness and Nairn Railway* (Highland Railway Society, 2005).
Fenwick, K and Sinclair, NT	*The Perth and Dunkeld Railway* (Highland Railway Society, 2006).
Fenwick, K	*Railways of Keith* (Great North of Scotland Railway Association, 2006).
Fenwick, K and Geddes, H	*The Highland Railway, Railway History in Old Photographs* (Stroud, 2009).
Fletcher, P	'Strategy, solvency and the state: the development of the railway system of northern Scotland, 1844-74' (PhD thesis, University of York, 2007).
Fletcher, P	'The Great North and the Aberdeen Railway Web', *Great North Review,* vol.45, No.177 (March 2008), 24-29.
Fletcher, P	'Caledonian conundrums in the Highlands', *Highland Railway Journal,* vol.6, No,88 (early 2009), 4-15.
Fletcher, P	'Inverness and the Railway Mania of 1845', *Highland Railway Journal,* vol.6, No.90 (summer 2009), 4-11.
Fraser, JB	*The Perth and Inverness Railway: its importance as a national and commercial enterprise* (London, 1846).
Fryer, CEJ	*The Callander and Oban Railway* (Headington, 1989).
Gourvish, TR	'The Bank of Scotland, 1830-1845', *Scottish Journal of Political Economy,* vol.16 (November 1968), 288-305.
Gourvish, TR	*Railways and the British Economy 1830-1914* (London and Basingstoke, 1980).
Gourvish, TR	'Railways 1830-1870: the formative years', in MJ Freeman and DH Aldcroft (eds.), *Transport in Victorian Britain* (Manchester, 1988), 57-67.
Gourvish, TR and Red, MC	'The financing of Scottish railways before 1860 – a comment', *Scottish Journal of Political Economy,* vol.18 (1971), 209-219.
Hawke, GR	*Railways and Economic Growth in England and Wales 1840-1870* (Oxford, 1970).
Hawke, GR and Reed, MC	'Railway capital in the UK in the nineteenth century'. *Economic History Review,* new series, vol. XXII (1969), 269-286.
Irving, RJ	'The capitalisation of Britain's railways 1830-1914', *Journal of Transport History,* 3rd series, vol.5, No.1 (March 1984), 1-24.
Jackson, D	*The Speyside line* (Great North of Scotland Railway Association, 1996, revised 2006).
Jackson, D	*Royal Deeside's Railway* (Great North of Scotland Railway Association, 1999, revised 2001).
Jackson, D	*Rails to Alford* (Great North of Scotland Railway Association, 2006).
Jones, KG	*The Railways of Aberdeen: 150 years of history* (Great North of Scotland Railway Association, 2000).

Keith, A	*The North of Scotland Bank Limited, 1836-1936* (Aberdeen, 1936).
Keith, A	*A Thousand Years of Aberdeen* (Aberdeen, 1972).
Kellett, JR	*The Impact of Railways on Victorian Cities* (London, 1969).
Kenwood, AG	'Railway investment in Britain 1835-1875', *Economica*, vol.32, No.127 (1965), 313-322.
Kostal, RW	*Law and English Railway Capitalism 1825-1875* (Oxford, 1994).
Leckie, J	'The Circumbendibus', *Great North Review*, vol.4, No.14 (August 1967), 45-49.
Lee, CH	'Some aspects of the coastal shipping trade: the Aberdeen Steam Navigation Company 1835-1880, *Journal of Transport History*, new series, vol.III, No.2 (September 1975), 94-107.
Lenman, B	*An Economic History of Modern Scotland 1660-1976* (London, 1977).
Lewin, HG	*The Railway Mania and its Aftermath, 1845-52* (London 1936, republished Newton Abbot 1968).
Lindsay, J	'The Aberdeenshire Canal 1805-1845, *Journal of Transport History*, vol.VI, No.3 (May 1964), 150-65.
Lindsay, J	*The Canals of Scotland* (Newton Abbot, 1968).
Loch, J	*An Account of the Improvements on the Estates of the Marquess of Stafford in the Counties of Stafford and Salop, and on the Estate of Sutherland, with remarks* (London, 1820).
McGregor, J	*The West Highland Railway: Plans, Politics and People* (Edinburgh, 2005).
McKean, C	*Battle for the North: The Tay and Forth Bridges and the 19th-Century Railway Wars* (London, 2006).
Marshall, PF	*The Scottish Central Railway* (Witney, 1998).
Mason, R and MacDougall, N (eds.)	*People and Power in Scotland: Essays in honour of TC Smout* (Edinburgh, 1992).
Mellor, REH (ed.)	*The Railways of Scotland: the papers of Andrew C O'Dell* (Aberdeen, 1984).
Michie, RC	*Money, Mania and Markets: Investment: Company Formation and the Stock Exchange in Nineteenth Century Scotland* (Edinburgh, 1981).
Michie, RC	'Investment and railways in nineteenth-century Scotland', *Scottish Industrial History*, vol.5, No.1 (1982), 45-53.
Mitchell, BR	'The coming of railway and United Kingdom economic growth', *Journal of Economic History,* 1st series, vol.24 (1964), 315-36; also in MC Reed (ed.), *Railways in the Victorian Economy* (Newton Abbot, 1969), 13-32.
Mitchell, J	*Reminiscences of My Life in the Highlands* (2 volumes, privately published, 1883 and 1884, reprinted Newton Abbot, 1971).
Mitchell, J	*The Construction and Works of the Highland Railway,* a paper read to the British Association in Dundee (September, 1867).
Munn, CW	*The Scottish Provincial Banking Companies 1747-1864* (Edinburgh, 1981).
Munn, CW	'The emergence of joint stock banking in the British Isles: a comparative approach'. *Business History,* vol. XXX, No.1 (1988), 69-83.
Munn, CW	'The emergence of Edinburgh as a financial centre', in AJG Cummings and TM Devine (eds.), *Industry, Business and Society in Scotland since 1700* (Edinburgh, 1994), 125-41.
Newlands, A	*The Scottish Railways: a sketch of their growth and recent development* (London, 1921).
Nock, OS	*The Caledonian Railway* (London, 1963; 2nd edition 1964).
Nock, OS	*The Highland Railway* (London, 1965).
O'Dell AC and Richards, PS	*Railways and Geography* (London 1956, republished 1971).
Parris, H	*Government and the Railways in Nineteenth-Century Britain* (London, 1965).
Pearson, D	'The Aberdeenshire Canal', *Great North Review,* vol.41, No.162 (September 2004), 84-87.
Pollins, H	'The marketing of railway shares in the first half of the nineteenth century', *Economic History Review,* vol.7, No.2 (1954), 230-39.
Pollins, H	'Aspects of Railway Accounting before 1868', in Reed, MC (ed.), *Railways in the Victorian Economy,* (Newton Abbot, 1969), 138-161.
Ramsey, A	*Guide to the Great North of Scotland Railway* (Banff, 1854).
Reed, MC	'Railways and the growth of the capital market' in MC Reed (ed.), *Railways in the Victorian Economy* (Newton Abbot, 1969), 162-183.
Reed, MC	*'Railways in the Victorian Economy* (Newton Abbot, 1969).
Reed, MC	*Investment in Railways in Britain, 1820-1844: a Study in the Development of the Capital Market* (London, 1975).
Reed, MC	'Railway Investment' in RW Ambler (ed.), *The history and practice of Britain's railways: a new research agenda* (Aldershot, 1999), 7-20.
Richards, E	*The Leviathan of Wealth (The Sutherland fortune in the Industrial Revolution)* (London, 1973).
Richards, E	'An anatomy of the Sutherland Fortune: Income, Consumption, Investments and Returns, 1780-1880', *Business History,* vol. XXI (1979), 45-78.
Richards, E	*A History of the Highland Clearances* (2 volumes, London, 1982 and 1985).
Roake, J	'The Inverness and Ross-shire Railway Act 1860'. *Highland Railway Journal,* vol.4, No.62 (summer 2002),

8-12.

Robertson, CJA	'The Cheap Railway Movement in Scotland: the St Andrews Railway Company', *Transport History*, vol.7, No.1 (March 1974), 1-40.
Robertson, CJA	*The Origins of the Scottish Railway System 1722-1844* (Edinburgh, 1983).
Robertson, CJA	'Railway Mania in the Highlands: the Marquis of Breadalbane and the Scottish Grand Junction Railway', in R Mason and N MacDougall (eds.), *People and Power in Scotland: Essays in honour of TC Smout* (Edinburgh, 1992), 189-217.
Ross, D	*The Highland Railway* (Stroud, 2005).
Ross, D	'The enigmatic Mr Dougall', *Highland Railway Journal*, vol.5, No.75 (Autumn 2005), 12-14.
Ross, J	*The Travellers' Joy 1852* (Elgin, 2001).
Simmons, J	*The Railway in England and Wales, 1830-1914*, (Leicester, 1978).
Simmons J	'Railways, Hotels and Tourism in Great Britain', *Journal of Contemporary History*, vol. 18, No. 2 (April 1984), 201-222.
Simmons, J	*The Railway in Town and Country 1830-1914*, (Newton Abbot, 1986).
Simmons, J	*The Victorian Railway* (London, 1995).
Simmons, J and Biddle, G	*The Oxford Companion to British Railway History* (Oxford, 1997, re-issued 1999).
Sinclair, N	*The Highland Main Line* (Penryn, 1998).
Sinclair, N	'The Aviemore Line: Railway Politics in the Highlands, 1882-1898, *Highland Railway Journal*, vol.3, No.46 (summer 1998), 4-12, and vol.3, No.47 (autumn 1998), 7-11.
Sinclair, N	*Highland Railway: People and Places* (Derby, 2005).
Slaven, A and Checkland, S (eds.)	*Dictionary of Scottish Business Biography* (2 volumes, Aberdeen, 1986 and 1990).
Smout, T	*A Century of the Scottish People 1830-1950* (London, 1986).
Stirling, D	'The Morayshire Connection', *Highland Railway Journal*, vol.1, No.7 (winter 1988), 4-7.
Stirling, D	'Land, Railways and the Dukes of Sutherland', *Highland Railway Journal*, vol.4, No.56 (early 2001), 4-7.
Thomas, J	*The Callander and Oban Railway* (Newton Abbot, 1966).
Thomas, J	*The North British Railway* (two volumes, Newton Abbot, 1969 and 1975).
Thomas, J	*A Regional History of the Railways of Great Britain, vol.6 Scotland (the Lowlands and the Borders)* (Newton Abbot, 1971, revised edition 1984).
Thomas, J and Turnock, D	*A Regional History of the Railways of Great Britain, vol.15: North of Scotland* (Newton Abbot, 1989).
Turnock, D	*An Historical Geography of Railways in Great Britain and Ireland* (Aldershot, 1998).
Vallance, HA	*The Highland Railway* (first published 1938, revised 1963, 3rd edition 1969, 4th edition, Newton Abbot, 1985).
Vallance, HA	*The Great North of Scotland Railway* (Newton Abbot, 1965, 2nd edition, Newton Abbot, 1989).
Vamplew, W	'Sources of Scottish railway share capital before 1860', *Scottish Journal of Political Economy*, vol.17 (1970), 425-40.
Vamplew, W	'Railway investment in the Scottish Highlands', *Transport History*, vol.3, No.2 (July 1970), 141-53.
Vamplew, W	'The financing of Scottish railways before 1860 – a reply', *Scottish Journal of Political Economy* vol.18 (1971), 221-23.
Vamplew, W	'Banks and railway finance: a note on the Scottish experience', *Transport History*, vol.4, No.2 (July 1971), 166-82.
Vamplew, W	'Railways and the transformation of the Scottish economy', *Economic History Review*, 2nd series, vol.24 (1971), 37-54.
Vamplew, W	'Railways and the Scottish transport system in the nineteenth century', *Journal of Transport History*, new series, vol.I, No.3 (February 1972), 133-45.
Waterman, JJ	*The Coming of the Railway to Aberdeen in the 1840s* (Aberdeen, 1975).
Whatley, CA	*The Industrial Revolution in Scotland* (Cambridge, 1997).
Whatley, CA	*Scottish Society 1707-1830: beyond Jacobitism, towards industrialisation* (Manchester, 2000).
Wheeler, PT	'The development of shipping services to the east coast of Sutherland', *Journal of Transport History*, vol.VI, No.2 (November 1963), 110-17.

REFERENCES

References to records held in the National Archives of Scotland are given in the catalogue form of NAS/BR/reference/number. For example, the reference NAS/BR/GNS/1/1 relates to the minutes of proprietors, directors and committees of the Great North of Scotland Railway, volume 1 (1845-54).

The first reference within the text includes the place and date of publication; subsequent references give only the author, title and page.

Chapter 1 : Preface

1   *Herapath's Railway Journal,* 21 April 1855, p.415.
2   TR Gourvish in J Simmons and G Biddle (eds.), *The Oxford Companion to British Railway History* (Oxford, 1997, re-issued 1999), appendix 3, p.579.

Chapter 2 : A Region of Contrasts

3   TM Devine, *The Scottish Nation, 1700-2007* (London 1999, new edition, London, 2006), pp.174-78.
4   TM Devine, *Clanship to Crofters' War: The social transformation of the Scottish Highlands* (Manchester, 1994), pp.36-37.
5   J Loch, *An Account of the Improvements on the Estates of the Marquess of Stafford in the Counties of Stafford and Salop, and on the Estate of Sutherland, with remarks* (London, 1820), p.4.
6   Thomas Sellar, *The Sutherland Clearances of 1814,* (1883), containing a letter from Patrick Sellar to James Loch, Commissioner of the Duke of Sutherland, 1 May 1850, and quoted in RH Campbell and JBA Dow (eds.), *Source Book of Scottish Economic and Social History* (Oxford, 1968), p.42.
7   TM Devine, *The Potato Famine in the Scottish Highlands, 1840-1860* (Report to the Economic and Social Science Research Council, March 1985), p.7; TM Devine, *The Scottish Nation 1700-2007,* pp.413-14; TM Devine and WJ Orr, *The Great Highland Famine* (Edinburgh, 1988), p.35 and p.41.
8   I McCrorie, *Royal Road to the Isles: 150 years of MacBrayne Shipping* (Gourock, 2001), p.5.
9   J Simmons, 'Railways, Hotels and Tourism in Great Britain 1839-1914', *Journal of Contemporary History,* 19, No 2, April 1984, p.211.
10 Railway News, 7 October 1882, pp.487-88.

Chapter 3 : The Financial Framework of Railways

11 CJA Robertson, 'The Cheap Railway Movement in Scotland: the St Andrews Railway Company', *Transport History,* 7, No.1 (March 1974), p.1.
12 TR Gourvish, 'The Bank of Scotland, 1830-1845', *Scottish Journal of Political Economy,* 16 (1969), pp.288-305.
13 CJA Robertson, *The Origins of the Scottish Railway System 1722-1844* (Edinburgh, 1983), p.98 and table 25, pp.101-102.
14 RC Michie, 'Investment and railways in nineteenth-century Scotland', *Scottish Industrial History,* 5, No.1 (1982), p.50.
15 CJA Robertson, *The Origins of the Scottish Railway System 1722-1844,* p.77.
16 GR Hawke and MC Reed, 'Railway capital in the United Kingdom in the nineteenth century' *Economic History Review,* new series, XXII, No.2 (1969), p.282; J Simmons and G Biddle (eds.), *The Oxford Companion to British Railway History* (Oxford 1997, re-issued 1999), entry on 'Capital' by MC Reed, p 69.
17 MC Reed, *Investment in Railways in Britain, 1820-1844 : a Study in the Development of the Capital Market* (London, 1975), p.72, p. 56, table 9 and p.60.
18 CJA Robertson, *The Origins of the Scottish Railway System 1722-1844,* p.334; W Vamplew, 'Sources of Scottish railway share capital before 1860', *Scottish Journal of Political Economy,* 17 (1970), pp.430-31 and p.434-35 and p.439; TR Gourvish and MC Reed, 'The financing of Scottish railways before 1860 – a comment', *Scottish Journal of Political Economy,* 18 (1971), p.211 and pp.218-19; W Vamplew, 'The financing of Scottish railways before 1860 – a reply', *Scottish Journal of Political Economy,* 18 (1971), p.222.
19 RJ Irving, 'The capitalization of Britain's railways, 1830-1914', *Journal of Transport History,* 3rd series, 5, No.1 (March 1984), p.6; MC Reed, *Investment in Railways in Britain, 1820-1844,* p.58; W Vamplew, 'Sources of Scottish railway share capital before 1860', p.427.
20 CJA Robertson, *The Origins of the Scottish Railway System 1722-1844,* p.147.
21 CJA Robertson, *The Origins of the Scottish Railway System 1722-1844,* p.178; MC Reed, *Investment in Railways in Britain, 1820-1844,* p.80; H Pollins, *British Railways: an industrial history* (Newton Abbot, 1971), p.35.
22 26&27 Vic. cap.118, The Company Clauses Act, 1863, s.22: if the creation of debenture stock had not been specifically included within previous private acts obtained by the company, the maximum rate of interest that could be offered on debenture stock was set at 4%. This limit of 4% was removed in 30&31 Vic. cap.127, The Railway Companies Act, 1867, s.24, and 30&31 Vic. cap.126, The Railway Companies (Scotland) Act., 1867.
23 TL Alborn, *Conceiving Companies: joint stock politics in Victorian England* (London, 1998), p.213 and p.215.
24 19&20 Vic. cap.47, The Joint Stock Companies Act, 1856.
25 RH Campbell, 'The Law and the Joint Stock Company in Scotland', PL Payne (ed.), *Studies in Scottish Business History* (London, 1967), p.136, quoting Acts of the Parliament of Scotland, 1661, VII, 285 and 261, and 1641, V, 497.
26 SG Checkland, *Scottish Banking, a History 1695-1973* (Glasgow, 1975), p.46.
27 SG Checkland, *Scottish Banking, a History 1695-1973,* p.283, and pp.306-307; CW Munn, *The Scottish Provincial Banking Companies* (Edinburgh, 1981), p.75.
28 CW Munn, 'The emergence of Edinburgh as a financial centre', in AJG Cummings and TM Devine (eds.), *Industry, Business and Society in Scotland since 1700* (Edinburgh, 1994), pp.133-34.
29 A Keith, *The North of Scotland Bank Ltd, 1836-1936* (Aberdeen, 1936), pp.23-24.
30 SG Checkland, *Scottish Banking, a History 1695-1973,* p.339; J Mitchell, *Reminiscences of My Life in the Highlands, vol.II* (2 volumes privately published, London 1883 and 1884, reprinted Newton Abbot, 1971), p.69.
31 CW Munn, 'The emergence of joint stock banking in the British Isles: a comparative approach', *Business History,* XXX, No.1 (1988),

pp.78-79; CW Munn, 'The emergence of Edinburgh as a financial centre', p.134.

32   MC Reed, *Investment in Railways in Britain, 1820-1844*, pp.229-30.

33   SG Checkland, *Scottish Banking, a History 1695-1973*, p.349; A Keith, *The North of Scotland Bank, 1836-1936* (Aberdeen, 1936), pp.50-55 and p.59.

34   8&9 Vic. cap. 20, The Railway Clauses Consolidation Act 1845; 8&9 Vic. cap. 33, The Railway Clauses Consolidation (Scotland) Act 1845; H Pollins, 'Aspects of Railway Accounting before 1868', in MC Reed (ed), *Railways and the Victorian Economy* (Newton Abbot, 1969), pp.138-161.

35   31&32 Vic. cap. 119, The Regulation of Railways Act, 1868; PL Cottrell, 'Railway finances and the crisis of 1866: contractor's bills of exchange and finance companies', *Journal of Transport History*, new series, III, No.1 (February 1975), pp.33-35.

36   31&32 Vic. cap.119, The Regulation of Railways Act, 1868; G Alderman, *The Railway Interest* (Leicester, 1973), p.31.

Chapter 4 : The Great Railway Mania and Scotland, 1845-46

37   WE Aytoun, 'The Railways', *Blackwood's Edinburgh Magazine*, 58 (November 1845), p.634.

38   HJ Dyos and DH Aldcroft, *British Transport* (Leicester, 2nd impression, 1971), p.127; CJA Robertson, *The Origins of the Scottish Railway System 1722-1844*, Table 32, p.164.

39   RW Kostal, *Law and English Railway Capitalism 1825-1875* (Oxford, 1994), p.12 and p.56; RC Michie, 'Investment and railways in nineteenth-century Scotland', p.52; J Simmons, *The Railway in England and Wales 1830-1914* (Leicester, 1978), p.41; H Parris, *Government and the Railways in Nineteenth-Century Britain* (London 1965), p.88.

40   SA Broadbridge, 'Sources of railway share capital', in MC Reed (ed.), *Railways in the Victorian Economy*, p.191; MC Reed, *Investment in Railways in Britain, 1820-1844*, p.75; G Channon, *Railways in Britain and the United States, 1830-1914* (Aldershot, 2001), p.38.

41   MC Reed, *Investment in Railways in Britain, 1820-1844*, p.105 and p.194.

42   WE Aytoun, 'How we got up the Glenmutchkin Railway, and how we got of it', Blackwood's *Edinburgh Magazine*, 58 (October 1845), 453-66.

43   CJA Robertson, 'Railway Mania in the Highlands: The Marquis of Breadalbane and the Scottish Grand Junction Railway', in R Mason and N MacDougall (eds.), *People and Power in Scotland* (Edinburgh, 1992), pp.198-99.

44   *Scottish Railway Gazette*, 27 September 1845, quoted in CJA Robertson, 'Railway Mania in the Highlands: The Marquis of Breadalbane and the Scottish Grand Junction Railway', p.203.

45   *Bradshaw's Railway Almanac*, 1850, p.131 and 1852, p.162; J McGregor, *The West Highland Railway: Plans, Politics and People* (Edinburgh, 2005), p.3; CJA Robertson, 'Railway Mania in the Highlands: The Marquis of Breadalbane and the Scottish Grand Junction Railway', pp.198-211.

46   Examples include *Railway Journal*, 14 May 1853, available in National Archives of Scotland (NAS)/BR/HR/4/3/2; *Railway Times*, 10 November 1860, p.1262.

47   WE Aytoun, 'How we got up the Glenmutchkin Railway, and how we got of it', p.455.

48   J Simmons, *The Railway in England and Wales 1830-1914*, p.41, footnote 7; CJA Robertson, *The Origins of the Scottish Railway System 1722-1844*, p.335; W Vamplew, 'Sources of railway share capital before 1860', p.427.

49   CJA Robertson, *The Origins of the Scottish Railway System 1722-1844*, p.334.

50   CJA Robertson, *The Origins of the Scottish Railway System 1722-1844*, p.334; W Vamplew, 'Sources of Scottish railway share capital before 1860', p.431.

51   BR Mitchell, 'The coming of the railway and United Kingdom economic growth', in MC Reed (ed.), *Railways in the Victorian Economy*, p.26; GR Hawke, *Railways and Economic Growth in England and Wales, 1840-1870* (Oxford, 1970), p.364 and p.370; HG Lewin, *The Railway Mania and its Aftermath, 1845-52* (London, 1936, republished Newton Abbot 1968), p.282.

52   *Bradshaw's Railway Gazette*, 13 December 1845; *The Times*, 9 January 1846, quoted in RW Kostal, *Law and English Railway Capitalism 1825-1875* (Oxford 1994), pp.40-41.

53   *Bradshaw's Railway Gazette*, 13 June 1846, p. 1230.

54   9&10 Vic. cap.28, An Act to facilitate the dissolution of certain Railway Companies, 1846.

55   *Herapath's Railway Journal*, 23 October 1847, p.1205.

56   W Vamplew, 'Sources of Scottish railway share capital before 1860', p.426.

57   *Railway Times*, 10 April 1841, p.415.

58   TM Devine, *The Scottish Nation 1700-2007*, p.417; TM Devine and WJ Orr, *The Great Highland Famine*, pp.93-94; TM Devine, *Clanship to Crofters' War: the social transformation of the Scottish Highlands*, pp.58-59 and p.66.

59   J Mitchell, *Reminiscences of My Life in the Highlands*, vol.II, p.116.

60   J Mitchell, *Reminiscences of My Life in the Highlands*, vol.I, p.31; J Lindsay, *The Canals of Scotland* (Newton Abbot, 1968), pp.142-43 and p.160.

61   TC Smout, 'Scottish landowners and economic growth, 1650-1850', *Scottish Journal of Political Economy*, 11 (1964), pp.229-30; W Vamplew, 'Railway Investment in the Scottish Highlands', *Transport History*, 3, No.2, (July 1970), p.147; TM Devine, *The Scottish Nation 1700-2007*, pp.451-52.

62   The Perth and Inverness Railway Bill, 9&10 Vic, session 1846; The Inverness and Elgin Railway Bill: 9&10 Vic, session 1846, NAS/BR/PYB(S)/1/477/1 and 1/477/3.

63   *Bradshaw's Railway Gazette*, 7 January 1846, p.1083.

64   Prospectus of the Great North of Scotland Railway, 1845, NAS/PYB(S)/1/477/1; The Great North of Scotland Railway Bill, 9&10 Vic. session 1846, NAS/BR/PYB(S)/1/477/3.

65   K Fenwick, 'Genesis of the Great North', Part 2, *Great North Review*, 33, No.129 (May 1996), p.288.

66   *Bradshaw's Railway Gazette*, 7 January 1846, pp.1090-92, and 24 January 1846, p.166.

67   Conference between the Great North of Scotland and Perth and Inverness Railway companies at Elgin, 21 October 1845, NAS/BR/PYB(S)/1/477/2.

68   Conference between the Great North of Scotland and Perth and Inverness Railway companies at Elgin, 21 October 1845, NAS/BR/PYB(S)/1/477/2.

69   *Inverness Courier* quoted in *Bradshaw's Railway Gazette*, 7 January 1846, p.1083.

70   M Casson, *The Evolution of the British Railway Network, 1825-1914*, Economic and Social Research Council Report, R000239586

(January 2005), pp.7-8; CJA Robertson, *The Origins of the Scottish Railway System 1722-1844*, p.296; H Parris, *Government and the Railways in Nineteenth-Century Britain*, p.84.

71   Board of Trade report on Schemes for extending Railway Communication in Scotland, 1845, paragraph 72.

72   *Bradshaw's Railway Gazette*, vol.I, 1845, showing share prices on the Liverpool exchange on 1 November 1845, and vol.II, 1846, showing share prices on the Glasgow exchange on 8 April 1846.

73   *Railway Times*, 18 April 1846, p.557.

74   *Railway Times*, 16 May 1846, p.697.

75   *Railway Times*, 16 May 1846, p.698.

76   *Bradshaw's Railway Gazette*, 16 May 1846, p.1054; *Railway Times*, 16 May 1846, p.698; Minutes of the Great North of Scotland Railway, 7 July 1846, NAS/BR/GNS/1/1, p.99.

77   Minutes of the Great North of Scotland Railway, 31 March 1845, NAS/BR/GNS/1/1, pp.24-25.

78   Report of Special General Meeting of the Shareholders of the Aberdeen Railway, 30 May 1846, NAS/BR/RAC(S)/1/36.

79   10&11 Vic. cap.195, The Great North of Scotland Railway Act, 1847.

80   Minutes of the Great North of Scotland Railway, 2 September 1845, NAS/BR/GNS/1/1, p.39; 9&10 Vic. cap.135, The Great North of Scotland Railway (Eastern Extension) Act, 1846; 9&10 Vic. cap.178, The Morayshire Railway Act, 1846.

81   *Railway Times*, 25 July 1846, p.1017.

82   *Railway Chronicle*, 23 May 1846, in NAS/BR/HR/4/3, item 9.

83   Minutes of the Inverness and Nairn Railway, 6 October 1853, NAS/BR/INR/1/1, p.18.

84   Minutes of the Great North of Scotland Railway, 3 March 1845, NAS/BR/GNS/1/1, p. 22; Prospectus of the Great North of Scotland Railway, 1845, NAS/BR/PYB(S)/1/477/1.

85   Minutes of the Great North of Scotland Railway, 31 March 1845, NAS/BR/GNS/1/1, p.24.

86   Minutes of the Great North of Scotland Railway, 31 March 1845, NAS/BR/GNS/1/1, p.25.

87   *Aberdeen Journal*, 9 April 1845, p.2, quoted in JJ Waterman, *The Coming of the Railway to Aberdeen in the 1840s* (Aberdeen 1975), p.28.

88   P Fletcher, 'The Great North and the Aberdeen Railway Web', *Great North Review*, 45, No.177 (March 2008), p.24; Sir M Barclay-Harvey, *A History of the Great North of Scotland Railway* (London, 2nd edition 1949, reprinted Shepperton, 1998), p.6.

89   Minutes of the Great North of Scotland Railway, 1 April 1845 and 4 June 1845, NAS/BR/GNS/1/1. p.26 and p.27.

90   Prospectus of the Great North of Scotland Railway, 1846, NAS/BR/PYB(S)/1/477/1; 9&10 Vic. cap.103, The Great North of Scotland Railway Act, 1846.

91   J Mitchell, *Reminiscences of My Life in the Highlands*, vol.II, p.168.

92   A Keith, *The North of Scotland Bank Ltd, 1836-1936*, pp.49-51.

93   A Keith, *The North of Scotland Bank Ltd, 1836-1936*, p.66.

94   Minutes of the Great North of Scotland Railway, 19 May 1846, NAS/BR/GNS/1/1, pp.96-98.

Chapter 5 : The Route to Inverness: the Great North's Perspective

95   Report to the first Ordinary General Meeting of the Great North of Scotland Railway, 21 August 1846, NAS/BR/GNS/1/1, pp.102-134.

96   Accounts of the Great North of Scotland Railway for the period April 1844 to 12 August 1846, NAS/BR/GNS/1/1, pp.106-34.

97   MC Reed, *Investment in Railways in Britain, 1820-44*, p.80; Minutes of the Great North of Scotland Railway, 29 September 1845 and 31 January 1849, NAS/BR/GNS/1/1, p.40 and p.174; A Keith, *The North of Scotland Bank Ltd, 1836-1936*, p.50.

98   *Herapath's Railway Journal*, 1 May 1847, p.533.

99   Report to the Ordinary General Meeting of the Great North of Scotland Railway, 20 November 1847, NAS/BR/RAC(S)/1/14.

100   *Herapath's Railway Journal*, 4 December 1847, p.1352.

101   11&12 Vic. cap.3, The Railways (Extension of Time) Act, 1848.

102   Minutes of the Great North of Scotland Railway, 14 October 1845, NAS/BR/GNS/1/1, p.43; Minutes of the Great North of Scotland Railway, 4 August 1848, NAS/BR/GNS/1/1, p.159.

103   Minutes of the Great North of Scotland Railway, 17 February 1854, NAS/BR/GNS/1/1, p.490.

104   Ordinary General Meeting of 30 November 1847, NAS/BR/RAC(S)/1/36; 11&12 Vic. cap.67, The Aberdeen Railway Act, 1848; 13&14 Vic. cap.78, The Aberdeen Railway Act, 1850.

105   *Bradshaw's Railway Almanac*, 1875, appendix 12, p.83.

106   Scroll minutes of the Aberdeen Railway, 4 July 1848, NAS/BR/ABN/1/5, and 29 August 1848, 27 September 1848 and 25 October 1848, NAS/BR/ABN/1/6.

107   *Aberdeen Journal*, 4 October 1848, p.6 and 25 October 1848, p.4, quoted in JJ Waterman, *The Coming of the Railway to Aberdeen in the 1840s*, p.20.

108   *Railway Chronicle*, 4 November 1848, p.782; Report of the Ordinary General Meeting of the Aberdeen Railway, 29 November 1848, NAS/BR/RAC(S)/1/36; *Railway Times*, 4 November 1848, p.1162 and 9 December 1848, p.1285.

109   Report of the Ordinary General Meeting of the Aberdeen Railway, 29 November 1848, NAS/BR/RAC(S)/1/36; *Railway Times*, 9 December 1848, p.1162.

110   P Fletcher, 'The Great North and the Aberdeen Railway Web', *Great North Review*, 45, No.177 (March 2008), pp.24-29.

111   *Bradshaw's Railway Almanac*, 1848; Scroll minutes of the Directors of the Aberdeen Railway, 25 December 1848, NAS/BR/ABN/1/6; *Railway Times*, 6 January 1849, p.7.

112   *Railway Times*, 6 January 1849, p.7.

113   Report of the directors to the Ordinary General Meeting of the Aberdeen Railway, 29 November 1849, NAS/BR/RAC(S)/1/36.

114   Minutes of the Great North of Scotland Railway, Special General Meeting, 24 June 1850, NAS/BR/GNS/1/1, pp.246-47.

115   13&14 Vic. cap.78, The Aberdeen Railway Act, 1850, which repealed 10&11 Vic. cap.195, The Great North of Scotland Railway Act, 1847 that had authorised amalgamation of the Great North and Aberdeen Railway companies.

116   Report to shareholders for the Ordinary General Meeting of the Great North of Scotland Railway Company, 28 November 1849, NAS/BR/RAC(S)/1/14.

117   Minutes of the Great North of Scotland Railway, 11 and 24 February 1849, NAS/BR/GNS/1/1, p.17 and p.181; Report to the Ordinary General Meeting of the Great North of Scotland Railway. 28 November 1849, NAS/BR/RAC(S)/1/14.

118   Minutes of the Great North of Scotland Railway, 29 March 1849, NAS/BR/GNS/1/1, p.187.
119   Minutes of the Great North of Scotland Railway, 28 August 1849 and 31 August 1849, NAS/BR/GNS/1/1, p.198 and pp.200-201; Report to the Ordinary General Meeting of the Great North of Scotland Railway, 28 November 1849, NAS/BR/RAC(S)/1/14.
120   Minutes of the Great North of Scotland Railway, 15 March 1851, NAS/BR/GNS/1/1, p.288.
121   Minutes of the Great North of Scotland Railway, 11 April 1849, NAS/BR/GNS/1/1, p.192; Circular to landowners reported in the minutes of the Great North of Scotland Railway, 30 August 1849, NAS/BR/GNS/1/1, pp.202-203, Report to the Ordinary General Meeting of the Great North of Scotland Railway, 28 November 1849, NAS/BR/RAC(S)/1/14; Letter from the chairman and directors of the Great North to landowners dated 20 February 1850, NAS/BR/RAC(S)/1/14.
122   Railway Times, 6 December 1851, p.1218.
123   Minutes of the Great North of Scotland Railway, 7 September 1849 and 15 March 1850, NAS/BR/GNS/1/1, p.209 and p.240.
124   Minutes of the Great North of Scotland Railway, 22 August 1850, NAS/BR/GNS/1/1, p.258; Report to the Ordinary General Meeting of the Great North of Scotland Railway, 29 November 1850, p.270.
125   14&15 Vic. cap.75, The Great North of Scotland Railway Amendment Act, 1851; Report to the Ordinary General Meeting of the Great North of Scotland Railway, 28 November, 1851, NAS/BR/GNS/1/1, p.313.
126   Minutes of the Great North of Scotland Railway, 1 September 1852, NAS/BR/GNS/1/1, p.353.
127   Minutes of the Great North of Scotland Railway, 1 September 1852, NAS/BR/GNS/1/1, p.353; Sir M Barclay-Harvey, A History of the Great North of Scotland Railway, p.14.
128   Report of the Aberdeen Railway directors into the affairs of the Great North of Scotland Railway Company, 16 July 1852, NAS/BR/RAC(S)/1/14.
129   Report of the Aberdeen Railway directors into the affairs of the Great North of Scotland Railway Company, 16 July 1852, NAS/BR/RAC(S)/1/14; Minutes of the Great North of Scotland Railway, 16 July 1852, NAS/BR/GNS/1/1, pp.338-42.
130   Report of the Aberdeen Railway directors into the affairs of the Great North of Scotland Railway Company, 16 July 1852, NAS/BR/RAC(S)/1/14.
131   Prospectus of the Great North of Scotland Railway, amended scheme 1852, NAS/BR/PROS(S)/1/9; Minutes of the Great North of Scotland Railway, 29 November 1852, NAS/BR/GNS/1/1, p.372 and p.375.
132   Report to the Ordinary General Meeting of the Great North of Scotland Railway, 29 November 1852, NAS/BR/GNS/1/1. p.372; Accounts of the Great North of Scotland Railway, 29 November 1852, NAS/BR/RAC(S)/1/14.
133   Aberdeen Herald, 2 December 1852, recorded in minutes of the Great North of Scotland Railway, 2 December 1852, NAS/BR/GNS/1/1, p.376.
134   Report of chairman's statement to shareholders of the Great North of Scotland Railway, 29 November 1852, NAS/BR/RAC(S)/1/14.
135   Report to the Ordinary General Meeting of the Great North of Scotland Railway, 25 November, 1853, NAS/BR/GNS/1/1, p.463.
136   17&18 Vic. cap.187, The Great North of Scotland Railway Amendment Act, 1853.
137   Minutes of the Great North of Scotland Railway, 20 July 1853 and 27 August 1853, NAS/BR/GNS/1/1, p.409 and pp,.420-22.
138   Report to the Ordinary General Meeting of the Great North of Scotland Railway, 25 November 1853, NAS/BR/GNS/1/1, p.463.
139   17&18 Vic. cap.176, The Inverness and Nairn Railway Act, 1854.
140   Minutes of the Inverness and Nairn Railway, 25 February 1854, pp.83-84; minutes of the Great North of Scotland Railway, 25 February 1854, NAS/BR/GNS/1/1, p.497.
141   HA Vallance, The Great North of Scotland Railway (Newton Abbot, 1965), p.29 and p.131; Sir M Barclay-Harvey, A History of the Great North of Scotland Railway (2nd edition, London, 1949), p.26: Barclay-Harvey asserts that the Great North ultimately lost their copy of the unsigned agreement.
142   Minutes of the Great North of Scotland Railway, 26 October 1855, NAS/BR/GNS/1/1, pp.318-19.
143   Report to the Ordinary General Meeting of the Great North of Scotland Railway, 29 October 1855, NAS/BR/RAC(S)/1/14.
144   Minutes of the Great North of Scotland Railway, 17 May 1854, NAS/BR/GNS/1/1, p.553.
145   Minutes of the Great North of Scotland Railway, 18 May 1854, NAS/BR/GNS/1/2, p.2.
146   Minutes of the Great North of Scotland Railway, 11 August, 1854, NAS/BR/GNS/1/2, p.48.
147   Report to the Ordinary General Meeting of the Great North of Scotland Railway, 30 November 1854, NAS/BR/RAC(S)/1/14.
148   Accounts of the Great North of Scotland Railway, 31 August 1855, NAS/BR/RAC(S)/1/14.
149   18 Vic. cap.28, The Great North of Scotland Railway Extension Act, 1855.
150   Report to the Ordinary General Meeting of the Great North of Scotland Railway, 28 November 1849, NAS/BR/RAC(S)/1/14 and NAS/BR/GNS/1/1, p.220; CJA Robertson, 'The Cheap Railway Movement in Scotland: the St Andrews Railway Company', p.2.
151   Herapath's Railway Journal, 3 November 1855, pp.1117-18.
152   Minutes of the Great North of Scotland Railway, 21 March 1856, NAS/BR/GNS/1/2.p.389.
153   Report of the Directors to the Ordinary General Meeting of the Aberdeen Railway, 26 October 1854, NAS/BR/RAC(S)/1/36; Scroll minutes of the Scottish North Eastern Railway, 22 December 1858, NAS/BR/SNE/1/5.
154   CH Lee, 'Some aspects of the coastal shipping trade: the Aberdeen Steam Navigation Company 1835-1880', Journal of Transport History, new series, III, No.2 (September 1975), p.102.
155   Minutes of the Great North of Scotland Railway, 4 January 1859, NAS/BR/GNS/1/2, p.298; Journal and Ledger of the Inverness and Edinburgh Steam Packet Company, 1859-60, NAS/BR/GNS/23/57-58, p.86.
156   Herapath's Railway Journal, 5 April 1862, p.376.

Chapter 6 : The Route from Aberdeen: The Inverness Perspective

157   A Ramsay, Guide to the Great North of Scotland Railway (Banff, 1854), p.(v).
158   J Mitchell, Reminiscences of My Life in the Highlands, vol.II, p.168.
159   J Fraser, The Perth and Inverness Railway: its importance as a national and commercial enterprise (London, 1846), p.2.
160   Railway Times, 17 December 1853, p.1300.
161   Railway Times, 23 April 1853, p.426.
162   CJA Robertson, 'The Cheap Railway Movement in Scotland: the St Andrews Railway Company', p.2.
163   Railway Times, 23 April 1853, p.434.
164   Herapath's Railway Journal, 16 January 1858, p.69.

165 TM Devine and WJ Orr, *The Great Highland Famine* (Edinburgh, 1988), p.77 and pp.93-94; J Mitchell, *Reminiscences of My Life in the Highlands*, vol.I, p.115.

166 J Mitchell, *Reminiscences of My Life in the Highlands*, vol.II, p.21; A Slaven, *The Development of the West of Scotland: 1750-1960*, p.46 and p.124.

167 A Slaven, 'Sir Alexander Matheson', in A Slaven and S Checkland, *Dictionary of Scottish Business Biography, 1860-1960* (two volumes, Aberdeen, 1986 and 1990), vol.2, pp.301-302; HCG Matthew and B Harrison (eds.), *The Oxford Dictionary of National Biography*, vol.37 (Oxford, 2004), pp.280-81.

168 TM Devine, *Clanship to Crofters' War: the social transformation of the Scottish Highlands* (Manchester, 1994), p.82.

169 *Railway Magazine,* 4 (January-June, 1899), p.10.

170 'Statement with regard to the Perth and Inverness and Inverness and Elgin Railways by the deputation appointed at a meeting held in Inverness on 16 December 1852', dated February 1853, NAS/BR/PROS(S)/1/15.

171 'Statement with regard to the Perth and Inverness and Inverness and Elgin Railways by the deputation appointed at a meeting held in Inverness on 16 December 1852', dated February 1853, NAS/BR/PROS(S)/1/15.

172 *Inverness Courier,* 14 April 1853 in the file of prospectuses of the Perth and Inverness and Inverness and Elgin Railways, 1852-53, NAS/BR/PROS(S)/1/15; *Railway Times,* 23 April, 1853, pp. 425-27.

173 J Mitchell, *Reminiscences of My Life in the Highlands,* vol.II, p.180.

174 Letter headed 'Perth and Inverness and Inverness and Elgin Railways' to JR Mowat, Secretary, Great Northern Railway, London, 14 April 1853, and Inverness Courier, 14 April 1853, in the file of prospectuses of the Perth and Inverness and Inverness and Elgin Railways, 1852-53 NAS/BR/PROS(S)/1/15.

175 *Inverness Advertiser,* 19 April 1853.

176 *Railway Journal,* 14 May 1853, in 'Miscellaneous memoranda on the history of the Highland Railway', NAS/BR/HR/4/3/11.

177 G and P Anderson, *Handbook to the Inverness and Nairn Railway and scenes adjoining it* (Inverness, 1856), p.29.

178 *Inverness Advertiser,* 8 December 1853, in the minute book of the Inverness and Nairn Railway, NAS/BR/INR/1/1, p.47-48, reporting a public meeting held in Nairn.

179 *Inverness Advertiser,* 26 September 1854, in the minute book of the Inverness and Nairn Railway, NAS/BR/INR/1/1, p.147.

180 Prospectus of the Inverness and Nairn Railway, 1853, NAS/BR/PROS(S)/1/10; 17&18 Vic. cap.176, The Inverness and Nairn Railway Act, 1854.

181 P Fletcher, 'Strategy, solvency and the state: the development of the railway system of northern Scotland, 1844-74' (PhD thesis, University of York, 2007), Table 49, p.243.

182 *Herapath's Railway Journal,* 9 May 1857, p.475.

183 24&25 Vic. cap.8, The Inverness and Aberdeen Junction Railway Act, 1861.

184 *Herapath's Railway Journal,* 24 November 1855, p.1193.

185 *Herapath's Railway Journal,* 1856; Accounts of the Inverness and Nairn Railway, 1855-61, in NAS/BR/INR/1/1.

186 Minutes of the Inverness and Nairn Railway, 12, 19 and 26 January, 9 February, 9 and 20 August, and 6 September 1856, NAS/BR/INR/1/1, pp.346-408.

187 *Railway Times,* 7 May 1859, p.525.

188 *Herapath's Railway Journal,* 28 April 1856, p.462.

189 P Fletcher, 'Strategy, solvency and the state: the development of the railway system of northern Scotland, 1844-74', Appendix, table 13(a).

190 Minutes of the Inverness and Nairn Railway, 2 November 1853, NAS/BR/INR/1/1, pp.25-26.

191 Accounts of the Inverness and Nairn Railway, 31 August 1857, NAS/BR/INR/1/2, p.50; Accounts of the Great North of Scotland Railway, 1857, NAS/BR/RAC(S)/1/14.

192 Scroll minutes of the directors of the Inverness and Nairn Railway, 9 August 1859, NAS/BR/INR/1/4, item 3.

193 Minutes of an Extra-ordinary General Meeting of the Inverness and Nairn Railway, 14 July 1857, NAS/BR/INR/1/1, p.488; 20&21 Vic. cap. 5, The Inverness and Nairn Railway Act, 1857.

194 Minutes of the Great North of Scotland Railway, 25 August and 30 November 1854, NAS/BR/GNS/1/2, p.54 and p.149.

195 *Railway Times,* 4 November 1854, p.1199.

196 Minutes of the Great North of Scotland Railway, 30 November 1854, NAS/BR/GNS/1/2, p.149.

197 Minutes of the Great North of Scotland Railway, 5 February 1855, NAS/BR./GNS/1/2, p.194 and p.211; 18 Vic. cap.28, The Great North of Scotland Railway Extension Act, 1855

198 Minutes of the Great North of Scotland Railway, 26 October 1855, NAS/BR/GNS/1/1, pp.318-19.

199 Minutes of the Inverness and Aberdeen Junction Railway, 14 June 1855, NAS/IAJ/1/2, p.2.

200 19&20 Vic. cap.110, The Inverness and Aberdeen Junction Railway Act, 1856.

201 Minutes of the Great North of Scotland Railway, 2 June 1857, NAS/BR/GNS/1/3, p.13.

202 Minutes of the Inverness and Aberdeen Junction Railway, 19 and 25 May 1857, NAS/BR/IAJ/1/1, pp.276-77 and p.282.

203 Minutes of the Highland Railway, 30 January 1866, NAS/BR/HR/1/1, pp.101-103.

204 Minutes of the Inverness and Aberdeen Junction Railway, 16 October 1857 and 3 August 1858, NAS/BR/IAJ/1/1, p.337 and p.457; Order of Business Book, Inverness and Aberdeen Junction Railway, 31 October 1857.

205 Minutes of the Great North of Scotland Railway, 2 and 9 June 1857, NAS/BR/GNS/1/3, p.15 and p.19.

206 Letter from Sir James Elphinstone to Alexander Matheson, 8 June 1857, in minutes of the Great North of Scotland Railway, 12 June 1857, NAS/BR/GNS/1/3, p.28.

207 Minutes of the Great North of Scotland Railway, 19 June 1857, NAS/BR/GNS/1/3, p.35.

208 *Bradshaw's Railway Almanac,* 1857 edition, p.126.

209 Register of Dividends, 31 July 1864, Inverness and Aberdeen Junction Railway, NAS/BR/IAJ/2/1.

210 Minutes of the Extra-ordinary General Meeting of the Inverness and Aberdeen Junction Railway, 21 July 1857, NAS/IAJ/1/1, p.306; Minutes of the Great North of Scotland Railway, 24 July 1857, NAS/BR/GNS/1/3, p.53.

211 Minutes of the Great North of Scotland Railway, 14 August 1857, NAS/BR/GNS/1/3, p.63; Minutes of the Great North of Scotland Railway, 21 August 1857, NAS/BR/GNS/1/3, p.70.

212 Minutes of the adjourned Extra-ordinary General Meeting of the Inverness and Aberdeen Junction Railway, 18 August 1857, NAS/

BR/IAJ/1/1, p.313; Minutes of the Great North of Scotland Railway, 21 August 1857, NAS/BR/GNS/1/3, p.70.

213   *Herapath's Railway Journal,* 14 November 1857, p.1180.

214   Report to the Ordinary General Meeting of the Inverness and Aberdeen Junction Railway, 28 October 1859, NAS/BR/IAJ/1/2, pp.40-42; Minutes of an Extra-ordinary General Meeting of the Inverness and Aberdeen Junction Railway, 20 December 1859, NAS/BR/IAJ/1/2, p.68; 23 Vic. cap.9, The Inverness and Aberdeen Junction Railway Act, 1860.

215   Minutes of the Inverness and Aberdeen Junction Railway, 25 January 1860, NAS/BR/IAJ/1/2, p.75.

216   Letter of law agents Adam and Anderson to R Milne, secretary of the Great North, in the minutes of the Traffic and Finance Committee of the Great North of Scotland Railway, 17 January 1860, NAS/BR/GNS/1/3, p.425; Minutes of the Inverness and Aberdeen Junction Railway, 25 January 1860, NAS/BR/IAJ/1/2, p.76.

217   Report of the chairman of the meeting, John Stewart, to the Ordinary General Meeting of the Great North of Scotland Railway, 2 April 1860, NAS/BR/GNS/1/3, p.451 and page 3 of printed report.

218   Minutes of the Inverness and Nairn Railway, 14 February, 1857, NAS/BR/INR/1/1, p.443 and 17 March 1857, NAS/BR/INR/1/1, p.458; Minutes of the Inverness and Aberdeen Junction Railway, 19 February 1857, NAS/BR/IAJ/1/1, p.240; Minutes of the Inverness and Aberdeen Junction Railway, 16 March 1857, NAS/BR/IAJ/1/1, pp.244-45.

219   Minutes of the Inverness and Ross-shire Railway, 27 October 1859, NAS/BR/IRR/1/2, p.40; Minutes of the Inverness and Perth Railway, 3 December 1861, NAS/BR/IPJ/1/1, p.11; Minutes of the Inverness and Aberdeen Junction Railway, 27 October 1859 and 3 December 1861, NAS/BR/IAJ/1/2, p.39 and p.290.

220   24&25 Vic. cap.8, The Inverness and Aberdeen Junction Railway Act, 1861; 25&26 Vic. cap. 113, The Inverness and Aberdeen Junction Railway Act, 1862.

221   Minutes of the Inverness and Aberdeen Junction Railway, 25 June 1859, NAS/BR/IAJ/1/1, p.564; Accounts of the Inverness and Aberdeen Junction Railway to 29 February 1859 and 31 August 1859, reported to the Ordinary General Meeting held on 29 October 1859, NAS/BR/IAJ/1/2, pp.40-42.

222   P Fletcher, 'Strategy, solvency and the state: the development of the railway system of northern Scotland, 1844-74', Appendix, table 12(a).

223   *Railway Times,* 4 November 1865, p.1407.

224   *Railway Times,* 5 May 1866, p.515.

225   Minutes of the Inverness and Aberdeen Junction Railway, 17 February 1860, NAS/BR/IAJ/1/2, p.94.

226   Minutes of the Inverness and Aberdeen Junction Railway, 22 February 1860, NAS/BR/IAJ/1/2, p.101.

227   Minutes of the Inverness and Aberdeen Junction Railway, 29 February 1860, NAS/BR/IAJ/1/2, p.102; J Lindsay, *The Canals of Scotland,* p.129 and p.171.

228   *Bradshaw's Railway Gazette,* 13 December 1845, p.843; 7 January 1846, pp.1090-92.

229   Minutes of the Inverness and Aberdeen Junction Railway, 2 November 1858, NAS/BR/IAJ/1/2, p.495; Minutes of the Inverness and Ross-shire Railway, 18 January 1859, NAS/BR/IRR/1/2, p.1.

230   Minutes of the Inverness and Aberdeen Junction Railway, 2 November 1858, NAS/BR/IAJ/1/2, p.495; Minutes of the Inverness and Ross-shire Railway, 18 January 1859, NAS/BR/IRR/1/2, p.1.

231   Minutes of the Inverness and Ross-shire Railway, 18 January 1859, NAS/BR/IRR/1/2, pp.2-4, inserted press report of the meeting.

232   *Herapath's Railway Journal,* 4 November 1865, p.1217.

233   Minutes of the Inverness and Ross-shire Railway, 22 October 1859, NAS/BR/IRR/1/2, p.36; Minutes of the Inverness and Nairn Railway, 27 October 1859, NAS/BR/INR/1/2, p.48; Minutes of the Inverness and Aberdeen Junction Railway, 27 October 1859, NAS/BR/IAJ/1/2, p.38.

234   Register of Dividends, 1864-65, Inverness and Aberdeen Junction Railway, NAS/BR/IAJ/2/1.

235   *Railway Times,* 4 November 1865, p.1407.

236   Minutes of the Inverness and Aberdeen Junction Railway, 2 September 1859 and 27 October 1859, NAS/BR/IAJ/1/2, p.17 and p.39; also scroll minutes of the directors of the Inverness and Nairn Railway, 27 October 1859, NAS/BR/INR/1/4, item 2, which repeat the conditions set by the Inverness and Aberdeen Junction board.

237   Minutes of the Inverness and Ross-shire Railway, 27 October 1859, NAS/BR/IRR/1/2, p.39, recording the minutes of the Inverness and Nairn and Inverness and Aberdeen Junction Railways, both dated 27 October 1859.

238   Report to the Ordinary General Meeting of the Inverness and Nairn Railway, 28 October 1859, NAS/BR/INR/1/2, p.50; Minutes of the Inverness and Nairn Railway, 27 October 1859, NAS/BR/INR/1/2, p.48.

239   Minutes of the Inverness and Ross-shire Railway, 4 November 1859, NAS/IRR/1/2, pp.42-44,; Scroll minutes of the directors of the Inverness and Nairn Railway, 7 November 1859, NAS/BR/INR/1/4, item 2.

240   Minutes of the Inverness and Aberdeen Junction Railway, 4 November 1859, NAS/BR/IAJ/1/2, p.45; Minutes of the Inverness and Ross-shire Railway, 8 January 1859, 27 October 1859, 2 February 1860, and 23 July 1860, NAS/BR/IRR/1/2, p.5, p.39, p.66, and p.106.

241   Minutes of the Inverness and Ross-shire Railway, 31 December 1859 and 23 June 1860, NAS/BR/IRR/1/2, p.60 and p.101.

242   23&24 Vic. cap.131, The Inverness and Ross-shire Railway Act, 1860.

243   *Inverness Courier,* 20 September 1860, contained in the minute book of the Inverness and Ross-shire Railway, NAS/BR/IRR/1/2, p.126.

244   Minutes of the Inverness and Ross-shire Railway, 11 March 1861, NAS/BR/IRR/1/2.

245   25&26 Vic. cap. 113, The Inverness and Aberdeen Junction Railway Act, 1862.

246   Minutes of the Inverness and Ross-shire Railway, 16 October 1861, minute 12, NAS/BR/IRR/1/2; Minutes of the Inverness and Aberdeen Junction Railway, 16 October 1861, NAS/BR/IAJ/1/2, p.274.

247   Accounts of the Inverness and Aberdeen Junction Railway to 31 August 1862, NAS/BR/IAJ/1/2, p.375.

248   Minutes of the Inverness and Ross-shire Railway, 28 May 1861, NAS/BR/IRR/1/2.

249   Minutes of the Inverness and Ross-shire Railway, 13 April 1861, NAS/BR/IRR/1/2.

250   Minutes of the Inverness and Ross-shire Railway, 29 April 1861, NAS/BR/IRR/1/2.

251   Resolution of the Ordinary General Meeting of the Ross-shire Railway, 29 October 1861, NAS/BR/IRR/1/2.

252   MC Reed, *Investment in Railways in Britain, 1820-1844,* p 27; CJA Robertson, The *Origins of the Scottish Railway System 1722-1844,* p.81.

253   Minutes of the Inverness and Ross-shire Railway, 16 October 1861, minute 3, NAS/BR/IRR/1/2.

254   Minutes of the Inverness and Aberdeen Junction Railway, 16 October 1861, NAS/BR/IAJ/1/2, p.274.

255 Minutes of the Inverness and Ross-shire Railway, 8, 14 and 23 November 1861, 27 and 28 December 1861, 17 and 31 January 1862, and 18 February 1862, NAS/BR/IRR/1/2; Order of Business Book 1860-1862, Inverness and Ross-shire Railway, NAS/BR/IRR/1/1.

256 Minutes of the Inverness and Ross-shire Railway, 18 February 1862, NAS/BR/IRR/1/2; Minutes of the Inverness and Aberdeen Junction Railway, 18 February 1862, NAS/BR/IAJ/1/2, p.308.

257 Data to 31 July 1864 complied from the Register of Dividends, 1864-65, Inverness and Aberdeen Junction Railway, NAS/BR/IAJ/2/1.

258 *Railway Times*, 4 November 1865, p.1407.

259 Register of Dividends, 1864-65, Inverness and Aberdeen Junction Railway, NAS/BR./IAJ/1/2.

260 Minutes of the Inverness and Aberdeen Junction Railway, 2 January 1864, NAS/BR/IAJ/1/2, p.521.

261 *Inverness Courier*, 15 August 1903, reproducing an article dated 9 September 1863, NAS/BR/HR/4/3/2; 26&27 Vic. cap.32, The Inverness and Aberdeen Junction Railway (Bonar Bridge Extension) Act 1863; Minutes of the Inverness and Aberdeen Junction Railway, 18 March 1862, NAS/BR/IAJ/1/2, p.314.

262 J Mitchell, *Reminiscences of My Life in the Highlands*, vol. II, p.79 and p.116.

263 E Richards, 'An anatomy of the Sutherland Fortune: Income, Consumption, Investments and Returns, 1780-1880', *Business History*, XXI (1979), p.54; D Stirling, 'Land, Railways and the Dukes of Sutherland', *Highland Railway Journal*, 4, No.56 (early 2001), p.5: these sources quote investment by the Duke of £322,064, although *Railway News*, 1 August 1874, p.138, calculates a figure of £341,000.

264 E Richards, 'An anatomy of the Sutherland Fortune: Income, Consumption, Investments and Returns, 1780-1880', p.49.

265 J Mitchell, *Reminiscences of My Life in the Highlands*, vol.II, p.204; JAR Smith, 'From Isolation to Integration: the development of roads in the northern Highlands of Scotland, 1800-1850' (PhD thesis, Aberdeen University, 2001), p.110.

266 Minutes of the Inverness and Aberdeen Junction Railway, 18 March 1862, NAS/BR/IAJ/1/2, p.314; PT Wheeler, 'The development of shipping services to the east coast of Sutherland', *Journal of Transport History*, VI, No.2 (November 1963), p.115.

267 Minutes of the Inverness and Aberdeen Junction Railway, 18 March 1862, NAS/BR/IAJ/1/2, p.314.

268 Minutes of the Inverness and Ross-shire Railway, 18 March 1862, NAS/BR/IRR/1/2; Order of Business Book, Inverness and Ross-shire Railway, 18 March 1862, NAS/BR/IRR/1/1.

269 25&26 Vic. cap.113, The Inverness and Aberdeen Junction Railway Act, 1862; 26 Vic. cap.32, The Inverness and Aberdeen Junction Railway (Bonar Bridge Extension) Act, 1863.

270 Dividends paid to 31 January 1865, Register of Dividends, 1864-65, Inverness and Aberdeen Junction Railway, NAS/BR/IAJ/2/1: £445.14s.7d was paid as guaranteed 3% dividend for the first four months since the line opened.

271 Register of Dividends, 31 January 1865, Inverness and Aberdeen Junction Railway, NAS/BR/IAJ/2/1.

272 Accounts of the Inverness and Aberdeen Junction Railway, 31 January 1865, NAS/BR/IAJ/1/3, p.100.

273 *Railway Times*, 4 November 1865, p.1407.

Chapter 7 : An Uneasy Alliance

274 Examples of various disputes reported in 1859 alone can be found in minutes of the Great North of Scotland Railway, 15 April and 27 September 1859, NAS/BR/GNS/1/3, p.326 and p.376, and minutes of the Inverness and Aberdeen Junction Railway, 23 August 1859, NAS/BR/IAJ/1/2, p.8.

275 Minutes of the Great North of Scotland Railway, 22 September 1854, NAS/BR/GNS/1/2, p.82.

276 Minutes of the Inverness and Aberdeen Junction Railway, 13 July 1859, NAS/BR/IAJ/1/2, p.5.

277 Minutes of the Great North of Scotland Railway, 4 January 1859, NAS/BR/GNS/1/2, p.298; Journal and Ledger of the Inverness and Edinburgh Steam Packet Company, 1859-60, NAS/BR/GNS/23/57-58, p.86; Report to the Ordinary General Meeting of the Great North of Scotland Railway, 20 September 1861, NAS/BR/GNS/1/4, pp.180-81: *Herapath's Railway Journal*, 28 September 1861, pp.996-99.

278 Sir M Barclay-Harvey, *A History of the Great North of Scotland Railway*, pp.70-71.

279 *Aberdeen Journal*, 3 April 1861; *Herapath's Railway Journal*, 28 September 1861, p.997.

280 Report of the Ordinary General Meeting of the Great North of Scotland Railway, 26 September 1862, NAS/BR/GNS/1/4, pp.414-15; *Herapath's Railway Journal*, 11 October 1862, p.1060.

281 *Aberdeen Journal*, 1 October 1862.

282 *Aberdeen Journal*, 30 September 1863.

283 19&20 Vic. cap.134, The Scottish North Eastern Railway Act, 1856.

284 Minutes of the Scottish North Eastern Railway, 19 May 1860, NAS/BR/SNE/1/1, pp.292-93.

285 Minutes of the Great North of Scotland Railway, 6 August 1858, NAS/BR/GNS/1/2, pp.218-19.

286 Report to the Ordinary General Meeting of the Inverness and Aberdeen Junction Railway, 30 October 1860, NAS/BR/IAJ/1/2, p.185; Scroll minutes of the Inverness and Perth Junction Railway, 10 July 1860, NAS/BR/IPJ/1/2.

Chapter 8 : The Great North and its Branches

287 15 Vic. cap.61, The Deeside Railway Act, 1852.

288 *Herapath's Railway Journal*, 1 July 1848, p.687.

289 *Railway Times*, 20 July 1850, p.710.

290 14&15 Vic. cap.75, The Great North of Scotland Railway Amendment Act, 1851

291 Prospectus of the Great North of Scotland Railway, amended scheme 1852, NAS/BR/PROS(S)/1/9.

292 Minutes of the Formartine and Buchan Railway, 7 September 1857, NAS/BR/FBR/1/1, pp.43-44.

293 Accounts of the Great North of Scotland Railway, July 1857, NAS/BR/RAC(S)/1/14.

294 *Bradshaw's Railway Almanac*, 1875, appendix 12, p.83.

295 Capital accounts of the Great North of Scotland Railway, 1857-58, NAS/BR/RAC(S)/1/14.

296 *Bradshaw's Railway Almanac*, 1875, appendix 12, p.83

297 Report to the Ordinary General Meeting of the Great North of Scotland Railway, 29 October 1855, NAS/BR/RAC(S)/1/14.

298 *Herapath's Railway Journal*, 3 November 1855, pp.1117-18.

299 *Railway Times*, 25 November 1854, pp.1269-70.

300 *Railway Times*, 6 January 1855, p.15.

301 *Herapath's Railway Journal*, 5 April 1862, pp.364-65.

302   *Herapath's Railway Journal,* 25 May 1861, p.527.
303   *The Economist,* 8 December 1860, p.1360; *Herapath's Railway Journal,* 13 July, 1861, p.702.
304   Report of the Ordinary General Meeting of the Great North of Scotland Railway, 14 November 1856, NAS/BR/RAC(S)/1/14; *Herapath's Railway Journal,* 22 November 1856, p.1203.
305   *Herapath's Railway Journal,* 12 September 1857, p.959.
306   *Herapath's Railway Journal,* 21 November 1857, pp.1187-89; Report of the Ordinary General Meeting of the Great North of Scotland Railway, 13 November 1857, NAS/BR/GNS/1/3, pp.122-23.
307   *Railway Times,* 21 November 1857, p.1562.
308   Report of the Ordinary General Meeting of the Great North of Scotland Railway, 13 November 1857, NAS/BR/GNS/1/3, pp.112-23.
309   AC O'Dell, 'Railway Routes of the North-East' in RA Mellor (ed.), *The Railways of Scotland: the papers of Andrew C O'Dell* (Aberdeen 1984), p.40.
310   18&19 Vic. cap.65, The Inverury and Old Meldrum Junction Railway Act, 1855; 21&22 Vic cap.45, The Inverury and Old Meldrum Junction Railway Lease Act, 1858.
311   *Railway Times,* 21 November 1857, p.1563.
312   Minutes of the Banff, Macduff and Turriff Junction Railway, 23 October 1854, NAS/BR/ABT/1/1, pp.1-2.
313   18 Vic. cap.57, The Banff, Macduff and Turriff Junction Railway Act, 1855.
314   Minutes of the Banff, Macduff and Turriff Junction Railway, 23 October 1854, NAS/BR/ABT/1/1, p.2; Report to the Ordinary General Meeting of the Banff, Macduff and Turriff Junction Railway, 14 September 1855. NAS/BR/ABT/1/1, p.13.
315   Minutes of the Great North of Scotland Railway, 24 October 1856, NAS/BR/GNS/1/2, p.474, confirming a £10,000 guarantee; Minutes of the Banff, Macduff and Turriff Junction Railway, 31 October 1855, NAS/BR/ABT/1/1, p.21.
316   Minutes of the Traffic and Finance Committee of the Banff, Macduff and Turriff Junction Railway, 8 December 1857, NAS/BR/ABT/1/1, p.62.
317   Minutes of the Banff, Macduff and Turriff Junction Railway, 8 December 1857, NAS/BR/ABT/1/1, p.61.
318   Minutes of the Banff, Macduff and Turriff Junction Railway, 2 January and 20 March, 1857, NAS/BR/ABT/1/1, p.29 and p.32.
319   Minutes of the Banff, Macduff and Turriff Junction Railway, 31 July 1857, NAS/BR/ABT/1/1, p.45.
320   *Railway Times,* 20 November 1858, p.1364.
321   Accounts of the Banff, Macduff and Turriff Junction Railway, 1858-1865, NAS/BR/ABT/1/1.
322   Report to the Ordinary General Meeting of the Aberdeen and Turriff Railway, 29 November 1861, NAS/BR/ABT/1/1, p.165.
323   Report to the Ordinary General Meeting of the Aberdeen and Turriff Railway, 28 November 1862, NAS/BR/ABT/1/1, p.181.
324   As previous note.
325   22&2 Vic. cap.11, The Aberdeen and Turriff Junction Railway Act, 1859.
326   20&21 Vic. cap.50, The Banff, Macduff and Turriff Extension Railway Act, 1857.
327   Minutes of the Aberdeen and Turriff Railway, 29 November 1859, NAS/BR/ABT/1/1, pp.126-27.
328   Minutes of the Aberdeen and Turriff Railway, 9 December 1859, NAS/BR/ABT/1/1, pp.128.
329   P Fletcher, 'Strategy, solvency and the state: the development of the railway system of northern Scotland, 1844-74', Appendix, table 4(a).
330   Minutes of the Banff, Macduff and Turriff Extension Railway, 16 January 1858, NAS/BR/BMEX/1/1, p.10.
331   Minutes of the Banff, Macduff and Turriff Extension Railway, 9 February 1858, NAS/BR/BMEX/1/1, pp.20-22..
332   Minutes of the Banff, Macduff and Turriff Extension Railway, 20 April 1858, NAS/BR/BMEX/1/1, p.12.
333   Minutes of the Banff, Macduff and Turriff Extension Railway, 10 July 1858, NAS/BR/BMEX/1/1, p.39.
334   Minutes of the Banff, Macduff and Turriff Extension Railway, 31 May and 13 December 1861, NAS/BR/BMEX/1/1, p.145, and p.165.
335   Accounts of the Banff, Macduff and Turriff Extension Railway, 1860-1866, NAS/BR/BMEX/1/1.
336   9&10 Vic. cap.134, The Alford Valley Railway Act, 1846; *Railway Times,* 6 December 1851, p.1218.
337   *Herapath's Railway Journal,* 20 October 1855, p.1081; Report to the Ordinary General Meeting of the Deeside Railway, 24 October 1855, NAS/BR/DEE/1/1, p.343.
338   19&20 Vic. cap.40, The Alford Valley Railway Act, 1856.
339   Minutes of the Alford Valley Railway, 23 September 1856, NAS/BR/ALF/1/1, p.3.
340   Minutes of the Alford Valley Railway, 16 February 1858, NAS/BR/ALF/1/1, p.23.
341   Minutes of the Alford Valley Railway, 28 February, 5 March and 12 March 1858, NAS/BR/ALF/1/1, p.30, p.32 and p.34.
342   Accounts and report to the Ordinary General Meeting of the Alford Valley Railway, 29 November, 1859, NAS/BR/ALF/1/1, p.130 and p.135.
343   Accounts and report to the Ordinary General Meeting of the Alford Valley Railway, 30 November 1860, NAS/BR/ALF/1/1, p.161.
344   Accounts and report to the Ordinary General Meeting of the Alford Valley Railway, 30 November 1860, NAS/BR/ALF/1/1, p.161.
345   Report to the Ordinary General Meeting of the Alford Valley Railway, 29 November 1861, NAS/BR/ALF/1/1, p.189.
346   Report of the Ordinary General Meeting of the Aberdeen and Turriff Railway, 30 November 1860, NAS/BR/ABT/1/1, p.145.
347   Accounts of the Alford Valley Railway to 31 August 1861, NAS/BR/ALF/1/1, pp.183-89.
348   25&26 Vic. cap.87, The Alford Valley Railway Amendment Act, 1862; Extra-ordinary General Meeting of the Alford Valley Railway, 19 August 1862, NAS/BR/ALF/1/1, p.205.
349   Report to the Ordinary General Meeting of the Alford Valley Railway, 28 November 1862, p.216.
350   25&26 Vic. cap.62, The Great North of Scotland Railway Amendment Act, 1862.
351   Minutes of the Alford Valley Railway, 3 July 1863, p.222.
352   P Fletcher, 'Strategy, solvency and the state: the development of the railway system of northern Scotland, 1844-74', Appendix, table 3(a).
353   9&10 Vic. cap.135, The Great North of Scotland (Eastern Extension) Railway, 1846.
354   *Herapath's Railway Journal,* 10 November 1855, p.1157.
355   Report to the Ordinary General Meeting of the Great North of Scotland Railway, 14 November 1856, NAS/BR/GNS/1/2. p.490; 21&22 Vic. cap.107, The Formartine and Buchan Railway Act, 1858.
356   Minutes of the Formartine and Buchan Railway, 7 September 1857, NAS/BR/FBR/1/1, p.43 and p.45.
357   Minutes of the Formartine and Buchan Railway, 10 August 1858, NAS/BR/FBR/1/1, pp.64-65.

358   Report to the Ordinary General Meeting of the Great North of Scotland Railway, 12 November 1858, NAS/BR/GNS/1/3, p.260 and page 3 of printed report of the meeting.

359   *Herapath's Railway Journal*, 20 November 1858, p.1181.

360   Minutes of the Formartine and Buchan Railway, 10 September 1858, NAS/BR/FBR/1/1, pp.67-68.

361   Minutes of the Formartine and Buchan Railway, 10 September 1858, NAS/BR/FBR/1/1, p.68.

362   Minutes of the Formartine and Buchan Railway, 21 December 1858 and 11 March 1859, NAS/BR/FBR/1/1, pp.86-87 and p.88.

363   Accounts of the Formartine and Buchan Railway, 31 August 1859, NAS/BR/FBR/1/1, p.129.

364   Minutes of the Formartine and Buchan Railway, 28 November, 1859, NAS/BR/FBR/1/1, p.128.

365   Minutes of the Formartine and Buchan Railway, 19 November 1860, NAS/BR/FBR/1/1, p.178.

366   Minutes of the Formartine and Buchan Railway, 14 October and 4 November 1862, NAS/BR/FBR/1/1, pp.326-27 and p.328.

367   Minutes of the Extra-ordinary General Meeting of the Formartine and Buchan Railway, 25 September 1863, NAS/BR/FBR/1/1, pp.383-85; 26&27 Vic. cap.189, The Formartine and Buchan Railway Act, 1863; 25&26 Vic. cap.62, The Great North of Scotland Railway Amendment Act, 1862.

368   P Fletcher, 'Strategy, solvency and the state: the development of the railway system of northern Scotland, 1844-74', Appendix, table 9(a).

369   Minutes of the Formartine and Buchan Railway, 2 October 1863, NAS/BR/FBR/1/1, p.385-86.

370   *Railway Times,* 6 December 1862, p.1702.

371   *Railway Times*, 30 March 1861, p.409.

372   *Herapath's Railway Journal,* 5 April 1862, p.376.

373   *Herapath's Railway Journal,* 21 April 1860, p.397.

374   Report of the Ordinary General Meeting of the Great North of Scotland Railway, 2 April 1860, NAS/BR/GNS/1/3, pp.464-65.

375   20&21 Vic. cap.87, The Keith and Dufftown Railway Act, 1857.

376   Minutes of the Keith and Dufftown Railway, 3 December 1856, NAS/BR/KDR/1/1, p.4.

377   Report from the Committee for the Keith and Dufftown (No.2) Bill, 11 June 1857, inserted as a loose leaf at the back of the minute book of the Keith and Dufftown Railway, NAS/BR/KDR/1/1.

378   Report to the Ordinary General Meeting of the Keith and Dufftown Railway, 19 October 1858, NAS/BR/KDR/1/1, p.22.

379   Report to the Extra-ordinary General Meeting of the Keith and Dufftown Railway, 2 July 1859, NAS/BR/KDR/1/1, pp.27-28.

380   Report of the Ordinary General Meeting of the Morayshire Railway. 30 October 1847, NAS/BR/MOR./1/1; Minutes of the Inverness and Aberdeen Junction Railway, 9 July 1855, NAS/BR/IAJ/11, pp.11-20; Minutes of the Great North of Scotland Railway, 20 July 1855, NAS/BR/GNS/1/2, p.290.

381   Minutes of the Morayshire Railway, 31 August 1859, BR/NAS/MOR/1/2.

382   23&24 Vic. cap. 63, The Keith and Dufftown Railway (Deviation) Act; 1860 Minutes of the Great North of Scotland Railway, 26 August and 2 December 1859, NAS/BR/GNS/1/3. p.367 and p.408; Minutes of the Keith and Dufftown Railway, 6 June 1860, NAS/BR/KDR/1/1, p.53.

383   Minutes of the Great North of Scotland Railway, 16 October 1860, NAS/BR/GNS/1/4, pp.4-9.

384   Report to the Ordinary General Meeting of the Keith and Dufftown Railway, 29 October 1859, NAS/BR/KDR/1/1, pp.38-39.

385   Minutes of the Keith and Dufftown Railway, 6 June 1860, NAS/BR/KDR/1/1, p.53.

386   Minutes of the Keith and Dufftown Railway, 28 November 1860, NAS/BR/KDR/1/1, pp.63-64.

387   Accounts of the Keith and Dufftown Railway, 1862-1866, NAS/BR/KDR/1/1.

388   Minutes of the Great North of Scotland Railway, 19 August 1864, NAS/BR/GNS/1/5, p.186; Minutes of the Keith and Dufftown Railway, 29 July 1864 and 24 February 1865, NAS/BR/KDR/1/1, p.131 and p.146.

389   Minutes of the Banff, Macduff and Turriff Extension Railway, 6 July and 17 October 1860, NAS/BR/BMEX/1/1, p.117, p.119 and p.123.

390   Minutes of the Inverness and Aberdeen Junction Railway, 7 February 1859, NAS/BR/IAJ/1/1, p.524, *Herapath's Railway Journal*, 10 October 1863, p.1078.

391   Report to the Ordinary General Meeting of the Great North of Scotland Railway, 30 March 1864, NAS/BR/GNS/1/5, p.128.

392   *Aberdeen Journal*, 6 April 1864.

393   EL Ahrons, *Locomotive and Train Working in the later part of the Nineteenth Century* (Cambridge, 1952), p.101.

394   *Herapath's Railway Journal,* 28 September 1861, p.997.

395   *Railway Times*, 22 September 1860, p.1067.

396   *Herapath's Railway Journal*, 28 September 1861, p.1008.

397   Minutes of the Scottish North Eastern Railway, 5 September 1861, NAS/BR/SNE/1/1, p.560.

398   Minutes of a special meeting of the Great North of Scotland Railway, 6 November 1861, NAS/BR/RAC(S)/1/14; Minutes of the Scottish North Eastern Railway, 16 October 1861, NAS/BR/SNE/1/1, p.584.

399   Minutes of the Scottish North Eastern Railway, 4 December 1861, p.593; Minutes of the Great North of Scotland Railway, 13 December 1861, NAS/BR/GNS/1/4, p.222.

400   *Railway Times*, 5 April 1862, p.477.

401   *Railway Times*, 6 April 1861, p.450.

Chapter 9 : The Gale of Competition, 1860-65

402   *Herapath's Railway Journal,* 3 May 1862, p.471.

403   *Herapath's Railway Journal,* 3 May 1862, p.466 and p.471.

404   *Railway Times*, 10 April 1862, p.547.

405   *Railway Times,* 26 April 1862, p.578.

406   Minutes of the Morayshire Railway, 12 November 1855, NAS/MOR/1/1; Minutes of the Inverness and Aberdeen Junction Railway, 18 December 1855, NAS/BR/IAJ/1/1, pp.108-13.

407   17&18 Vic. cap.148, The Perth and Dunkeld Railway Act, 1854.

408   20&21 Vic. cap.53, The Banff, Portsoy and Strathisla Railway Act, 1857.

409   19&20 Vic. cap.86, The Morayshire Railway (Extension) Act, 1856.

410   Minutes of the Inverness and Aberdeen Junction Railway, 21 September 1858, NAS/BR/IAJ/1/1, pp.472-73.

411   Minutes of the Inverness and Aberdeen Junction Railway, 3 August 1859, NAS/BR/IAJ/1/2, p.8; Order of Business Book, Inverness and

Aberdeen Junction Railway, 3 August 1858, NAS/BR/IAJ/1/5, item 5.

412 Minutes of the Morayshire Railway, 31 August 1859, and resolution of a Special General Meeting of the Morayshire Railway, 31 October 1859, NAS/BR/MOR/1/2.

413 Minutes of the Inverness and Aberdeen Junction Railway, 6 February 1860, NAS/BR/IAJ/1/2, p.80.

414 *Railway Times*, 12 November 1859, p.1245.

415 23&24 Vic. cap.116, The Morayshire Railway (Junction) Act, 1860; Minutes of the Great North of Scotland Railway, 16 October 1860, NAS/BR/GNS/1/4, pp.4-9; Minutes of the Special General Meeting of the Morayshire Railway, 31 October 1860, NAS/BR/MOR/1/2.

416 *Herapath's Railway Journal*, 7 July 1860, p.679, Minutes of the Inverness and Aberdeen Junction Railway, 18 and 30 October 1860, NAS/BR/IAJ/1/2, p.181 and p.182; Minutes of the Great North of Scotland Railway, 16 October 1860, NAS/BR/GNS/1/4, p.12, Minutes of the Morayshire Railway, 25 October 1860, NAS/BR/MOR/1/2.

417 Minutes of a Special General Meeting of the Morayshire Railway, 31 October 1860, NAS/BR/MOR/1/2; *Herapath's Railway Journal*, 17 November 1860, pp.1164-65.

418 Prospectus of the Inverness and Perth Junction Railway, 1860, NAS/BR/PROS(S)/1/18; Minutes of the Inverness and Aberdeen Junction Railway, 30 October 1860, NAS/BR/IAJ/1/12, p.185; *Railway Times*, 1 December 1860, p.1367.

419 *Inverness Courier*, 8 November 1860.

420 *Railway Times*, 10 November 1860, p.1262.

421 Minutes of the Morayshire Railway, 5 October 1860, NAS/BR/MOR/1/1; Prospectus of the Morayshire and Perthshire Direct Junction Railway, 1860, NAS/BR/PROS(S)/1/22.

422 Engineer's report on the proposed Morayshire and Perthshire Direct Junction Railway, 1 September 1860, NAS/BR/PROS(S)/1/22; Report to a Special General Meeting of the Great North of Scotland Railway, 17 July 1860, p.502.

423 *Railway Times*, 7 July 1860, p.773.

424 Shareholder list for the Morayshire Railway, 1869, NAS/BR/MOR/2/1.

425 *Railway Times*, 1 December 1860, p.1364.

426 Minutes of the Morayshire Railway, 2 July 1862, NAS/BR/MOR/1/3, p.86.

427 Accounts of the Morayshire Railway, 1853-1874, NAS/BR/MOR/1/1-4; company data is incomplete and has been supplemented with data published in *Bradshaw's Railway Almanac, Herapath's Railway Journal* and *Railway Times*.

428 *Railway Times*, 16 June 1860, p.685.

429 *Railway Times*, 1 December 1860, p.1363.

430 Minutes of the Morayshire Railway, 25 September, 12 and 18 November 1866, NAS/BR/MOR/1/3, p.409, pp.418-19 and p.,421, 29&30 Vic. cap.288, The Great North of Scotland Railway (Amalgamation) Act, 1866, section 52; 29&30 Vic. cap.20, The Morayshire Railway Act, 1866.

431 Minutes of the Morayshire Railway, 16 November 1866, NAS/BR/MOR/1/3, p.421.

432 Minutes of the Highland Railway, 11 January, 5 April, and 10 May 1867, NAS/BR/HR/1/1, p.258, p.275, and p.298; Minutes of the Morayshire Railway, 31 January, 26 March, and 9 April 1867, NAS/BR/MOR/1/3, p.438, pp.443-44, and p.448.

433 44&45 Vic. cap.201, The Great North of Scotland Railway Act, 1881.

434 *Herapath's Railway Journal*, 10 November 1860, p.1136.

435 *Railway Times*, 10 November, 1860, p.1262.

436 Report to the Ordinary General Meeting of the Inverness and Aberdeen Junction Railway, 30 October 1860, NAS/BR/IAJ/1/2, p.185; *Railway Times*, 10 November 1860, p.1262.

437 Scroll minutes of the Inverness and Perth Junction Railway, 20 September 1860 and 6 October 1860, NAS/BR/IPJ/1/2.

438 *Herapath's Railway Journal*, 4 November 1865, p.1217.

439 Minutes of the Great North of Scotland Railway, 23 December 1859, NAS/BR/GNS/1/3, pp.418-19.

440 Report to the Ordinary General Meeting of the Scottish Midland Junction Railway, 26 August 1846, NAS/BR/RAC(S)/1/37.

441 17&18 Vic. cap.148, The Perth and Dunkeld Railway Act, 1854.

442 Report to the Ordinary General Meeting of the Inverness and Aberdeen Junction Railway, 30 October 1860, NAS/BR/IAJ/1/2, p.185; Minutes of the Perth and Dunkeld Railway, 23 October 1860, NAS/BR/PDR/1/1; Minutes of the Scottish North Eastern Railway, 19 October 1860, NAS/BR/SNE/1/1, p.364.

443 Minutes of the Perth and Dunkeld Railway, 10 November 1860, NAS/BR/PDR/1/1.

444 Minutes of the Locomotive Committee of the Scottish North Eastern Railway, 5 November 1860, NAS/BR/SNE/1/1, p.367.

445 Minutes of the Perth and Dunkeld Railway, 23 January 1861, NAS/BR/PDR/1/1; Chairman's notes, Perth and Dunkeld Railway, 23 January (minute 3) and 13 February 1861 (minute 2), NAS/BR/PDR1/5; Minutes of the Scottish North Eastern Railway, 19 October and 17 December 1860, 7 and 21 February and 8 March 1861, NAS/BR/SNE/1/1, p.364, p.381, p.397, p.400, p.407 and p.419.

446 Minutes of the Scottish North Eastern Railway, 25 September 1860, NAS/BR/SNE/1/1, pp.352-53.

447 Accounts of the Perth and Dunkeld Railway, 1858-1863, NAS/BR/PDR/1/1-2.

448 *Herapath's Railway Journal*, 12 October 1861, p.1045; Minutes of the Inverness and Perth Junction Railway, 4 and 23 October 1862, NAS/BR/IPJ/1/1, p.66 and p.70; Report to the Ordinary General Meeting of the Inverness and Perth Junction Railway, 28 October 1862, NAS/BR/IPJ/1/1, p.72.

449 *Railway Times*, 5 October 1861, p.1256.

450 Minutes of the Perth and Dunkeld Railway, 12 February 1863, NAS/BR/PDR/1/1.

451 Report to the Ordinary General Meeting of the Perth and Dunkeld Railway, 30 September 1863; 26&27 Vic. cap.58, The Inverness and Perth Junction and Perth and Dunkeld Railways Amalgamation Act, 1863.

452 *Herapath's Railway Journal*, 10 October 1863, p.1096.

453 Prospectus of the Inverness and Perth Junction Railway, 1860, NAS/BR/PROS(S)/1/18.

454 Report of the Ordinary General Meeting of the Great North of Scotland Railway, 1 October 1860, NAS/BR/GNS/1/3, p.548.

455 Minutes of the Great North of Scotland Railway, 24 July and 25 September 1860, NAS/BR/GNS/1/3, p.505, p.529 and p.531.

456 Minutes of the Great North of Scotland Railway, 27 November 1860, NAS/BR/GNS/1/4, pages 21 and 24; Minutes of the Great North of Scotland Railway, 22 March 1861, NAS/BR/GNS/1/4, p.75; Scroll minutes of the Inverness and Perth Junction Railway, 7 December 1860, NAS/BR/IPJ/1/2.

457 Minutes of the Great North of Scotland Railway, 20 December 1860, NAS/BR/GNS/1/4, p.31; Scroll minutes of the Inverness and

Perth Junction Railway, 13 December 1860, NAS/BR/IPJ/1/2.

458   NT Sinclair, 'Boat of Garten in the nineteenth century', *Great North Review*, 12, No.46 (August 1975), p.122.

459   Scroll minutes of the Inverness and Perth Junction Railway, 31 August, 1861, NAS/IPJ/1/2; Report of the Ordinary General Meeting of the Inverness and Perth Junction Railway, 19 September 1861, NAS/BR/IPJ/1/2.

460   *Railway Times,* 24 November 1860, pp.1316-17.

461   24&25 Vic. cap.186, The Inverness and Perth Junction Railway Act, 1861.

462   *Railway Times,* 9 March 1861, p.306.

463   Scroll minutes of the Ordinary General Meeting of the Inverness and Perth Junction Railway, 19 September 1861, NAS/BR/IPJ/1/2; NT Sinclair, *The Highland Main Line* (Penryn, 1998), p.22.

464   *Herapath's Railway Journal,* 24 November 1860, p.1172.

465   *Railway Times,* 24 November 1860, pp.1316-17 and p.1339.

466   Scroll Minutes of the Inverness and Perth Junction Railway, 15 October 1860, NAS/BR/IPJ/1/2; Minutes of the Scottish North Eastern Railway, 29 November 1860, NAS/BR/SNE/1/1, p.378.

467   Scroll minutes of the Inverness and Perth Junction Railway, 28 December 1860, NAS/BR/IPJ/1/2.

468   Scroll minutes of the Inverness and Perth Junction Railway, 26 March 1861, NAS/BR/IPJ/1/2; Minutes of the Inverness and Aberdeen Junction Railway, 27 October 1863, NAS/BR/IAJ/1/2, p.490.

469   Minutes of the Inverness and Perth Junction Railway, 23 April 1862, NAS/BR/IPJ/1/1, p.34.

470   Minutes of the Inverness and Perth Junction Railway, 10 July 1862, NAS/BR/IPJ/1/1, p.51, and Special General Meeting of the Inverness and Perth Junction Railway, 28 October 1862, pp.75-76.

471   Minutes of the Inverness and Perth Junction Railway, 6 and 17 November and 1 December, 1862, NAS/BR/IPJ/1/1, pp.80-84, p.85 and p.87.

472   Minutes of the Inverness and Perth Junction Railway, 6 November 1862 to 10 January 1863, NAS/IPJ/1/1, pp.80-99.

473   Minutes of the Inverness and Perth Junction Railway, 27 October 1863, NAS/IPJ/1/1, p.167.

474   Minutes of the Inverness and Perth Junction Railway, 25 August 1863, NAS/BR/IPJ/1/1, p.149.

475   Minutes of the Inverness and Perth Junction Railway, 2 January and 30 March 1864, NAS/BR/IPJ/1/1, p.181 and p.195.

476   Special General Meeting of the Inverness and Perth Junction Railway, 27 October 1863, NAS/BR/IPJ/1/1, p.169.

477   J Mitchell, *Reminiscences of My Life in the Highlands*, vol.II, p.197; NT Sinclair, *The Highland Main Line*, p. 28, quoting the *Illustrated London News* dated 19 September 1863.

478   Report to the Ordinary General Meeting of the Inverness and Perth Junction Railway, 28 March 1865, NAS/BR/IPJ/1/1, p.260.

479   Prospectus of the Inverness and Perth Junction Railway, 1860, NAS/BR/PROS(S)/1/18; 24&25 Vic. cap.186, The Inverness and Perth Junction Railway Act, 1861: the planned system comprised the Forres-Dunkeld main line (103¾ miles) and the Aberfeldy branch (8¾ miles).

480   *Railway Times,* 4 November, 1865, p.1407; Herapath's Railway Journal, 4 November 1865, p.1218.

481   *Railway Times,* 4 November, 1865, p.1407; Herapath's Railway Journal, 4 November 1865, p.1217-19.

482   *Railway Times,* 4 November, 1865, p.1407.

483   J Mitchell, *The Construction and Works of the Highland Railway*, a paper read to the British Association in Dundee, British Association records (September 1867), p.159, NAS/BR/HR/4/100.

484   The capital cost per mile of £9,387 is calculated from Matheson's statement of expenditure of £1,056,000 and based on the 112½ miles of the Forres-Dunkeld and Aberfeldy lines. If, however, Matheson's estimate of expenditure included the £96,000 capital cost of the Perth and Dunkeld Railway, originally planned to be subject to a working agreement which was to be paid from revenue, the capital cost for the Forres-Stanley and Aberfeldy lines comprising 120¾ miles falls to £8,745 per mile, close to Mitchell's assessment of £8,860 per mile.

485   Report to the Ordinary General Meeting of the Great North of Scotland Railway, 28 November 1849, NAS/BR/RAC(S)/1/14.

486   Report to the Ordinary General Meeting of the Inverness and Perth Junction Railway, 30 March 1864, NAS/BR/IPJ/1/1, p.201.

487   Minutes of the Inverness and Perth Junction Railway, 10 January – 27 March 1864, and 3 July – 18 September 1864, NAS/BR/IPJ/1/1, pages 186-205 and 218-29.

488   Report to the Ordinary General Meeting of the Inverness and Perth Junction Railway, NAS/BR/IPJ/1/1. 30 March 1864, p.201.

489   Report to the Ordinary General Meeting of the Great North of Scotland Railway, 28 September 1864, NAS/BR/GNS/1/5, pp.224-25, page 2 of printed report of the meeting.

490   *Railway Times,* 2 November 1861, p.1349.

491   *Railway Times,* 28 September 1861, p.1215.

492   *Herapath's Railway Journal,* 16 March 1861, p.301.

493   Minutes of the Scottish North Eastern Railway, 10 January 1861, NAS/BR/SNE/1/1, p.390.

494   Minutes of the Scottish North Eastern Railway, 5 September 1861, NAS/BR/SNE/1/1, p.560.

495   *Railway Times,* 28 September 1861, p.1221.

496   *Herapath's Railway Journal,* 22 November 1856, p.1203.

497   *Herapath's Railway Journal,* 15 March 1862, p.291.

498   T Cook, *Scottish Tourist Practical Directory* (London, 1866), p.59.

499   Special meeting of the board of the Great North of Scotland Railway, 6 November 1861, NAS/BR/RAC(S)/1/14.

500   Minutes of the Scottish North Eastern Railway, 16 October 1861, NAS/BR/SNE/1/1, p.584.

501   15 Vic. cap.61, The Deeside Railway Act, 1852.

502   Reports and accounts of the Caledonian Railway, 1845-68, NAS/BR/RAC(S)/1/3; Minutes of the Deeside Railway, 9 September, 26 November 1851 and 1 March 1853, NAS/BR/DEE/1/1, pp.74-75, p.92, and p.178.

503   *Railway Times,* 22 October 1859, p.1173.

504   20&21 Vic. cap.49, The Deeside Railway Extension Act, 1857.

505   Minutes of an Extra-Ordinary General Meeting of the Deeside Railway, 17 November 1856, NAS/BR/DEE/1/1. pp.454-57; Minutes of the Ordinary General Meeting of the Deeside Railway, 27 October 1857, NAS/DEE/1/2, pp.50-58.

506   Minutes of the Great North of Scotland Railway, 11 February, 1862, NAS/BR/GNS/1/4, pp.259-60; Minutes of the Deeside Railway, 18 February 1862, NAS/BR/DEE/1/3, pp.100-101.

507   29&30 Vic. cap 288, The Great North of Scotland (Amalgamation) Act, 1866; Report to the Ordinary General Meeting of the Deeside Railway, 24 October 1866, NAS/BR/DEE/1/3, pp.308-10.
508   39&40 Vic. cap.124, The Great North of Scotland (Further Powers) Act, 1876.
509   Accounts of the Scottish North Eastern Railway, 31 July 1861, NAS/BR/SNE/1/1, p.540-58.
510   Accounts of the Great North of Scotland Railway, 31 July 1861, NAS/BR/RAC(S)/1/14.
511   *Herapath's Railway Journal*, 27 September 1862, p.1022.
512   *Herapath's Railway Journal*, 28 September 1861, pp.996-97.
513   Report to the Ordinary General Meeting of the Great North of Scotland Railway, 20 September 1861, NAS/BR/GNS/1/3, p.171; *Herapath's Railway Journal*, 28 September 1861, pp.996-97.
514   Minutes of the Scottish North Eastern Railway, 4 December 1861, NAS/BR/SNE/1/1, p.593; 25&28 Vic. cap.79, The Scottish Northern Junction Act, 1862; 25&26 Vic. cap.64, The Scottish North Eastern Railway Amendment Act, 1862.
515   Minutes of the Scottish North Eastern Railway, 7 February 1862, NAS/BR/SNE/1/1, pp.623-24; Minutes of the Great North of Scotland Railway, 22 January 1862, NAS/BR/GNS/1/4, p.250.
516   Minutes of the Great North of Scotland Railway, 11 and 21 February 1862, NAS/BR/GNS/1/4, pp.259-60, p, .262 and p.263; Minutes of the Deeside Railway, 18 February 1862, NAS/BR/DEE/1/2, p.107.
517   *Herapath's Railway Journal*, 13 September 1862, p.980; Report to the Ordinary General Meeting of the Scottish North Eastern Railway, 12 September 1862, NAS/BR/SNE/1/1, p.738; 29&30 Vic. cap 288, The Great North of Scotland (Amalgamation) Act, 1866.
518   28&29 Vic. cap.79, The Scottish Northern Junction Railway Act, 1862.
519   *Railway Times*, 13 September 1862, p.1365.
520   Minutes of the Scottish North Eastern Railway, 15 August, 2, 12 and 13 September, and 7 October 1862, NAS/BR/SNE/1/1, pages 726, 727, 760 and 766.
521   Minutes of the Scottish North Eastern Railway, 23 October 1862, NAS/BR/SNE/1/1. p.769; J Leckie, 'The Circumbendibus', *Great North Review*, 4, No.14 (August 1967), pp.45-49.
522   Minutes of the Scottish North Eastern Railway, 17 March 1863, NAS/BR/SNE/1/2, p.8.
523   Minutes of the Scottish North Eastern Railway, 5 November 1862, NAS/BR/SNE/1/1, p.772.
524   *Railway Times*, 8 November 1862, p.1590 and p.1594.
525   *Herapath's Railway Journal*, 10 October 1863, p.1079.
526   26&27 Vic. cap.164, The Great North of Scotland (Aberdeen Junction) Railway Act, 1863; Minutes of the Scottish North Eastern Railway, 20 May 1863, NAS/BR/SNE/1/2, p.38.
527   Report to the Ordinary General Meeting of the Scottish North Eastern Railway, 17 September 1863, NAS/BR/SNE/1/2, p.88.
528   27&28 Vic. cap.111, The Denburn Valley Railway Act, 1864.
529   Minutes of the Scottish North Eastern Railway, 22 September 1864, NAS/BR/SNE/1/2. p.383.
530   Minutes of the Scottish North Eastern Railway, 22 September 1864, NAS/BR/SNE/1/2, p.379; Minutes of the Great North of Scotland Railway, 23 September 1864, NAS/BR/GNS/1/5, p.214-15.
531   Minutes of the Great North of Scotland Railway, 14 November 1864, NAS/BR/GNS/1/5, p.253; Minutes of the Scottish North Eastern Railway, 24 November 1864, NAS/BR/SNE/1/2, p.417.
532   Minutes of the Scottish North Eastern Railway, 16 March 1865, NAS/BR/SNE/1/2, p.475.
533   28&29 Vic. cap.287, The Caledonian and Scottish Central Railways Amalgamation Act, 1865; 29&30 Vic. cap.350, The Caledonian and Scottish North Eastern Railways Amalgamation Act, 1866.
534   *Railway Times*, 7 April 1866, p.420.

Chapter 10 : Defence and Collapse of the Aberdeen Monopoly

535   Minutes of the Great North of Scotland Railway, 13 July 1860, NAS/BR/GNS/1/3, p.500 and p.501.
536   Report to the Ordinary General Meeting of the Great North of Scotland Railway, 1 October 1860, NAS/BR/GNS/1/3, p.548.
537   *Railway Times*, 1 December 1860, p.1363.
538   *Railway Times*, 1 December 1860, pp.1367-68.
539   Minutes of the Great North of Scotland Railway, 20 December 1860, NAS/BR/GNS/1/4, p.29 and p.31; Scroll minutes of the Inverness and Perth Junction Railway, 6 October and 7 December 1860, NAS/BR/IPJ/1/2.
540   *Herapath's Railway Journal*, 5 October 1861, p.1020.
541   24&25 Vic. cap.16, The Strathspey Railway Act, 1861.
542   Minutes of the Strathspey Railway, 16 August 1861, NAS/BR/STY/1/1, p.6.
543   Minutes of the Strathspey Railway, 22 and 26 November 1861, NAS/BR/STY/1/1, p.8 and p.9.
544   Accounts of the Strathspey Railway, 31 August 1862, NAS/BR/STY/1/1, pp.75-76.
545   Minutes of the Strathspey Railway, 16 December 1862 – 4 September 1863, NAS/STY/1/1, pp.83 onwards.
546   Minutes of the Strathspey Railway, 27 January 1863, NAS/STY/1/1, p.86.
547   Minutes of a Special General Meeting of the Great North of Scotland Railway, 31 March 1862, NAS/BR/GNS/1/4, p.291.
548   Accounts of the Strathspey Railway, 1863-1865, NAS/BR/STY/1/1.
549   Report to the Ordinary General Meeting of the Great North of Scotland Railway, 28 September 1864, NAS/BR/GNS/1/5, pp.222-23; 27&28 Vic. cap.26, The Great North of Scotland Railway Act, 1864.
550   Report of the Extra-ordinary General Meeting of the Great North of Scotland Railway, 23 June 1866, NAS/BR/GNS/1/6, pp.39-40; 29&30 Vic. cap.288, The Great North of Scotland Railway (Amalgamation) Act, 1866.
551   Report to the Ordinary General Meeting of the Great North of Scotland Railway, 7 April 1865, NAS/BR/GNS/1/6. pp.332-33.
552   *Herapath's Railway Journal*, 25 April 1863, p.440, reporting John Stewart's address to the Ordinary General Meeting of the Great North of Scotland Railway on 27 March 1863; Report to the Ordinary General Meeting of the Great North of Scotland Railway, 27 March 1863, NAS/BR/GNS/1/4, p.492 and page 3 of printed report.
553   Minutes of the Great North of Scotland Railway, 30 December 1863, NAS/BR/GNS/1/5, pp.69-70.
554   Letter of Sir James Elphinstone, dated 21 December 1863, in minutes of the Great North of Scotland Railway, 30 December 1863, NAS/BR/GNS/1/5, pp.71-73.
555   *Burke's Peerage, Baronetage and Knightage*, 104th edition (London, 1967), p.679: entry for Sir James Dalrymple-Horn-Elphinstone, 2nd

Baronet of Logie.

556   *Herapath's Railway Journal,* 10 October 1863, p.1078.

557   Report of the Ordinary General Meeting of the Strathspey Railway, 13 November 1863, NAS/BR/STY/1/1, p.127.

558   Minutes of the Great North of Scotland Railway, 30 December 1863, NAS/BR/GNS/1/5, p.74.

559   Minutes of the Great North of Scotland Railway, 30 December 1863, NAS/BR/GNS/1/5, p.75.

560   Minutes of the Great North of Scotland Railway, 10 March 1864, NAS/BR/GNS/1/5, pp.114-15.

561   Minutes of the Great North of Scotland Railway, 23 and 28 September 1864, NAS/BR/GNS/1/5, p.211 and p.218.

562   Minutes of the Great North of Scotland Railway, 28 September 1864, NAS/BR/GNS/1/5, p.225.

563   Report to the Ordinary General Meeting of the Great North of Scotland Railway, 28 September 1864, NAS/BR/GNS/1/5, pp.222-23; 27&28 Vic. cap.28, The Great North of Scotland Railway Act, 1864.

564   Minutes of the Strathspey Railway, 31 March 1865, NAS/BR/STY/1/1, p.148.

565   *Herapath's Railway Journal,* 7 October 1865, p.1091.

566   28&29 Vic. cap.345, The Strathspey Railway (Extension) Act, 1865; Report of the Ordinary General Meeting of the Strathspey Railway, 29 November 1865, NAS/BR/STY/1/1, p.151.

567   Minutes of the Great North of Scotland Railway, NAS/BR/GNS/1/2, 24 October 1856, p.476, and 12 December 1856, NAS/BR/GNS/1/2. p.508.

568   20&21 Vic. cap.53, The Banff, Portsoy and Strathisla Railway Act, 1857.

569   Minutes of the Ordinary General Meeting of the Banff, Portsoy and Strathisla Railway, NAS/BR/BAN/1/1, 24 September 1857, p.1; Minutes of the Banff, Macduff and Turriff Extension Railway, 24 September 1857, NAS/BR/BMEX/1/1. p.2.

570   Minutes of the Banff, Portsoy and Strathisla Railway, 24 September 1857, 12 January and 4 February 1859, NAS/BR/BAN/1/1, p.4, p.143 and p.149.

571   Accounts of the Banff, Portsoy and Strathisla Railway, 31 August 1859, NAS/BR/BAN/1/1, pp.232-38; Minutes of the Banff, Portsoy and Strathisla Railway, 24 August 1859, NAS/BR/BAN/1/1, p.221.

572   Minutes of the Extra-ordinary General Meeting of the Banff, Portsoy and Strathisla Railway, 23 July 1859, NAS/BR/BAN/1/1, pp.214-15; Minutes of the Banff, Portsoy and Strathisla Railway, 21 September 1859 and 3 January 1860, NAS/BR/BAN/1/1, p.224 and p.248.

573   Minutes of the Banff, Portsoy and Strathisla Railway, 24 December 1860 and 1 March 1861, NAS/BR/BAN/1/1, p.296 and p.299.

574   Minutes of the Inverness and Aberdeen Junction Railway, 23 April 1862, NAS/BR/IAJ/1/2, p.322; Minutes of the Banff, Portsoy and Strathisla Railway, 3 July 1862, NAS/BR/BAN/1/1, p.351; Minutes of the Great North of Scotland Railway, 24 June 1862, NAS/BR/GNS/1/4, p.336; Minutes of the Banff, Portsoy and Strathisla Railway, 18 November 1862, NAS/BR/BAN/1/2, pp.18-23.

575   26&27 Vic. cap.170, The Banffshire Railway Act, 1863.

576   30&31 Vic. cap.190, The Great North of Scotland Railway (Further Powers) Act, 1867.

577   26&27 Vic. cap.65, The Fochabers and Garmouth Railway Act, 1863.

578   Minutes of the Great North of Scotland Railway, 16 September 1864, NAS/BR/GNS/1/5, pp.209-10; Minutes of the Banffshire Railway, 22 September 1864, NAS/BR/BAN/1/2, pp.64-65; Report of the Committee of Investigation to the Ordinary General Meeting of the Great North of Scotland Railway, 26 April 1865, NAS/BR/GNS/1/5, pp. 342-46, page 5 of printed report.

579   Warrant for the abandonment of the Fochabers and Garmouth Railway, 1869, NAS/BR/AP(S)/1/123; Minutes of the Highland Railway, 25 September 1867, NAS/BR/HR/1/1, p.319, minute 6.

580   Accounts of the Great North of Scotland Railway, 1863-1874, NAS/BR/RAC(S)/1/14.

581   *Railway Times,* 1 April 1865, p.410.

582   Report from the *Buchan Observer,* published in *Railway Times,* 8 April 1865, p.444.

583   *Herapath's Railway Journal,* 1 April 1865, pp.378-79.

584   Report of the Ordinary General Meeting of the Great North of Scotland Railway, 7 April 1865, NAS/BR/GNS/1/5, p.332-333, pages 2-4 of printed report.

585   *Herapath's Railway Journal,* 15 April 1865, p.419.

586   Report of the Ordinary General Meeting of the Great North of Scotland Railway, 7 April 1865, NAS/BR/GNS/1/5, p.334-35, page 5 of printed report.

587   Report to the Ordinary General Meeting of the Great North of Scotland Railway, 7 October 1869, NAS/BR/GNS/1/8. pp.213-14 and page 4 of printed report.

588   *Railway Times,* 1 October 1864, p.1314.

Chapter 11 : Great North and Highland Finances, 1865-67

589   *Herapath's Railway Journal,* 10 December 1864, p.1411.

590   *Herapath's Railway Journal,* 8 October 1864, p.1177; *Railway Times,* 8th April 1865, p.439.

591   28&29 Vic. cap.287, The Caledonian and Scottish Central Railways Amalgamation Act, 1865; 29&30 Vic. cap.350, The Caledonian and Scottish North Eastern Railways Amalgamation Act, 1866.

592   *Railway News,* 9 July 1864, pp.30-31.

593   Minutes of the Inverness and Aberdeen Junction Railway, 13 December 1860, NAS/BR/IAJ/1/2, pp.199-200; 28&29 Vic. cap.168, The Highland Railway Act, 1865.

594   28&29 Vic. cap.168, The Highland Railway Act, 1865: section 82.

595   *Herapath's Railway Journal,* 17 June 1865, p.648.

596   *Railway Times,* 4 November 1865, pp.1406-1407.

597   Minutes of the Inverness and Aberdeen Junction Railway, 7 July 1865, NAS/BR/IAJ/1/3, p.148; 28&29 Vic. cap.287, The Caledonian and Scottish Central Railways Amalgamation Act, 1865.

598   Letters of 27 and 30 June 1865 in minutes of the Inverness and Aberdeen Junction Railway, 7 July 1865, NAS/BR/IAJ/1/3, p.150.

599   *Railway Times,* 15 April 1865, pp.450-53.

600   *Herapath's Railway Journal,* 15 April 1865, p.419.

601   29&30 Vic. cap.288, The Great North of Scotland Railway (Amalgamation) Act, 1866; 30&31 Vic. cap.190, The Great North of Scotland (Further Powers) Act, 1867; 44&45 Vic. cap.201, The Great North of Scotland Railway Act, 1881.

602   Minutes of an Extra-ordinary General Meeting of the Great North of Scotland Railway, 23 June 1866, NAS/BR/GNS/1/6, p.34.

603 *Railway News,* 16 May 1868, p.531; Railway News, 31 August 1867, p.218.

604 HA Vallance, *The Highland Railway,* p.29; HA Vallance, *The Great North of Scotland Railway,* p.66: these data include leased and worked lines.

605 *Railway Times,* 15 April 1865, pp.450-53.

606 Report to the Ordinary General Meeting of the Great North of Scotland Railway, 7 April 1865, NAS/BR/GNS/1/5, pp.332-33.

607 Report of the Ordinary General Meeting, 7 April 1865, NAS/BR/GNS/1/5, p. 330.

608 *Railway Times,* 15 April 1865, p.466.

609 Report by the Committee of Investigation to the shareholders of the Great North of Scotland Railway, dated 22 April 1865, NAS/BR/GNS/1/32, subsidiary document 5, and minutes of the adjourned Ordinary General Meeting of the Great North of Scotland Railway, 26 April 1865, NAS/BR/GNS/1/5, pp.346-47.

610 Report by the Committee of Investigation to the shareholders of the Great North of Scotland Railway, 22 April 1865, NAS/BR/GNS/1/32, subsidiary document 5, pp.4-5.

611 Recommendations to the adjourned Ordinary General Meeting of the Great North of Scotland Railway, 26 April 1865, NAS/BR/GNS/1/5, p.345.

612 *Railway Times,* 29 April 1865, p.522.

613 *Railway Times,* 29 April 1865, p.505.

614 Minutes of the Great North of Scotland Railway, 2 January 1866, NAS/BR/GNS/1/5, p.503.

615 Minutes of the Finance Committee of the Great North of Scotland Railway, 13 March 1866, NAS/BR/GNS/1/5, pp.538-39.

616 Minutes of the Great North of Scotland Railway, 13 February 1866, NAS/BR/GNS/1/5, p.521; Report of the Extra-ordinary General Meeting of the Great North of Scotland Railway, 23 June 1866, pp.39-40.

617 29&30 Vic. cap.288, The Great North of Scotland Railway (Amalgamation) Act, 1866; *Railway Times,* 30 June 1866, p.783.

618 Report to the Ordinary General Meeting of the Great North of Scotland Railway, 2 October 1866, NAS/BR/GNS/1/6, pp.85-86.

619 Report of the Ordinary General Meeting of the Great North of Scotland Railway, 2 October 1866, NAS/BR/GNS/1/6, pp.85-86, page 3 of printed report.

620 Minutes of the Great North of Scotland Railway, 1 October 1866, NAS/BR/GNS/1/6, p.78; Report of the Ordinary General Meeting of the Great North of Scotland Railway, 2 October 1866, NAS/BR/GNS/1/6, pp.87-88, page 3 of printed report.

621 Minutes of the reconvened Ordinary General Meeting of the Great North of Scotland Railway, 4 December 1866, NAS/BR/GNS/1/6, p143; Minutes of the Great North of Scotland Railway, 5 February 1867, NAS/BR/GNS/1/6, p.212.

622 Accounts of the Great North of Scotland Railway, 31 January 1867, NAS/BR/RAC(S)/1/14.

623 Minutes of the Great North of Scotland Railway, 14 November 1866, NAS/BR/GNS/1/6, pp.121-22.

624 Report of Robert Fletcher in minutes of the Great North of Scotland Railway, 14 November 1866, NAS/BR/GNS/1/6, p.4 and p.7.

625 Report of Robert Fletcher in minutes of the Great North of Scotland Railway, 14 November 1866, NAS/BR/GNS/1/6, p.7 and p.10.

626 Report of Robert Fletcher in minutes of the Great North of Scotland Railway. 14 November 1866, NAS/BR/GNS/1/6, p.17.

627 Letter from the National Bank of Scotland, 16 November 1866, reported to the board of the Great North of Scotland Railway, 23 November 1866, NAS/BR/GNS/1/6, p.126.

628 Minutes of the Great North of Scotland Railway, 23 November 1866, NAS/BR/GNS/1/6, p.128.

629 Minutes of the Great North of Scotland Railway, 11 December 1866, NAS/BR/GNS/1/6, p.149.

630 Minutes of the Great North of Scotland Railway, 18 December 1866, NAS/BR/GNS/1/6, pp.158-59 and p.162.

631 Bank letters of 19 and 20 December 1866, in minutes of the Great North of Scotland Railway, 26 December 1866, NAS/BR/GNS/1/6, pp.168-69.

632 National Bank of Scotland letter of 26 December 1866, in minutes of the Great North of Scotland Railway, 2 January 1867, NAS/BR/GNS/1/6, p.171.

633 Letter of the Caledonian Railway to the Great North of Scotland Railway, 22 January 1867, in minutes of the Great North of Scotland Railway, 29 January 1867, NAS/BR/GNS/1/6, pp.202-203.

634 *Railway Times,* 19 November 1864, p.1482.

635 *Herapath's Railway Journal,* 17 June 1865, p.648.

636 *Railway Times,* 1 April 1865, p.410.

637 Report to the Ordinary General Meeting of the Inverness and Perth Junction Railway, 28 March 1865, NAS/BR/IPJ/1/1, p.260.

638 Minutes of the Inverness and Aberdeen Junction Railway, 1 March 1865, NAS/BR/IAJ/1/3, p.90.

639 *Railway Times,* 20 May 1865, p.641.

640 *Herapath's Railway Journal,* 22 November 1862, p.1208.

641 *Herapath's Railway Journal,* 7 November 1863, p.1181; Railway Times, 7 November 1863, p.1434.

642 *Herapath's Railway Journal,* 8 October 1864, p.1166.

643 As previous reference.

644 As previous reference.

645 *Railway Times,* 8 October 1864, p.1323.

646 *Railway Times,* 8 October 1864, p.1323; *Herapath's Railway Journal,* 8 October 1864, p.1166.

647 *Railway Times,* 8 October 1864, p.1323, reporting the Ordinary General Meeting of the Inverness and Aberdeen Junction Railway held on 28 September 1864.

648 28&29 Vic. cap.168, The Highland Railway Act, 1865.

649 Accounts of the Highland Railway to 31 August 1865 in the report to the Ordinary General Meeting of the Highland Railway, 27 October 1865, NAS/BR/HR/1/1, pp.42-43.

650 *Railway Times,* 4 November 1865, p.1407.

651 *Herapath's Railway Journal,* 4 November 1865, p.1219.

652 *Railway Times,* 5 May 1866, pp.514-15; Report of the Ordinary General Meeting of the Highland Railway, 27 April 1866, NAS/BR/HR/1/1, pp.148-49.

653 *Bradshaw's Railway Almanac,* 1875 edition, appendix 12, p.83.

654 Accounts of the Highland Railway to 31 August 1865, reported on 27 October 1865, NAS/BR/HR/1/1, pp.42-43: preference stock (£750,687) and debenture loans (£565,241) total £1,315,928, 54.76% of the £2,402,892 capital raised.

655 *Railway Times*, 5 May 1866, p.515.
656 *Railway Times*, 5 May 1866, p.515.
657 Report of the Ordinary General Meeting of the Highland Railway, 30 October 1866, NAS/BR/HR/1/1, pp.218-19, page 2 of printed report.
658 Report to the Ordinary General Meeting of the Highland Railway, 27 October 1865, NAS/BR/HR/1/1, pp.42-43, page 2 of printed report.
659 Minutes of the Highland Railway, 21 August 1865 and 22 February 1866, NAS/BR/HR/1/1, p.19 and p.115.
660 *Herapath's Railway Journal*, 4 November 1865, p.1217-18.
661 *Railway Times*, 4 November 1865, p.1407.
662 *Herapath's Railway Journal*, 4 November 1865, p.1218.
663 *Railway Times*, 4 November 1865, p.1407; *Herapath's Railway Journal*, 4 November 1865, p.1217.
664 *Railway Times*, 4 November 1865, p.1417.
665 *Railway News*, 17 September 1864, p.299.
666 PL Cottrell, 'Railway Finances and the Crisis of 1866: contractors' bills of exchange and finance companies', pp.24-26.
667 *Railway Times*, 12 May 1866, pp.563-64.
668 *Railway News*, 12 May 1866, p.510; Railway Times, 12 May 1866, pp.563-64; *Bradshaw's Railway Almanac*, 1875 edition, appendix 12, p.83.

Chapter 12 : Caledonian Lifelines

669 28&29 Vic. cap.287, The Caledonian and Scottish Central Railways Amalgamation Act, 1865; 29&30 Vic. cap.350, The Caledonian and Scottish North Eastern Railways Amalgamation Act, 1866.
670 Report to the Ordinary General Meeting of the Caledonian Railway, 12 September 1865, NAS/BR/RAC(S)/1/3; Minutes of the Scottish North Eastern Railway, 10 November 1865, NAS/BR/SNE/1/2, p.118; Report to the Ordinary General Meeting of the Caledonian Railway, 31 March 1866, NAS/BR/RAC(S)/1/3.
671 28&29 Vic. cap.266, The Callander and Oban Railway Act, 1865; Agreement between the promoters of the Callander and Oban Railway and the Scottish Central Railway, 17, 19 and 22 December 1864, NAS/BR/AP(S)/146.
672 24&25 Vic. cap.186, The Inverness and Perth Junction Railway Act, 1861.
673 Minutes of the Inverness and Aberdeen Junction Railway, 7 July 1865, NAS/BR/IAJ/1/3, p.148; Minute 589 of the Caledonian Railway, 25 July 1865, NAS/BR/CAL/1/15.
674 28&29 Vic. cap.223, The Dingwall and Skye Railway Act, 1865.
675 Minute 598, meetings of Directors and Committees of the Caledonian Railway, 25, July 1865, NAS/BR/CAL/1/14.
676 Minute 729, meetings of Directors and Committees of the Caledonian Railway, 22 August 1865, NAS/BR/CAL/1/14.
677 P Fletcher, 'Caledonian conundrums in the Highlands', *Highland Railway Journal*, 6, No.88 (early 2009), pp.1-15.
678 Minutes of the Highland Railway, 20 March 1866, NAS/BR/HR/1/1, minute 9, p.132; Order of Business Book, Inverness and Aberdeen Junction Railway, 20 March 1866, NAS/IAJ/1/6, item 10.
679 Minute 1151, meetings of Directors and Committees of the Caledonian Railway, 7 November 1865, NAS/BR/CAL/1/15.
680 *Railway Times*, 27 April 1867, p.429.
681 Letter from the Caledonian Railway dated 8 August 1866, in minutes of the Highland Railway, 10 August 1866, NAS/BR/HR/1/1, p.193.
682 Minute 1608, meetings of Directors and Committees of the Caledonian Railway, 11 June 1867, NAS/BR/CAL/1/15.
683 Minute 1795, meetings of Directors and Committees of the Caledonian Railway, 5 July 1867, NAS/BR/CAL/1/15.
684 Minute 1855, meetings of Directors and Committees of the Caledonian Railway, 20 August 1867, NAS/BR/CAL/1/15; Minute 1908, meetings of Directors and Committees of the Caledonian, 16 September 1867, NAS/BR/CAL/1/15.
685 Minute 170, meetings of Directors and Committees of the Caledonian Railway, 29 October 1867, NAS/BR/CAL/1/16.
686 Minute 402, meetings of Directors and Committees of the Caledonian Railway, 18 December 1867, NAS/BR/CAL/1/16.
687 *Railway Times*, 26 October 1867, p.1102.
688 Report of the Committee of Inquiry to the Shareholders of the Caledonian Railway Company, 3 January 1868, NAS/BR/RAC(S)/1/3, paragraphs 26 and 46.
689 *Railway Times*, 26 October 1867, p.1093.
690 *Railway Times*, 31 October 1868, p.1115-16.
691 *Railway Times*, 24 April 1869, p.409.
692 Accounts and reports to shareholders, in minutes of the Highland Railway, 1865-1871, NAS/BR/HR/1/1-2.
693 Accounts of the Great North of Scotland Railway, 1866-1868, NAS/BR/RAC(S)/1/14.
694 Accounts of the Great North of Scotland Railway, 31 January 1868, NAS/BR/RAC(S)/1/14; Accounts of the Highland Railway, 29 February 1868, NAS/BR/HR/1/1, pp.380-81.
695 *Railway Times*, 25 August 1866, p.1014; *Railway Times*, 15 December 1866, p.1437.
696 Minutes of the Finance Committee of the Great North of Scotland Railway, 23 November 1866, NAS/BR/GNS/1/6, p.126; Minute 711, minutes of Directors and Committees of the Caledonian Railway, 4 December 1866, NAS/BR/CAL/1/15.
697 Minutes of the Great North of Scotland Railway, 1 December 1866, NAS/BR/GNS/1/6, p.136.
698 Minutes of the Great North of Scotland Railway, 1 December 1866, NAS/BR/GNS/1/6, p.136 and p.139.
699 Letter from the Caledonian Railway dated 22 January 1867, in minutes of the Great North of Scotland Railway, 29 January 1867, NAS/BR/GNS/1/6, pp.202-203; Minute 995, minutes of Directors and Committees of the Caledonian Railway, 22 January 1867, NAS/BR/CAL/1/15.
700 Minute 1431 (9 April 1861), minute 1473 (1 May 1867), minute 298 (21 November 1867), in minutes of directors and committees of the Caledonian Railway, NAS/BR/CAL/1/15-16; 30&31 Vic. cap.190, The Great North of Scotland Railway (Further Powers) Act, 1867; 27&28 Vic. cap.111, the Denburn Valley Railway Act, 1864.
701 Minutes of the Great North of Scotland Railway, 3 December 1866, NAS/BR/GNS/1/6, p.141; Report of the adjourned Ordinary General Meeting of the Great North of Scotland Railway, 5 February 1867, NAS/BR/GNS/1/6, pp.211-12, page 1 of printed report.
702 *Railway News*, 16 March 1867, p.271.

703   Report of the Committee of Investigation to the Shareholders of the Caledonian Railway Company, 1849, NAS/BR/CAL/1/98, p.7 and p.18.
704   *Railway Times*, 11 December 1869, p.1210.
705   Report of the Committee of Inquiry to the Shareholders of the Caledonian Railway Company, 3 January 1868, NAS/BR/RAC(S)/1/3, paragraphs 45 and 46, pp.14-15.
706   Railway Times, 10 August 1872, pp.811-12; H Parris, Government and the Railways in Nineteenth-Century Britain, p.221.
707   *Railway Times*, 28 July 1866, p.886.
708   *Railway News*, 30 May 1868, p.568.
709   Minutes of the Great North of Scotland Railway, 4 June 1868, NAS/BR/GNS/1/7, p.290.

Chapter 13 : Refinancing the Great North of Scotland Railway

710   Report to the Ordinary General Meeting of the Great North of Scotland Railway, 2 October 1866, NAS/BR/GNS/1/6, pp.87-88 and page 3 of printed report.
711   Minutes of the reconvened Ordinary General Meeting of the Great North of Scotland Railway, 4 December 1866, NAS/BR/GNS/1/6, p.143.
712   *Herapath's Railway Journal*, 10 December 1864, p.1382.
713   Report of Robert Fletcher in minutes of the Great North of Scotland Railway, 14 November 1866, NAS/BR/GNS/1/6, p.7.
714   Minutes of the Great North of Scotland Railway, 12 December 1866, NAS/BR/GNS/1/6, pp.151-52.
715   Minutes of the Great North of Scotland Railway, 18 December 1866, NAS/BR/GNS/1/6, p.157.
716   Minutes of the Great North of Scotland Railway, 8 January 1867, NAS/BR/GNS/1/6, p.179 and 4 February 1867, NAS/BR/GNS/1/6, p.205.
717   Minutes of the Great North of Scotland Railway, 5 February 1867, NAS/BR/GNS/1/6, p.212: resignations were accepted from Elphinstone, Elmsly, Erskine, Jopp and Thompson; directors re-appointed were Burnett, Crombie, Duncan, Leslie, Ligertwood, and G Milne; new appointments were William Ferguson of Kilmundy, Ramsey, Longmore, Kaye, Nicolson, and Provost Adam of Banff.
718   *Aberdeen Journal*, 6 February 1867; Minutes of the adjourned Ordinary General Meeting of the Great North of Scotland Railway, 5 February, 1867, NAS/BR/GNS/1/6, p.212, pages 1 and 2 of printed report.
719   *Railway Times*, 22 March 1879, p. 242.
720   *Aberdeen Journal*, 6 February 1867.
721   *Aberdeen Journal*, 6 February 1867; Report of the Ordinary General Meeting of the Great North of Scotland Railway, 5 February 1867, NAS/BR/GNS/1/6, pp.211-12 and page 3 of printed report.
722   Minutes of the Great North of Scotland Railway, 12 February 1867, NAS/BR/GNS/1/6, p.216.
723   *Aberdeen Journal*, 6 February 1867.
724   Letter from Bruce of the Highland Railway, dated 28 December 1868, in minutes of the Finance, Works and Traffic Committee of the Great North of Scotland Railway, 7 January 1869, NAS/BR/GNS/1/7, p.545.
725   Minutes of the Finance, Works and Traffic Committee of the Great North of Scotland Railway, 18 February 1869, NAS/BR/GNS/1/8, p.7.
726   Report of the Ordinary General Meeting of the Great North of Scotland Railway, 5 February 1867, NAS/BR/GNS/1/6, pp.211-12 and page 1 of printed report; Railway Times, 13 July 1867, p.697.
727   Minutes of the Finance and Works Committee of the Great North of Scotland Railway. 14 February 1867, NAS/BR/GNS/1/6, p.220.
728   Minutes of the Great North of Scotland Railway, 28 February 1867, NAS/BR/GNS/1/6, p.240.
729   Report to the Special General Meeting of the Great North of Scotland Railway, 12 March 1867, NAS/BR/GNS/1/6, pp.248-50 and page 1 of printed report.
730   Circular to shareholders, 25 March 1867, in Accounts of the Great North of Scotland Railway, NAS/BR/RAC(S)/1/14.
731   *Railway Times*, 20 April 1867, p.398; *Aberdeen Journal*, 24 April 1867; Report to the Ordinary General Meeting of the Great North of Scotland Railway, 17 April 1867, NAS/BR/GNS/1/6, pp.299-300: net revenue for the half year to 31 January 1867 was £32,516, from which interest (£15,087) and interest on floating debt and Denburn Valley work (£11,706) was deducted. The total interest (£26,973) represents 82.4% of the net revenue of the half year.
732   Accounts of the Great North of Scotland Railway, 31 July 1867, NAS/BR/RAC(S)/1/14.
733   Minutes of the Great North of Scotland Railway, 28 March 1867, NAS/BR/GNS/1/6, pp.257-60.
734   Minutes of the Great North of Scotland Railway, 28 March 1867, NAS/BR/GNS/1/6, p.263; Report to the Ordinary General Meeting of the Great North of Scotland Railway, 17 April 1867, NAS/BR/GNS/1/6, pp.299-300 and page 2 of printed report, and letter 23 April 1867, within minutes of the board, 25 April 1867, NAS/BR/GNS/1/6, p.309.
735   Minutes of the Great North of Scotland Railway, 2 May 1867, NAS/BR/GNS/1/6, p.320.
736   30&31 Vic. cap.190, The Great North of Scotland Railway (Further Powers) Act, 1867; Report to the Ordinary General Meeting of the Great North of Scotland Railway, 3 October 1867, NAS/BR/GNS/1/6, pp.519-20 and page 2 of printed report.
737   *Railway Times*, 20 April 1867, p.413.
738   Report to the Ordinary General Meeting of the Great North of Scotland Railway, 3 October 1867, NAS/BR/GNS/1/6, pp.519-20 and pages 2 and 3 of printed report.
739   Minutes of the Finance and Works Committee of the Great North of Scotland Railway, 24 October 1867, NAS/BR/GNS/1/6, p.557.
740   Minutes of the Finance and Works Committee of the Great North of Scotland Railway, 29 August 1867 and 21 November 1867, NAS/BR/GNS/1/6, p.459 and NAS/BR/GNS/1/7, p.14.
741   Minutes of the Great North of Scotland Railway, 26 December 1867, NAS/BR/GNS/1/7, p.72.
742   Report to the Ordinary General Meeting of the Great North of Scotland Railway, 3 October 1867, NAS/BR/GNS/1/6, pp.519-20; Minutes of the Great North of Scotland Railway, 26 December 1867 and 9 January 1868, NAS/BR/GNS/1/7, p.73 and p.85.
743   Minutes of the Great North of Scotland Railway, 30 March 1868 and 1 April 1868, NAS/BR/GNS/1/7, p.210 and p.212.
744   Minutes of a special board meeting, Great North of Scotland Railway, 1 April 1868, NAS/BR/GNS/1/7, p.212.
745   Accounts of the Great North of Scotland Railway, 1868, NAS/BR/RAC(S)/1/14.
746   Minutes of the Great North of Scotland Railway, 23 April 1868, NAS/BR/GNS/1/7, p.238.
747   Report to the Ordinary General Meeting of the Great North of Scotland Railway, 8 October 1868, NAS/BR/GNS/1/7, p.447 and

page 4 of printed report.

748   Minutes of the Great North of Scotland Railway, 10 September 1868, NAS/BR/GNS/1/7, p.416.

749   CJA Robertson, entry on 'William Ferguson' in A Slaven and S Checkland (eds.), *Dictionary of Scottish Business Biography 1860-1960*, vol.2 (Aberdeen, 1990), p.279: William Ferguson was a director of the Great North from 1867 and chairman from 1879, and not to be confused with William B Ferguson, general manager of the Deeside Railway who became secretary of the Great North following its reconstitution in 1866 and served until 1880.

750   Minutes of the Finance and Works Committee of the Great North of Scotland Railway, 4 June 1868, NAS/BR/GNS/1/7, p.293.

751   Letter from the North of Scotland Bank dated 3 June 1868, in minutes of the Finance and Works Committee of the Great North of Scotland Railway, 4 June 1868, NAS/BR/GNS/1/7, p.294.

752   Minutes of the Great North of Scotland Railway, 23 July 1868, NAS/BR/GNS/1/7, p.362; *Bradshaw's Railway Almanac*, 1875 edition, appendix 12, p.83; Minutes of the Finance, Works and Traffic Committee of the Great North of Scotland Railway, 22 and 29 October 1868, NAS/BR/GNS/1/7, pp.471-72, and p.478.

753   Report of the Special General Meeting of the Great North of Scotland Railway, 10 October 1871, NAS/BR/GNS/1/9, p.72.

754   Report to the Ordinary General Meeting of the Great North of Scotland Railway, 8 April 1869, NAS/BR/GNS/1/8, pp.53-56, pages 2 and 3 of printed report.

755   *Railway Times*, 2 October 1869, p.970.

756   *Railway Times*, 7 January 1871, p. 9, and 18 November 1871, p.1121.

757   *Railway Times*, 18 April and 26 December 1874, p.408 and p.1278.

758   *Railway Times*, 8 April 1871, p.34.

759   *Railway News*, 30 September 1871, p.458.

760   Report of the Ordinary General Meeting of the Great North of Scotland Railway, 4 October 1870, NAS/BR/GNS/1/8, p.486.

761   Report to the Ordinary General Meeting of the Great North of Scotland Railway, 30 March 1871, NAS/BR/GNS/1/9, pp.7-10.

762   Report to the Ordinary General Meeting of the Great North of Scotland Railway, 28 March 1872, NAS/BR/GNS/1/9, pp.119-22.

763   Minutes of the Great North of Scotland Railway, 19 October 1871, NAS/BR/GNS/1/9, p.73; Report of the Ordinary General Meeting of the Great North of Scotland Railway, 28 March 1872, NAS/BR/GNS/1/9, pp.119-22, page 1 of printed report.

764   Report to the Ordinary General Meeting of the Great North of Scotland Railway, 4 October 1872, NAS/BR/GNS/1/9, pp.181-86, page 1 of printed report.

765   Report to the Ordinary General Meeting of the Great North of Scotland Railway, 4 October 1872, NAS/BR/GNS/1/9, pp.181-86, page 1 of printed report.

766   Report of the Extra-ordinary General Meeting of the Great North of Scotland Railway, 12 February 1873, NAS/BR/GNS/1/9, pp.237-38 and page 1 of printed report.

767   36&37 Vic cap.104, The Great North of Scotland Railway Act, 1873

768   Report to the Ordinary General Meeting of the Great North of Scotland Railway, 27 March 1874, pp.376-78, page 1 of printed report.

769   *Aberdeen Journal*, 24 April 1867.

770   *Railway News*, 21 March 1874, p.405.

771   Minutes of the Great North of Scotland Railway, 22 August 1872, NAS/BR/GNS/1/9, p.162; 30&31 Vic. cap.190, The Great North of Scotland Railway Act, 1867.

772   Minutes of the Great North of Scotland Railway, 11 July 1872 and 5 August 1875, NAS/BR/GNS/1/9, p.146 and p.530; 45&46 Vic. cap.126, The Great North of Scotland (Buckie Extension) Act, 1882.

773   Minutes of the Great North of Scotland Railway, 24 December 1874, NAS/BR/GNS/1/9, p.455.

Chapter 14 : Tackling the Debt of the Highland Railway

774   *Herapath's Railway Journal*, 4 November 1865, p.1218.

775   *Railway News*, 12 May 1866, p.505.

776   *Railway Times*, 5 May 1866, p.515.

777   *Railway Times*, 5 May 1866, p.514.

778   Report to the Ordinary General Meeting of the Highland Railway, 27 April 1866, NAS/BR/HR/1/1, pp.148-49; *Railway Times*, 5 May 1866, pp.514-15.

779   Report to the Ordinary General Meeting of the Great North of Scotland Railway, 30 March 1871, NAS/BR/GNS/1/9, p.10.

780   Minute of the Special General Meeting of the Highland Railway, 7 March 1906, NAS/BR/HR/1/17, p.372.

781   Minutes of the Scottish North Eastern Railway, 7 February 1861, NAS/BR/SNE/1/1, p.397-98.

782   Minutes of the Highland Railway, 22 September 1865, NAS/BR/HR/1/1, p.25; Minutes of the Directors of the Scottish North Eastern Railway, 8 September 1865, NAS/BR/SNE/1/3, p.59.

783   Minutes of the Highland Railway, 22 September 1865, NAS/BR/HR/1/1, p.25; *Railway Times*, 1 April 1865, p.194; *Herapath's Railway Journal*, 1 April 1865, p.364; NT Sinclair, The Highland Main Line, p.30.

784   *Herapath's Railway Journal*. 8 April 1865, p.394.

785   Minutes of the Highland Railway, 13 December 1865 and 8 May 1866, NAS/BR/HR/1/1, p.83 and p.154.

786   Minutes of the Highland Railway, 8 May and 7 June 1866, NAS/BR/HR/1/1, p.154 and p.167; 29&30 Vic. cap.350, The Caledonian and Scottish North Eastern Railways Amalgamation Act, 1866, sections 48-59.

787   Minutes of the Highland Railway, 22 September 1865, NAS/BR/HR/1/1, p.27.

788   Letters from the Commercial Bank dated 2 and 3 November 1865, in minutes of the Highland Railway, 7 November 1865, NAS/BR/HR/1/1, p.54.

789   Minutes of the Highland Railway, 7 November, 9 November 1865 and 5 December 1865, NAS/BR/HR/1/1, p.54, p.65 and p.79.

790   Minutes of the Highland Railway, 30 December 1865, NAS/BR/HR/1/1, p.89.

791   *Bradshaw's Railway Almanac*, 1875 edition, appendix 12, p.83.

792   Minutes of the Highland Railway, 2 and 12 January 1866, NAS/BR/HR/1/1, p.90 and p.97.

793   Minutes of the Highland Railway, 30 January 1866, NAS/BR/HR/1/1, pp.101-105; 28&29 Vic. cap.169, The Sutherland Railway Act, 1865.

794   Minutes of the Inverness and Aberdeen Junction Railway, 25 May 1857, NAS/NR/IAJ/1/1, p.282.

795   Minutes of the Sutherland Railway, 5 February 1866, NAS/BR/SLD/1/1, pp.14-16.
796   Minutes of the Highland Railway, 30 January 1866, NAS/BR/HR/1/1, pp.101-102.
797   Minutes of the Sutherland Railway, 5 February 1866, NAS/BR/SLD/1/1, pp.14-16.
798   Minutes of the Highland Railway, 19 June 1866, NAS/BR/HR/1/1, pp.168-69.
799   Minutes of the Highland Railway, 19 June 1866, NAS/BR/HR/1/1, p.170.
800   Minutes of the Highland Railway, 9 October 1866, NAS/BR/HR/1/1, p.213.
801   *Railway Times*, 22 October 1870, p.1053.
802   Minutes of the Highland Railway, 3 September 1867, NAS/BR/HR/1/1, p.318.
803   Minutes of the Highland Railway, 4 February 1868, NAS/BR/HR/1/1, p.363.
804   Minutes of the Highland Railway, 17 March and 5 August 1868, NAS/BR/HR/1/1, p.373 and p.413.
805   Minutes of the Highland Railway, 1 and 18 September and 5 October 1868, NAS/BR/HR/1/1, p.416, p.423 and p.427.
806   Report of the Special General Meeting of the Highland Railway, 28 April 1869, NAS/BR/HR/1/1, pp.492-96.
807   Minutes of the Highland Railway, 10 April 1866, NAS/BR/HR/1/1, p.140.
808   Minutes of the Highland Railway, 3 January 1871, NAS/BR/HR/1/2, p.44.
809   Minutes of the Highland Railway, 6 June, 4 July, 1 August 1871, NAS/BR/HR/1/2, pages 86, 92 and 97.
810   Accounts of the Highland Railway, 1869-1872, NAS/BR/HR/1/1-2.
811   Minutes of the Highland Railway, 5 September 1871, NAS/BR/HR/1/2, page 102.
812   Minutes of the Highland Railway, 18 October 1871, NAS/BR/HR/1/2, p.111; Report to the Ordinary General Meeting of the Highland Railway, 27 October 1871, NAS/BR/HR/1/2, p.116, page 2 of printed report.
813   Minutes of the Highland Railway, 5 December 1871, NAS/BR/HR/1/2, p.124.
814   Minutes of the Highland Railway, 2 January 1872, NAS/BR/HR/1/2, p.130.
815   Minutes of the Highland Railway, 2 January and 6 February 1872, NAS/BR/HR/1/2, p.130 and p.139.
816   *Railway Times*, 17 February 1872, p.177.
817   Minutes of the Highland Railway, 6 February 1872, NAS/BR/HR/1/2, p.141.
818   Report to the Ordinary General Meeting of the Highland Railway, 26 April 1872, NAS/BR/HR/1/2, pp.161-62, page 2 of printed report.
819   Report to the Ordinary General Meeting of the Highland Railway, 26 April 1872, NAS/BR/HR/1/2, p.169.
820   *Railway Times*, 4 May 1872, p.473.
821   *Railway Times*, 6 November 1875, p.1065.
822   *Railway Times*, 6 November 1875, p.1055; Minutes of the Highland Railway, 5 September 1876, NAS/BR/HR/1/3, p.9; Minutes of the Highland Railway, 4 March 1896, NAS/BR/HR/1/7, p.323.
823   *Railway Times*, 6 November 1875, p.1055.
824   *Railway Times*, 6 November 1875, p.1055.
825   Minutes of the Highland Railway, 1 April 1873 NAS/BR/HR/1/2, p.253; Report to the Ordinary General Meeting of the Highland Railway, 25 April 1873, NAS/BR/HR/1/2, pp.261-62, p.266, page 2 of printed report.
826   *Railway News*, 25 October 1873, p.552.

Chapter 15 : The Great North and the Highland Railways, 1874

827   *Herapath's Railway Journal*, 21 April 1855, p.415.
828   *Railway News*, 7 November 1874, p.626.